Soups

BY
THE EDITORS OF TIME-LIFE BOOKS

TIME-LIFE BOOKS/ALEXANDRIA, VIRGINIA

Cover: The first ladleful of a mixed vegetable soup (recipe, page 112) is lifted from a steaming casserole. Tomatoes simmered to a purée provided the soup with its rosy hue. Other vegetables have been added in stages according to their different cooking times—onions and a leek first, then carrots and zucchini, and finally shredded cabbage.

Time-Life Books Inc.
is a wholly owned subsidiary of
TIME INCORPORATED

Founder: Henry R. Luce 1898-1967

Editor-in-Chief: Henry Anatole Grunwald
Chairman of the Board: Andrew Heiskell
President: James R. Shepley
Editorial Director: Ralph Graves
Vice Chairman: Arthur Temple

TIME-LIFE BOOKS INC.

Managing Editor: Jerry Korn; Executive Editor: David Maness; Assistant Managing Editors: Dale M. Brown (planning), George Constable, George G. Daniels (acting), Martin Mann, John Paul Porter; Art Director: Tom Suzuki; Chief of Research: David L. Harrison; Director of Photography: Robert G. Mason; Senior Text Editor: Diana Hirsh; Assistant Art Director: Arnold C. Holeywell; Assistant Chief of Research: Carolyn L. Sackett; Assistant Director of Photography: Dolores A. Littles; Production Editor: Douglas B. Graham; Operations Manager: Gennaro C. Esposito, Gordon E. Buck (assistant); Assistant Production Editor: Feliciano Madrid; Quality Control: Robert L. Young (director), James J. Cox (assistant), Michael G. Wight (associate); Art Coordinator: Anne B. Landry; Copy Staff: Susan B. Galloway (chief), Tonna Gibert, Ricki Tarlow, Celia Beattie; Picture Department: Alvin Ferrell; Traffic: Jeanne Potter

Chairman: Joan D. Manley; President: John D. McSweeney; Executive Vice Presidents: Carl G. Jaeger, John Steven Maxwell, David J. Walsh; Vice Presidents: Nicholas Benton (public relations), John L. Canova (sales), Nicholas J. C. Ingleton (Asia), James L. Mercer (Europe/South Pacific), Herbert Sorkin (production), Paul R. Stewart (promotion), Peter G. Barnes; Personnel Director: Beatrice T. Dobie; Consumer Affairs Director: Carol Flaumenhaft; Comptroller: George Artandi

THE GOOD COOK

The original version of this book was created in London for Time-Life International (Nederland) B.V.
European Editor: Kit van Tulleken; Design Director: Louis Klein; Photography Director: Pamela Marke; Chief of Research: Vanessa Kramer; Text Director: Simon Rigge (acting); Chief Designer: Graham Davis; Chief Sub-Editor: Ilse Gray; Production Editor: Ellen Brush

Staff for Soups: Series Editor: Windsor Chorlton; Series Designer: Douglas Whitworth; Series Co-ordinator: Liz Timothy; Text Editor: Marguerite Tarrant; Anthology Editor: Markie Benet; Staff Writers: Gillian Boucher, Norman Kolpas; Researcher: Sally Crawford; Sub-Editors: Jay Ferguson, Nicoletta Flessati, Katie Lloyd; Permissions Researcher: Mary-Claire Hailey; Design Assistants: Mary Staples, Adrian Saunders; Editorial Department: Anetha Bessidone, Pat Boag, Debra Dick, Don Fragale, Philip Garner, Margaret Hall, Joanne Holland, Molly Sutherland, Julia West

U.S. Editorial Staff for Soups: Series Editor: Gerry Schremp; Picture Editor: Adrian Allen; Text Editor: Ellen Phillips; Designer: Peg Schreiber; Chief Researcher: Juanita James Wilson; Researchers: Christine Bowie Dove, Eleanor Kask; Art Assistant: Cynthia Richardson; Editorial Assistants: Audrey Keir, Patricia Kim

CHIEF SERIES CONSULTANT

Richard Olney is an American who has lived and worked since 1951 in France, where he is a highly regarded authority on food and wine. A regular contributor to such influential journals as *La Revue du Vin de France* and *Cuisine et Vins de France*, he also has written numerous articles for other gastronomic magazines in France and the United States, and is the author of *The French Menu Cookbook* and the award-winning *Simple French Food*. He has directed cooking courses in France and the United States, and is a member of several distinguished gastronomic societies, including La Confrérie des Chevaliers du Tastevin, La Commanderie du Bontemps de Médoc et des Graves and Les Amitiés Gastronomiques Internationales. Working in London with the series editorial staff, he has been basically responsible for the step-by-step photographic sequences in the techniques section of this volume and has supervised the final selection of recipes submitted by other consultants. The United States edition of *The Good Cook* has been revised by the Editors of Time-Life Books to bring it into complete accord with American customs and usage.

CHIEF AMERICAN CONSULTANT

Carol Cutler, who lives in Washington, D.C., is the author of the award-winning *The Six-Minute Soufflé and Other Culinary Delights*, as well as *Haute Cuisine for Your Heart's Delight*, a volume directed at those requiring low cholesterol diets. She is a contributing editor to *The International Review of Food & Wine* and *Working Woman* magazines, and frequently lectures about food and demonstrates cooking techniques.

PHOTOGRAPHERS

Alan Duns was born in 1943 in the north of England and studied at the Ealing School of Photography. He specializes in food, and has contributed to major British publications.
Aldo Tutino, a native of Italy, has worked in Milan, New York City and Washington, D.C. He has won a number of awards from the New York Advertising Club.

INTERNATIONAL CONSULTANTS

GREAT BRITAIN: *Jane Grigson* has written several books about food and has been a cookery correspondent for the London *Observer* since 1968. FRANCE: *Michel Lemonnier*, co-founder and vice president of Les Amitiés Gastronomiques Internationales, is a frequent lecturer on wine and vineyards. GERMANY: *Jochen Kuchenbecker* trained as a chef, but has worked for 10 years as a food photographer in several European countries. *Anne Brakemeirer* is the co-author of three cookbooks. THE NETHERLANDS: *Hugh Jans* has published two cookbooks and his recipes appear in a number of Dutch magazines. THE UNITED STATES: *François Dionot*, a graduate of L'École des Hôteliers de Lausanne in Switzerland, has worked as chef, hotel general manager and restaurant manager in France and the U.S. He now conducts his own cooking school. *José Wilson*, a former food editor of *House & Garden* magazine, has written many books on food and interior decoration.

Correspondents: Elisabeth Kraemer (Bonn); Margot Hapgood, Dorothy Bacon, Lesley Coleman (London); Susan Jonas, Lucy T. Voulgaris (New York); Maria Vincenza Aloisi, Josephine du Brusle (Paris); Ann Natanson (Rome).
Valuable assistance was also provided by: Jeanne Buys (Amsterdam); Hans-Heinrich Wellmann, Gertraud Bellon (Hamburg); Diane Asselin (Los Angeles); Bona Schmid, Maria Teresa Marenco (Milan); Carolyn T. Chubet, Miriam Hsia (New York); Michèle le Baube (Paris); Mimi Murphy (Rome).

For information about any Time-Life book, please write:
Reader Information, Time-Life Books
541 North Fairbanks Court, Chicago, Illinois 60611

Library of Congress CIP data, page 175.

CONTENTS

Cuisine's Kindest Course

Originally, soup was basic sustenance—a daily pot of warming nourishment that brought the family together in communion around the hearth where it was made. Soup was a meal in itself; and although nowadays it is more often served in small quantity as a first course, soup continues to represent the main body of a meal for many people. It may be a kidney-bean soup, a meaty Scotch broth, a vegetable-laden garbure, or a seafood chowder; or it may be the primordial soup for which there can be no recipe—a blend of foods chosen with common sense and a bit of discretion from whatever may be in the larder and the garden.

In its etymology and popular usage from one tongue to another, the word "soup" gives insights into the way our eating habits have evolved. The word itself derives from the Germanic "sop"—originally, the bread over which a pottage, broth or other liquid was poured. "Sup" and "supper" are related words; no doubt, in the rural tradition of comfortable but unsophisticated eating, a sop moistened with a broth represented the archetypal evening meal. In some regions of France, *la soupe* still refers to the crust of bread with which the liquid—*le potage*—is served. Indeed, bread is an inseparable accompaniment to soups: "... *et trempez votre soupe*" are the words that end many a soup recipe in French cookbooks, both old and recent. Literally, they mean "and moisten your soup," but in fact they mean "and pour the soup over your bread." The phrase is an incantation: it entreats one never to forget the sacred role of bread; it reminds one of the criminality of waste, of the luxury of being able to take pleasure in simple things; and it embodies ritual, which in cooking, as in all things, magnifies meaning and pleasure.

Although more sophisticated concepts of dining have altered the role of soup, the memory of soup as basic nourishment still lingers in the popular tongue. "Soup's on!", a familiar cry to American ears, means that the meal is ready to be served. Similarly, a French mother remonstrates with a child who dawdles over his food by saying, *"Mange ta soupe!"* Professional cooks in France speak affectionately of members of their trade as *marchands de soupes*—"soup peddlers."

Restaurant chefs, in fact, have particular cause to acknowledge the culinary influence of soups. The first eating establishment to be called a restaurant was opened by a Parisian soup vendor, M. Boulanger, in 1765, and served soups exclusively. The establishment, and all its successors, took its name from a motto inscribed in Latin above the entrance: *Venite ad me omnes qui stomacho laboratis et ego restaurabo*—"Come to me all of you whose stomachs cry out and I will restore you."

Now, as then, the restorative powers of soup are justly praised. Louis P. De Gouy, a European chef who worked in the United States during the first half of this century, sums up the appeal of soup in *The Soup Book,* published in 1949. "Soup is cuisine's kindest course," De Gouy wrote. "It breathes reassurance; it steams consolation; after a weary day it promotes sociability . . . there is nothing like a bowl of hot soup, its wisp of aromatic steam making the nostrils quiver with anticipation."

Although soups are part of the foundations of our cooking traditions, they are not always treated in today's kitchens with the respect they deserve. Many cooks, seduced by the plethora of canned, packaged and dehydrated products that pass under the guise of soup, have forgotten how delicious the real thing is. But anyone who can cut up a vegetable can make a soup in only a little more time than it takes to open a can and heat the contents. A perfect example is the leek and potato soup demonstrated on page 40: it is ready to serve 20 minutes after the water has been put on to boil. The fact is that fresh vegetables cooked in clean water count among the sublime things in this world; only a crust of bread and a last-minute dab of sweet, fresh butter are required for such a soup to be just as much at home at a formal dinner as it was in the farmhouse kitchen where it originated.

This volume starts with the premise that soups are the most versatile and variable item on the menu. Served hot, they will banish the cold on a winter evening; served chilled, they refresh the palate on a summer afternoon. They can be made with every category of food—meats, poultry, fish, fruits and vegetables. And they encourage the cook to experiment with the entire range of herbs, spices and seasonings.

The techniques that are demonstrated on the following pages will teach you how to explore all of these possibilities, and they will enable you to execute all of the recipes in the anthology that makes up the second half of the book. The recipes presented here include the best soups from more than two dozen national cuisines; among them, they provide both an introduction and a guide to an elemental aspect of cookery.

Broth, bouillon, stock and consommé

Most of the names by which different types of soup are known date only from the mid-19th Century and are frequently misapplied. In particular, a murky confusion surrounding the terms broth, bouillon, stock and consommé has led many people to believe that each must be different from the others. In fact, so far as mode of preparation is concerned, they are all one and the same thing: any differences among them reside in their respective roles and strength of flavor.

A broth is a clear, savory essence drawn from a combination of meats, aromatic vegetables and herbs that are simmered in water and then strained out when they have yielded their flavors. A broth makes a delicious soup in its own right and it can also be used as the moistening agent in other soups. Bouillon is merely the French word for broth.

The predominant flavor of a broth may come from beef, chicken, game, vegetables or fish; but for all general purposes, a broth is made with beef—frequently supplemented with chicken, and sometimes with veal as well. Chicken contributes a soft—almost sweet—flavor that, in effect, mellows the robustness of the beef; and mild-tasting but gelatinous veal lends some body to the finished, fragrant liquid.

Stocks—aptly named *fonds de cuisine,* meaning "foundations of cooking"—are made in the same way as broths. A stock is, however, meant to serve as a braising medium or a sauce base; it should give richness and body to a dish without masking the flavors of the basic ingredients. Stocks, therefore, are much more gelatinous than broths and somewhat less assertive in flavor. Since the flavors of beef or chicken would tend to overpower those of other ingredients, a stock might well be made with veal cuts only.

Stocks of this type are called *fonds blancs* because of their pale color. For certain dishes you may prefer a richer, deeper-colored liquid: a brown stock, or *fond brun.* To make it, simply brown the meat, bones and vegetables in the oven, as described on pages 46-47, before adding the water and simmering them. Browning caramelizes the vegetable and meat juices, which then add richness and color to the finished stock.

Definitions are necessary for a precise understanding of broth and stock, but they apply more to the world of highly refined restaurant cooking than to the practical demands of day-to-day living. The prototypal broth is that furnished by a pot-au-feu *(recipe, page 156),* a whole-meal soup that Auguste Escoffier praised as a "comfortable and thoroughly bourgeois dish that nothing may unseat." The meats used for pot-au-feu do not surrender all their flavor; they are served as a main course after the broth. And any broth that is left over from the meal may be saved and used to make another soup.

A consommé is a consummate, or perfectly prepared, beef broth: it should be richly flavored and completely clear. It is made with the same ingredients as a basic broth, but its flavor may be intensified by simmering the meats in a previously prepared broth rather than in water; in that case, it qualifies for the title of "double consommé." And whereas a few pearls of fat glistening on the surface of a pot-au-feu are in keeping with the homely nature of the dish, a consommé must be cleansed of every trace of fat. In addition, it should be only delicately gelatinous and perfectly limpid.

Many old cookbooks, and more than a few modern ones, insist that a consommé will not be perfectly translucent unless it is clarified by simmering in it egg whites and finely chopped beef and vegetables. These ingredients attract the tiny particles that may cloud a broth, and are strained out after simmering. Clarification has disadvantages, however. Even though the chopped meats and vegetables are added in the interest of great-er succulence, a consommé's initial delicacy of flavor is always lost in the process.

In fact, clarification is not necessary to convert a basic broth into a consommé. A faultlessly clear consommé can be produced simply by taking care when cooking. The meats and carcasses for a broth are placed on a rack to keep them from sticking on the bottom of the pot; they are covered with cold water and brought very slowly to a boil; the liquid is skimmed repeatedly to remove all traces of scum before the aromatic elements are added, then skimmed again after they are added. The heat is adjusted precisely so that, with the lid kept always ajar, the surface of the liquid barely trembles, never quite reaching a simmer.

Nevertheless, accidents do occur: a moment of inattention, or a well-meaning guest who sees the lid of the pot ajar and places it squarely on the pot, may produce a rolling boil and a muddy broth. The resulting liquid may serve passably as a stock, but it must be clarified after all if it is to be represented as a consommé. Accordingly, the technique of clarifying is demonstrated in this book. However, to underline the importance of avoiding the technique when it is not a necessity, clarifying is not presented in the demonstration of a basic broth *(pages 10-11),* but in the demonstration of a jellied madrilène *(pages 64-65),* a chilled consommé that is clarified to remove the tomato pulp that gives the soup its distinctive hue.

A crystalline consommé, unlike a basic broth, is not poured over bread crusts. It is a symbol of elegance and is garnished accordingly. It may be enlivened by jet-black wedges of truffle, pastel-colored custards or a filigree of chervil leaves—or by any of the hundreds of other classic garnish combinations, many named in honor of celebrities. La Belle Otéro, a celebrated turn-of-the-century music-hall artist, has been immortalized by the addition of frogs' legs, rice and little peas to her consommé. Her contemporary and rival, lovely Polaire, received a raw egg in her consommé. George Washington's memory has been rather amusingly honored in the form of a garnish of diced skin of calf's cheek and a truffle julienne.

An expanded vocabulary for soups

In addition to clear broths, there are thick or opaque soups (which may, of course, incorporate broth as a moistening agent). The categories within this larger group are often named for the way they are made. Purées, for example, whether based on vegetables, poultry or fish, are reduced to a uniform consistency by a sieve, a food mill, a blender or a food processor.

Cream soups are simply purées with cream added; if the main ingredient is shellfish, however, such a soup may be called a bisque—a term that was originally applied to game and poultry soups in addition to those made from shellfish. Veloutés, from the French word for velvet, are based—like a velouté sauce—on a broth thickened with flour, and they are enriched with egg yolks and cream.

In this volume, the term compound broth is given to soups in which solid ingredients are cut into pieces and served with the liquid. Included in this category are Scotch broth, minestrone, chowders and other soups that are akin to stews.

Bread soups, or panades—the latter name derives from the

French word for bread—form a category of soups that use bread not just as a garnish or for supplementary thickening, but as a central ingredient.

Many of the compound broths and some of the panades are nourishing enough to make meals in themselves. However, in this volume the term full-meal soup is reserved for preparations—such as *poule au pot,* garbure and borscht—that provide two courses from a single pot: a broth and a meat or fish course. All of the soups in this group share the simple yet bountiful spirit of a pot-au-feu.

In praise of simplicity

On the whole, soup-making is a relaxed process mercifully free of rules and dictums. A broth that is correctly set to simmer needs only to be left undisturbed; it will tend to itself. Indeed, many a soup has been ruined in the name of improvement.

Vegetable soups, in particular, are the victims of unnecessary refinements; the traditional belief that vegetables should be precooked in fat and simmered in beef broth has been responsible for masking and altering many a fresh garden flavor.

Another familiar mistake is salting and peppering a soup at the beginning of cooking. Common sense dictates caution when you are adding salt: an amount that seems barely sufficient to season a full pot may be far too much when the liquid has reduced by the end of cooking. And pepper should never be added at the start of *any* long cooking process. When it is freshly ground into a soup at the last moment, its clean, spicy perfume enhances the flavor of the other ingredients; but if pepper is cooked in the liquid for any length of time, its perfume dissipates and its taste becomes harsh and acrid.

A well-beloved overture

"Soup is to dinner what the portico or the peristyle is to an edifice. That is to say, not only is it the first part, but it should be conceived in such a way as to give an exact idea of the feast, very nearly as the overture to an opera should announce the quality of the whole work." The author of these words was Alexandre-Balthazar-Laurent Grimod de la Reynière, a 19th Century French lawyer who spent his life pleading the case for intelligent and enlightened gastronomy.

Not everybody agreed with de la Reynière's assessment. Another contemporary, the Marquis de Cussy, aide to Napoleon I, acknowledged that soup was the preface to dinner, but noted that a good work can do without a preface. When the great chef

Antonin Carême heard of this attack, he replied, with some puzzlement, "Why should the Marquis de Cussy wage war on soup? I cannot understand a dinner without it. I hold soup to be the well-beloved of the stomach."

During the lifetimes of these luminaries, the structure of a menu was, to say the least, an "edifice" of astounding complexity, often made up of more than a dozen courses. But Grimod de la Reynière's message is nonetheless relevant to the simpler menus of today. Imagine the cacophony if one were to follow a truffled consommé with a pot of Boston baked beans, or to precede a delicate turbot in champagne with a garlic-flavored *soupe au pistou*. And consider the dullness were a macaroni gratin to follow upon the heels of a pasta-laden minestrone.

Auguste Escoffier cites Grimod de la Reynière in *Le Guide Culinaire* and goes on to comment: "We agree with the illustrious gastronome. . . . Of all the elements that compose a menu, soups are those that demand the severest attention and the most delicate perfection, for the success of the rest of the dinner depends largely on the impression, good or bad, that they have produced on the guest." This is not to suggest that you may be careless in the preparation of other courses, but it is a psychological certainty that a brilliant opener will make your guests eager for the meal to come.

Not to forget the wine

Soup and wine are rarely associated. Most people hold the idea that a liquid should not accompany another liquid. If you believe, however, that one of the precepts of civilized dining is that one's guests' glasses should never be empty, there is no reason why you should not serve a wine with the soup course. If champagne or a dry white wine has been served as an apéritif, it is logical to continue the same service with most soups; if wine has not been served as an apéritif, the first wine planned on the menu may be served with the soup.

Consommés (in particular, game consommés) often are perfumed at the last moment by the addition of a few drops of fortified wine—perhaps a fine, dry, old sherry. In such a case, a glass of the wine used to flavor the soup would be the most appropriate accompaniment.

Most of the full-meal soups are rustic in spirit and robust in flavor; young and uncomplicated, but assertive, wines—such as a Crozes-Hermitage, Petite Sirah, or Valpolicella—are most comfortable in their presence. The exuberant and garlicky Mediterranean full-meal fish soups are usually accompanied by a dry white or rosé wine; but a cool, young red wine—Côtes-du-Rhône, Gamay, Chianti or Zinfandel, for example—will be as complementary. Most white wines would be annihilated by a garbure: a rough, country red wine is the best choice in this instance—a Gigondas, perhaps, or a Rioja. A *poule au pot* is equally at home with a sumptuous Chardonnay, a six-month-old Beaujolais or a venerable Bordeaux from one of the great vineyards of the Médoc.

These wines are suggestions only. As in all things associated with the table, make your decisions after you have judged with your own palate—and always be wary of rules, be they imposed by tradition or by today's prevailing culinary fashions.

Foundations for Good Soups

There is no mystery attached to the making of broths. The basic method is the same, whether you make the broth with meat, poultry, vegetables or fish: simply simmer the ingredients in water until they have yielded their flavors to the liquid. In each case, the fragrant broth that is produced can either be served as a soup in its own right or it can be used as the foundation of another soup.

Indeed, broths are so fundamental to soup making that you should choose only the best ingredients and exercise scrupulous care in their preparation. The ingredients for a meat broth (below, left; recipe, page 163) should contribute a mellow flavor and a smooth body to the liquid. The main ingredient must be a cut of stewing beef, such as chuck, which has

flavor to spare and enough natural gelatin to enrich the broth. Additional flavor and gelatin can be provided by a leftover chicken carcass, either raw or cooked, some chicken trimmings, a rolled veal breast, and/or a meaty veal shank. Some recipes call for beef bones, but these add little extra flavor or gelatin and take up valuable space in the cooking pot.

Aromatic vegetables and a mixture of herbs round out the flavor of the broth. The proportion of vegetables to meat is a matter of choice. Some cooks add a single carrot and an onion for discreet aromatic support; others prefer the fuller flavor and perceptible edge of sweetness that are contributed by additional vegetables. If you wish to add garlic to the broth, use unpeeled cloves or an unpeeled bulb; peeled garlic cloves cook to a purée that would cloud the broth.

To perfume the liquid, use an onion stuck with two or three whole cloves and add the classic herb combination of bay leaf, fresh parsley and thyme. Since the liquid is strained after cooking, you can leave the herbs loose. But for easy retrieval, you should wrap them in cheesecloth or tie them in a celery rib or leek leaves to form a bouquet garni.

To make a chicken broth (center, left; recipe, page 164), replace the mixture of meats with a trussed stewing chicken; a young roasting chicken lacks both the flavor and the gelatin of an older bird. A vegetable broth (center, right; recipe, page 164) includes the usual aromatic vegetables, but is supplemented by leafy vegetables, such as lettuce and cabbage, for extra flavor. Chop or slice the vegeta-

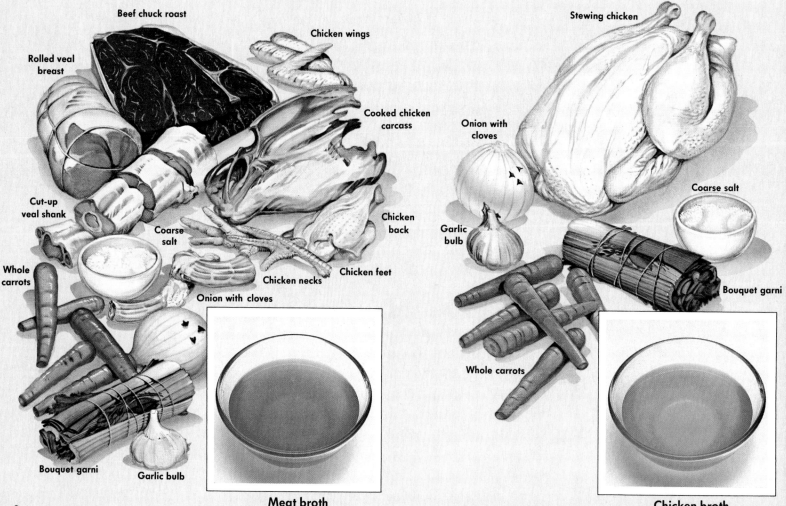

Beef chuck roast
Chicken wings
Rolled veal breast
Cooked chicken carcass
Cut-up veal shank
Coarse salt
Chicken back
Whole carrots
Chicken necks
Chicken feet
Onion with cloves
Bouquet garni
Garlic bulb

Meat broth

Stewing chicken
Onion with cloves
Coarse salt
Garlic bulb
Bouquet garni
Whole carrots

Chicken broth

bles so that they will yield the maximum flavor in a relatively short cooking time.

A fish broth (right; recipe, page 164) derives most of its flavor from the carcasses and trimmings of lean fish. The finished liquid will be less clear than a meat or vegetable broth. And, because fish yield much less gelatin than meat, a fish broth will have less body than meat broth. Supplement the basic herbs with chopped fennel leaves; the anise flavor goes especially well with fish.

The technique of preparing broths is demonstrated overleaf, using meat broth as an example; cooking chicken, vegetable and fish broths differs only in detail. In each case, make the broth in a heavy pan that will hold the ingredients snugly—an oval one is best for a whole fowl. Since the aim is to produce a broth rich in flavor, add only as much water as necessary to the pot; the closely packed ingredients should be covered by no more than about 1½ inches [4 cm.].

When meat is heated in water, it releases albuminous particles of protein that will cloud the broth if they are not removed. The water should therefore be heated very slowly to draw out the impurities; they will form a scum on the surface and can then be spooned off. Only after this skimming process is completed are the aromatic vegetables added: if they were included at the beginning of cooking, they would float to the surface of the liquid and interfere with skimming.

All broths are cooked at a bare simmer: boiling would cause the solid ingredients to disintegrate and muddy the liquid. During the first 30 minutes of cooking, look at the broth frequently and adjust the heat, if necessary, in order to prevent the broth from boiling too vigorously.

Once a simmer has been established, 5 to 6 hours of cooking are required to draw out the flavor of the meat. You can, however, make a meat broth in little more than an hour if you cut up the ingredients in fine pieces, as shown on page 10. A chicken broth should simmer for 1½ to 3 hours, depending on the age of the bird. Only 30 to 40 minutes' cooking is needed for a vegetable or fish broth; longer cooking would not draw much more flavor from the fish or vegetables.

After the cooking, the solids will be drained of flavor and should be discarded. You can, however, produce both a broth and a main course (pages 76-77) by poaching meat or chicken just long enough to flavor the liquid lightly.

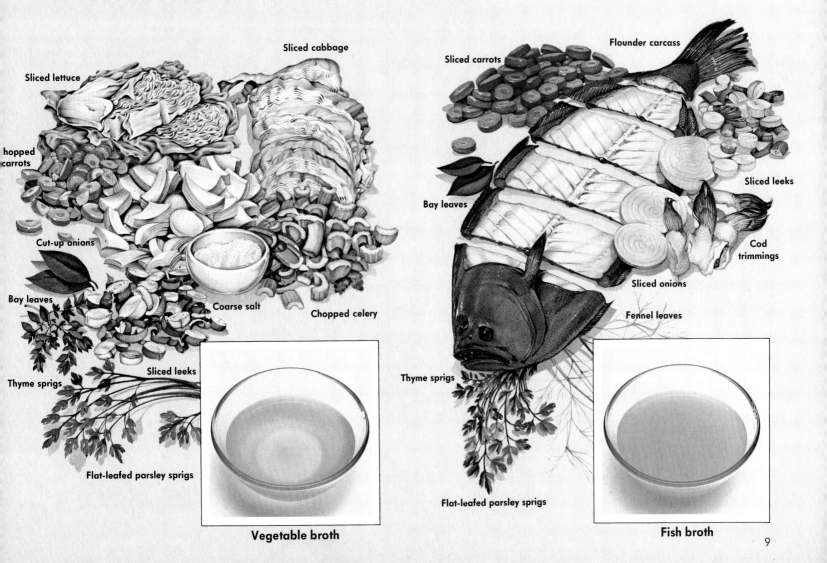

Sliced cabbage

Sliced lettuce

hopped carrots

Cut-up onions

Bay leaves

Coarse salt

Chopped celery

Thyme sprigs

Sliced leeks

Flat-leafed parsley sprigs

Vegetable broth

Sliced carrots

Flounder carcass

Bay leaves

Sliced leeks

Cod trimmings

Sliced onions

Thyme sprigs

Fennel leaves

Flat-leafed parsley sprigs

Fish broth

A Classic Meat Broth Rich in Flavor

1 **Packing the pot.** To prevent the meats from sticking, set a wire rack or a trivet in the pot. Add the bony pieces first — in this instance, a cooked chicken carcass and a cut-up veal shank. Pack in the meaty cuts — here, beef chuck and rolled veal breast. Then insert the small pieces — chicken feet, necks and such. Add cold water just to cover.

2 **Cleansing the liquid.** To encourage the meat to release albuminous scum, heat the water very slowly without stirring it; the water should take an hour or more to reach a boil. Using a ladle — preferably one with a shallow, tapered bowl *(above, left)* — remove the grayish scum as it collects on the surface while the water heats. When the liquid boils, pour in a cup or so of cold water *(center)* to encourage more scum to rise. Ladle off the cleaner scum that forms as the liquid returns to a boil *(right)*. Repeat until only a white froth forms on the surface.

A Shortcut Made by Chopping

The finer you cut meat and vegetables, the more surface area you expose and the more quickly those meats and vegetables will yield their flavors to a liquid. When ingredients are prepared in this way, broth *(recipe, page 89)* can be finished in only 1 hour.

Because fine-chopped meat will absorb the coagulated albumin particles that a rapid broth releases, the broth does not require scumming. Simply stir the broth as it heats up to keep the meat pieces separated; this allows the released albumin to cling to one of their many cut surfaces. When the broth is strained, the albumin will be filtered out with the meat.

The flavor of the broth is good and fresh. But because it is made without bones and trimmings, which require long cooking to release their gelatin, a rapid broth will be much lighter in body than the classic version shown above.

1 **Assembling the ingredients.** Cut up aromatic vegetables — in this demonstration, carrots and leeks. Finely chop or grind lean stew beef. If you prefer, ask the butcher to grind the meat for you, but be wary of already ground beef: it can be very fatty.

2 **Bringing to a boil.** Put the meat and vegetables in a pan and cover them with cold water. Add a little salt. Slowly heat the water, stirring to separate the bits of meat. Stop stirring when the water approaches a boil: any further stirring would cloud the liquid.

3 **Adding the vegetables.** Tuck in the vegetables: an onion stuck with three whole cloves, carrots, an unpeeled garlic bulb and a bouquet garni are used here. Salt very lightly, and remove any fresh scum that rises from the vegetables as the liquid returns to a boil. Partly cover the pan so that steam cannot build up and overheat the broth.

4 **Cooking and straining.** Simmer the broth gently for 5 to 6 hours without disturbing it; stirring would release protein and mineral particles that could cloud the broth. Double a large piece of muslin or cheesecloth and dampen it so that it will hold back fat. Line a colander with the fabric, then strain the broth into a bowl. Discard the solids.

5 **Removing the fat.** Let the broth cool to room temperature. If you want to use the broth immediately, blot up the remaining liquid fat from the surface by touching the globules lightly with a folded paper towel. If you do not intend to use the broth the same day, refrigerate it and spoon off the fat when it solidifies on the surface.

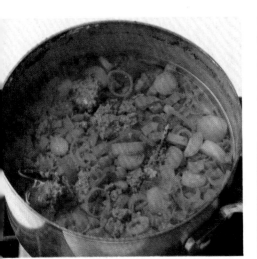

3 **Cooking the broth.** Partly cover the pan and adjust the heat so that the liquid simmers gently. Allow the broth to cook, undisturbed, for 1 hour. By the end of that time, the liquid should be completely clear (above).

4 **Straining.** Pour the broth into a bowl through a colander or strainer lined with a double layer of damp muslin or cheesecloth. Remove any fat from the surface of the broth (above, Step 5).

Neat Packages for Freezing

Freezing in bags. You may find it convenient to make large quantities of broth and freeze part of it. The easiest way to store broth is in plastic storage bags. Stretch the top of each bag over a straight-sided container; then ladle in 2 cups [½ liter] of broth. Keep the tied-up bag in the container until the broth freezes. To thaw, place the bag in a pan of warm water or under warm running water until the broth melts.

Diverse Ways to Embellish a Soup

As far as presentation is concerned, soup gives the cook a fine opportunity: a flat, shimmering surface that can be treated as a painter's canvas. That is why garnishes—those edible extras added to a soup before it is served—receive so much attention from professional chefs.

Almost any food, given the right preliminary treatment, can float on or in a soup. Among the many choices described on the following pages and later in this volume are vegetables and herbs; starches such as bread, pasta and dumplings; eggs; and spicy sauces. The challenge is to provide each soup with a garnish that offers a clear but complementary contrast in texture, taste or color without overwhelming the soup itself. The best guide is the cook's own imagination—directed by a few common-sense principles.

Flavor is the primary consideration, as illustrated by the simplest garnishes of all: chopped fresh herbs. These add little in the way of texture or body to a soup; they are there simply to provide flavor and color. Herbs can grace almost every soup, from a clear broth to a hearty garbure *(pages 82-83)*, but they must be used with discretion and chosen to complement the soup's primary ingredients.

Fennel, for example, is often used in cooking fish; its faint anise taste also complements a fish soup. Similarly, dill is a fine addition to a cucumber soup, but its sour-sweet flavor would be set off just as well by soups based on other traditional companions to the herb: a salmon bisque, for example. Basil, long used to flavor summer vegetables, will improve almost any vegetable soup, especially a tomato purée, where its green leaves provide a striking contrast to the red liquid.

With garnishes other than herbs, considerations become more complex. Vegetables, for example, lend not only flavor and color but also texture and—in some cases—body to a soup. Crisp, thinly cut vegetables give a delicate finish to a consommé, as shown below, without clouding the liquid. For another approach, a vegetable garnish can echo the flavor of a soup based on the same vegetable while providing a contrast in texture. A rich carrot purée, for example, is often topped by crisp julienne of raw carrot; a pear-and-watercress soup *(page 72)* will be enhanced by fresh sprigs of watercress.

A garnish should stand out clearly against its background, which is why vegetables, with their distinctive textures, are best suited to soups such as purées and consommés, which are essentially homogenous liquids. There would be little point in using carrots or onions to decorate a compound broth in which onions and carrots already float.

The same principles apply to garnishes based on starches or eggs; for contrast, these rich foods usually enhance light soups. Egg garnishes, for example, are almost always reserved for clear broths such as the consommé shown below, or for the broth from a whole-meal soup when it is served as a first course *(pages 76-77)*. A soft egg garnish would be lost in a thick cream soup and also would make the soup far too rich. Similarly, most pastas add too much starch to thick soups; pastas are best displayed in broths or in meat-and-vegetable soups that contain little starch themselves.

As a general rule, then, the more complex the garnish is, the simpler the soup should be. There are exceptions, however: for a grand occasion, the tiny, feathery, fish or meat dumplings called quenelles *(page 20)* can float on creamy purées based on the same ingredients.

The occasion when a soup is served should never be forgotten when choosing its garnish. A plain, hearty pea soup served for a Sunday-night supper deserves a plain, hearty garnish: toasted bread, for example, or croutons *(page 21)*. A consommé can be simply enhanced with a poached egg; or, for a more elegant effect, the egg might be turned into a meringue or a custard *(pages 14-15)*. The purpose of a garnish, after all, is to provide style as well as substance.

Pasta. Filled with ricotta cheese, spinach and egg yolks, these elaborate cases of pasta—known as tortellini or cappelletti—are a filling garnish that also attracts attention to the savory consommé beneath.

Julienned vegetables and meat. Cut into thin strips, lettuce, chicken, pepper and snow peas float in consommé with sliced mushrooms; they enhance its delicate flavor and bring a touch of crispness to it.

Egg. Poached separately and trimmed into a neat oval, an egg floats in solitary splendor on the steaming broth. When the egg is broken, its liquid yolk will enrich the soup without altering its subtle flavor.

Vegetables: Adding Colors and Textures

Julienne and Brunoise

1 Cutting. Thinly slice peeled root vegetables—here, carrots and turnips. For julienne, cut stacked slices into narrow strips. For *brunoise (right)*, cut the strips into cubes.

2 Parboiling. Drop the cut-up vegetables into boiling water or broth; let them cook about 1 minute, drain them and plunge them into cold water. Drain thoroughly.

A Vegetable Medley

1 Slicing. Trim the vegetables into small, even pieces. In this case, carrots, green beans, onions and peeled, seeded tomatoes are cut to the size of shelled peas.

2 Cooking. Leave the tomatoes raw. Parboil each firm vegetable in a strainer lowered into boiling water for 1 minute. Plunge the strainer into cold water and drain.

Whether vegetables are used singly or in combination to garnish a soup, the principles of preparation remain the same: the vegetables must be trimmed and—if necessary—cut into tiny pieces so that each spoonful of soup contains both vegetables and liquid.

Very small vegetables—peas or young snow peas, for example—may be left whole, of course. Green and wax beans should be cut into small cross sections. Asparagus and broccoli stalks should be peeled to prevent stringiness, and they, too, should be sliced crosswise. But leave the asparagus tips whole, and divide the broccoli heads into tiny florets. Leafy vegetables such as lettuce, spinach and sorrel *(shown below)* are sliced into thin ribbons known as chiffonade; the larger vegetables such as carrots, turnips and potatoes are cut either into narrow julienne or into the small cubes called *brunoise (left)*.

Almost all raw vegetables, except naturally soft tomatoes, require a brief parboiling before they can be served; doing so softens them slightly without removing their crispness. If the vegetables are to garnish a clear broth, they may be boiled in the broth itself, as shown below. If the soup to be garnished is a thick one such as a purée, parboil the vegetables separately in water, drain them thoroughly to avoid diluting the soup and add them just before serving.

Slicing a Chiffonade

1 Preparing leaves. Fold each sorrel leaf in half lengthwise, with the ridged stem outside. Pull the tough stem down the length of the leaf and discard it.

2 Slicing. Stack several trimmed leaves and roll them up lengthwise. For safety, curl your fingertips under. Slice across each roll at ¼-inch [6-mm.] intervals to make strips.

3 Softening the leaves. For a broth, drop the leaves into the boiling soup just before presenting it. For a purée, parboil the leaves in water for a few seconds and drain them.

A Sampler of Egg Toppings

Manifold as egg garnishes seem, they all depend for edibility on one rule: the cooking must be as gentle and as brief as possible; high temperatures and long exposure to heat produce rubbery results.

As long as the basic rule is kept in mind, though, beautiful garnishes can be made by the simplest techniques. A hard-boiled egg, for example, should have a firm—not tough—yellow yolk (*opposite, top left*). To produce that desirable result, simply cover a whole, room-temperature egg with cold water, bring the water just to a boil, immediately remove the pan from the heat and cover it. Let the egg stand for 15 minutes before plunging it into cold water to stop the cooking.

A perfectly poached egg—equally simple to make—has a still-liquid yolk completely wrapped in an oval of barely firm white (*below, top row*). For shapely results, buy freshly laid eggs at a shop that specializes in them and poach the eggs briefly in simmering—not boiling—water. You can store poached eggs in a bowl of ice water in the refrigerator for as long as 24 hours; reheat them in the soup just before serving.

The savory meringues called puffs are another poached garnish (*below, bottom row*). If the whites are to be beaten to stiffness, they must be at room temperature and they must not contain a trace of yolk. Whether the beating bowl is copper (this helps the whites hold air) or not, the bowl and all other utensils should be scrupulously clean and free of oil.

Threads of egg (*opposite, top right*) and savory custards, known in French as *royales* (*opposite, bottom*), require that you mix eggs with flour or with broth before cooking them—and then cook the mixture as gently as you would whole eggs or plain egg whites.

Secrets of Perfect Poaching

1 **Breaking.** To keep the yolk intact, break each egg into a saucer. Then slide the egg into a skillet containing 1½ inches [4 cm.] of simmering salted water.

2 **Shaping.** Immediately slide a large spoon under the egg and lift the white over the yolk to form a neat oval. Let the egg poach for 1 to 2 minutes or until the white becomes opaque.

3 **Trimming.** With a perforated spoon, transfer the poached egg to a bowl of cold water. Gently cut any ragged edges of white from the cooled egg.

Floating Savory Meringues

1 **Beating.** Using a circular, lifting motion, beat tepid egg whites with a whisk until a small amount stands up in a stiff peak when lifted on the whisk.

2 **Shaping.** Lift half a teaspoonful of egg white and, with another teaspoon, push it into a pan of simmering salted water. Quickly shape the rest of the whites; do not crowd the pan.

3 **Draining.** After about 3 minutes, the puffs will be firm. Lift each one with a perforated spoon or wire strainer and set it on a towel to drain.

Sieving the Yolks

Forming yellow grains. Use a spoon to press chilled hard-boiled egg yolk through a strainer (one with nonreactive stainless steel or nylon mesh) into a thoroughly dry bowl.

Pouring Golden Threads

1 **Making batter.** Break eggs into a bowl containing 1 to 2 tablespoons [15 to 30 ml.] of flour for each egg. Add salt. Beat the batter until smooth, then strain it to remove any membrane.

2 **Cooking.** Hold a perforated, stainless-steel spoon over a pan of simmering broth or water. Ladle batter into the spoon; fine streams will drip into the liquid and cook in 3 to 4 minutes.

Custards: An Elegant Touch

1 **Making custard.** Whisk yolks and whole eggs—3 yolks to each whole egg. Whisk in warm broth. Sieve this custard and divide it into batches.

2 **Flavoring.** Dilute puréed vegetables —tomatoes and peas are used here— with broth. Whisk each purée into a batch of custard, leaving one batch plain for contrast. Sieve the flavored mixtures.

3 **Baking.** Spoon the mixtures into buttered molds and set them in a pan on a wire rack. Pour hot water around the molds. Cover the pan and bake at 350° F. [180° C.] for 15 to 20 minutes.

4 **Unmolding.** Cool the custards in a shallow, ice-filled vessel. Run a small knife around the inside of each mold, then invert the mold over a plate and tap it sharply to turn out the custard.

5 **Cutting shapes.** Custards from small molds may be used as individual garnishes. Cut larger rectangular or square custards into strips or dice.

6 **Cutting fancy shapes.** To make decorative shapes for formal-dinner soups, use small cookie cutters or aspic cutters to stamp garnishes from larger slices of custard.

Pasta: Mixing, Shaping and Filling

Used from Italy to the Orient, pasta is a flour paste moistened with water or eggs that is cut into noodles, pressed into varied shapes or formed into packages to hold a stuffing. In some formulations oil is added for suppleness; in some, spinach or saffron is added for flavor and color.

Acceptable commercial pasta is widely available in dried form, as are fresh versions in ethnic markets. Commercial pasta should be made of durum-wheat flour—called *pura semolina* on Italian labels—to ensure that it will have the proper firm-but-tender texture.

Even the best commercial pasta, however, cannot match the homemade variety *(recipe, page 167)* in flavor and texture. It is made from flour mixed into eggs until the eggs have absorbed as much as they can hold: ¾ to 1 cup [175 to 250 ml.] of flour per egg. The crumbly paste thus formed is kneaded until it becomes smooth and elastic, then rolled and stretched paper-thin and, finally, cut into noodles or wrappers for stuffing.

The rolling, stretching and cutting can be done with a hand-cranked or an electric pasta machine, available at kitchen-equipment shops. Or you can make pasta by hand, provided you have a flat working space at least 2 feet [60 cm.] wide and 3 feet [90 cm.] long, in a cool place protected from drafts: heat and drafts encourage drying, and the dried-out pasta dough is too brittle to handle. For best control in rolling, use a wooden pastry pin at least 2½ feet [75 cm.] long. Cut pasta into strips or squares with a knife; to make tortellini—the packages stuffed with cheese and spinach shown opposite *(recipe, page 162)*—use a cookie cutter.

Before cutting hand-stretched pasta, dust its surface with semolina or cornmeal to keep the noodles from sticking together. As another precaution, ribbon-like noodles should dry for 5 minutes. To prevent cracking, however, tortellini should be shaped with moist dough; the packages will dry as you work.

The pasta can be cooked immediately; before adding it to soup, parboil it in large quantities of boiling salted water to prevent the cornmeal from clouding the broth. Or store the noodles in plastic bags; they will last a week in the refrigerator or several months in the freezer.

Handling the Basic Dough

1 **Mixing.** Make a well in a mound of all-purpose flour and put into it olive oil, beaten eggs and seasonings. Mix with your fingers to make a crumbly paste.

2 **Kneading.** Gather the dough into a ball, then flatten it by pressing it down and out with the heel of your hand. Form a ball and knead again until the dough is smooth and elastic.

3 **Rolling the dough.** To prevent sticking, lightly flour the work surface and the dough. With a pastry pin, roll out the dough into a large sheet about ⅛ inch [3 mm.] thick.

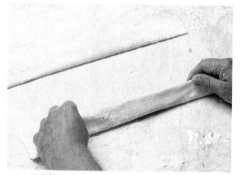

4 **Folding the dough.** Dust the top surface of the dough with cornmeal or semolina. Fold over 1½ inches [4 cm.] of dough on opposite sides of the sheet. Continue to fold in this way until both sides of the dough form a pair of tubes that meet in the center.

5 **Slicing noodles.** Slice across the tubes of dough with a sharp knife at ¼- to ½-inch [6-mm. to 1-cm.] intervals. To unfold the noodles, slip the blade of the knife into the middle of each folded slice and lift it.

6 **Precooking the noodles.** Drop the noodles into a large pot filled with rapidly boiling salted water. Let the water return to a boil and cook the noodles for 2 to 5 minutes—until they are only slightly resistant to the bite.

Preparing Stuffed Rings

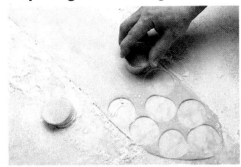

1 **Cutting rounds.** Roll out pasta dough *(opposite)*. Cut out 2¼- to 2½-inch [5½- to 6-cm.] circles with a cookie cutter or the rim of a glass, and stack the circles to limit air-drying.

2 **Stuffing.** Dab ½ teaspoon [2 ml.] of filling—in this case, spinach and cheese—on each circle. Moisten the edges of the circle, then fold it over the filling and pinch the ends to form a ring.

3 **Parboiling.** Drop the tortellini into a large pot of boiling salted water. After 4 or 5 minutes, lift them out with a wire strainer or perforated spoon and set them on paper towels to drain.

A Garnish from Central Europe

When thinned and lightened with milk or water, an egg-and-flour dough can be formed into the small, airy soup garnishes sometimes defined as pasta, and sometimes as dumplings. Popular in Germany and throughout Central Europe, this pasta is known in America as spaetzle *(recipe, page 160)*.

A spaetzle dough requires no kneading, stretching or rolling; making it is as simple as mixing a cake. Indeed, the mixture should have the consistency of a thick, gummy batter. It should cohere enough for the spaetzle to be malleable, but it should be light enough to produce a puffy result. Letting the dough rest for an hour or so after it is assembled will help ensure a tender finished product.

The spaetzle can be shaped in a variety of ways. Expert cooks use a sharp knife—repeatedly dipped in hot water to prevent sticking—to slice off minute bits of dough and drop them into simmering water or broth. Others use a spoon to press small amounts of dough through the holes of a colander. The easiest course, however, is to employ the inexpensive spaetzle-maker shown at right. Its base is a flat, perforated metal sheet. A small container for dough slides across the sheet, forcing just the right amount of dough through each hole to form the cylindrical spaetzle.

1 **Starting the dough.** Stir beaten eggs into all-purpose flour seasoned with nutmeg. Blend the ingredients until the mixture is smooth.

2 **Adjusting the texture.** Gradually stir in milk or water until the dough is very thick; when it is lifted on the spoon, the spaetzle dough should fall back into the bowl slowly in a thick ribbon.

3 **Shaping.** Set the spaetzle-maker over a pot of simmering water, pour dough into the container and slide the container across the flat base; spaetzle will drop into the water.

4 **Draining.** Cover the pot and cook the spaetzle for 5 to 8 minutes, until they rise to the surface of the liquid. Lift them out with a perforated spoon or strainer and drain them in a colander.

A Wide Choice of Dumplings

A soup dumpling mixture *(recipes, pages 160-162)* is either a batter based on a starch such as flour or matzo meal, or a purée based on potatoes, or on ground meat, fowl or seafood. The flavorings may be herbs, spices or aromatics; the enrichments may be butter, cream, marrow or even chicken fat. But all dumplings are bound together by eggs—or to ensure the lightest quenelles *(page 20)*, by egg whites—which swell airily during cooking. Starchy dumplings can be lightened by a leavening such as baking powder.

Any batter or purée—chilled so that the dumplings are easy to form—may be shaped in one of the ways shown here. To keep the dumplings light, however, work quickly so that the mixture does not soften, and handle the dumplings gently: a tightly packed dumpling cannot absorb the steam that should swell it.

Whether you poach the dumplings in water or soup, do not crowd the pan: the dumplings will stick together and cook unevenly. Keep the liquid at a simmer: high heat toughens the eggs. And cover the pot to trap the steam.

The dumplings will rise to the surface when finished; if you have cooked them in soup, serve it immediately to keep the dumplings from getting soggy. If you cook the dumplings separately in water, lift them out and drain on paper towels. Covered with plastic wrap, the dumplings will keep for as long as 3 hours.

Mashed Potatoes: Rolled and Cut

1 **Flavoring.** Into cooked, puréed potatoes mix a chopped onion that has been stewed in butter to soften it, plus chopped parsley and seasonings.

2 **Binding.** Stir in beaten eggs, then incorporate flour until the mixture is thick enough to shape. Chill the mixture for 1 hour in the refrigerator.

Chopped Marrow: Molded with a Spoon

1 **Removing the marrow.** With a sharp knife, pry the marrow from a beef or veal marrowbone sawed into 3- to 5-inch [8- to 13-cm.] lengths.

2 **Mixing.** Chop the marrow finely, and with your fingers mix in salt, nutmeg, chopped parsley, a raw egg and bread crumbs. Chill the mixture.

Ground Meat: Shaped by Hand

1 **Mixing.** Add chopped beef suet to ground meat—in this case, veal. Soak crustless white bread in milk for 10 minutes and squeeze out the excess milk.

2 **Enriching.** Add the bread to the meat and suet, then add chopped onions, eggs, nutmeg and a little cream. Mix the ingredients thoroughly.

3 **Pounding.** For the lightest dumplings, pound the mixture smooth in a mortar a little at a time. Or use first a food processor, then a sieve. Chill the mixture.

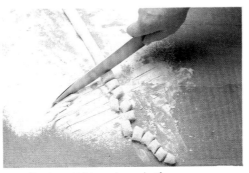

3 **Rolling.** On a floured surface, roll the mixture, a cupful at a time, into a sausage shape about 1 inch [2½ cm.] thick.

4 **Cutting.** With a sharp knife repeatedly dipped in hot water to prevent sticking, slice the rolls into dumplings 1 inch [2½ cm.] long.

5 **Cooking.** Add the dumplings to simmering liquid, cover and poach them for 10 minutes, until they float. Drain on paper towels before adding to soup.

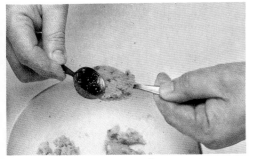

3 **Shaping.** With a pair of teaspoons repeatedly dipped in ice water to prevent sticking, shape oval dumplings and push each one onto a chilled, wet plate.

4 **Poaching.** Place the dumplings in simmering water, cover and poach for 10 minutes, or until they float.

5 **Draining.** Lift the dumplings from the pan with a perforated spoon or wire strainer. Add them to clear soup.

4 **Shaping.** Wet your hands. Roll a spoonful of the mixture between your palms to form a small ball. Place it on a plate of toasted bread crumbs.

5 **Coating.** When the plate is half-filled, shake it gently so that the dumplings roll around, picking up an even coating of crumbs.

6 **Poaching.** Lower the dumplings into simmering water and cover the pan. Cook for 10 minutes, until they float, and remove them with a perforated spoon.

Chicken Quenelles: Piped and Poached

1 **Pounding the flesh.** Trim raw meat, fish or poultry—chicken breasts, in this instance—of all skin, fat, bone and sinew, and cut it into small chunks. In a mortar, pound the chunks to a paste. Add egg whites and continue to pound until they have been incorporated.

2 **Sieving.** With a plastic scraper, gradually force the purée through a nylon-mesh drum sieve; scrape the purée from underneath the sieve. Place the purée in a metal bowl. Cover the bowl, set it in a larger, ice-filled bowl, and refrigerate it for 15 to 20 minutes.

3 **Adding cream.** Keep the bowl on ice and stir heavy cream into the purée. Spoon the mixture into a pastry bag equipped with a small tube or, as shown, into a cone made by rolling a sheet of parchment paper and cutting off the tip.

4 **Piping the quenelles.** Heavily coat the bottom of a large sauté pan or skillet with butter. Carefully squeeze the mixture from the open tip of the tube into the pan to pipe out tiny quenelles, shaped as you prefer.

5 **Adding water.** Pour boiling water into the pan until the quenelles are just covered. To avoid disturbing them, pour the water through a funnel held against the edge of the pan.

6 **Poaching.** Bring the water to a gentle simmer, cover the pan and poach the quenelles for 2 to 3 minutes, until they float to the surface. With a slotted spoon, lift and drain the quenelles, and reserve them on a warm, covered dish until they are needed.

Crisped Bread: A Universal Favorite

The bread that gives a soup an extra-hearty body should be full of flavor and very firm. For the right texture, choose a dense, homemade-type bread, either one you make yourself *(recipe, page 165)* or one you buy in a good bakery. (Commercially packaged breads are so soft they simply disintegrate in the liquid.) Crisp-crusted, white French or Italian breads make an excellent garnish; for variety of flavor and color, so do pumpernickel, rye and whole-wheat loaves.

Garnish bread should be stale and dry; very fresh bread is too absorbent to survive a dousing. If you must use fresh bread, dry it out by baking the slices on an ungreased baking sheet for 5 minutes in a preheated 325° F. [160° C.] oven.

For the crunchiest texture, bread garnishes usually are sautéed or toasted. And any number of other ingredients can be spread on the bread: butter or olive oil, if the bread has not already been sautéed in one or the other; freshly grated cheese, such as a Parmesan or Swiss that will melt smoothly; chopped fresh herbs; or puréed cooked vegetables. All will add special interest to both garnish and soup.

Cubes Fried in Butter

1 Cutting. Cut a loaf of bread into slices about ½ inch [1 cm.] thick and trim off the crusts. Cut each slice into strips and cut the strips into cubes.

2 Frying. Heat a little butter or oil in a frying pan and add the cubes. Fry them slowly until they are crisp, tossing occasionally for even browning.

Slices Flavored with Garlic and Olive Oil

1 Flavoring. Rub a peeled, sliced garlic clove over one side of French bread slices that have been toasted in the oven until they are golden.

2 Enriching. Dribble olive oil sparingly over the toast; to regulate the flow of oil, pour it from a bottle fitted with a slotted cork, as described on page 51.

Three Options from a French Loaf

Toasting bread. After slicing bread ¼ inch [6 mm.] thick, place the slices on an ungreased baking sheet and broil them for ½ minute per side, until they are golden.

Topping with cheese. Cut large, diagonal slices ¼ inch [6 mm.] thick. Brush each slice with melted butter, sprinkle with grated cheese and toast under the broiler.

Stuffing. Cut a loaf into thick slices and halve them. Hollow out each half, brush it with melted butter and fill it with puréed cooked vegetables, such as the carrots shown here.

1

Purées
Smooth Harmonies of Flavor

Characterized by a more or less uniform texture and a consistency like that of heavy cream, purée soups are made by breaking up solid ingredients into minuscule fragments that remain suspended in their cooking liquid. You can create smooth, rich purées—blends of cream with chicken, shellfish or asparagus, for example—to grace the most formal meal. Or you can make coarse-textured ones—such as the leek and potato soup illustrated on the opposite page—for family suppers.

Purées often include only one or two main ingredients presenting a single, dominant taste. If you add more ingredients, the flavors merge with one another, producing a soup of indeterminate origins. In addition to the main ingredient, purées include some liquid as well as an enrichment of butter or cream. If the main ingredient is a starch, one such as potatoes or beans, no further additions are required. Otherwise you must add a starchy element—flour or bread, for example—that will thicken the mixture and bind the solid ingredients in a stable suspension: without the starch, the purée would be thin and the solids would separate out from the liquid. As the chart on pages 36-37 shows, endless combinations of main ingredients, liquid, thickeners and enrichment are possible.

Coarse-textured purées may be produced with a masher, a mortar and pestle, or—more easily—a food mill. Fine-textured purées are made by pushing the ingredients through a strainer or sieve. A close-meshed sieve gives the smoothest result, since it not only breaks up solids into very small pieces but also holds back every scrap of fiber or membrane, such as the skin of peas. For easily discolored foods such as artichokes or celeriac, you will need a strainer or sieve with nylon or stainless-steel mesh; most metals would react with these vegetables, blackening them and giving them an acrid taste.

Food processors are invaluable for puréeing the resistant flesh of game birds and of mollusks—clams or scallops, for example. A food processor or blender can be used to make a fine or coarse purée, but the speed of these machines makes it difficult to control the soup's texture precisely. And the machines, like the food mill, do not eliminate fibers and membranes. To make a very smooth purée with a minimum of effort, however, first use a food processor, blender or food mill to break up the ingredients, then use a sieve to filter out any tough fragments.

Stirring in a chunk of butter adds a glossy finish to a purée of leeks and potatoes. The soup's granular texture is achieved by puréeing the cooked ingredients in a food mill; a smoother leek and potato soup, puréed through a strainer, is shown on pages 26-27.

Vegetables That Provide Their Own Thickener

When firm vegetables such as carrots, mature peas, lima beans or celeriac are cooked and then puréed, they become substantial soup bases. Because these vegetables are full of starch and cellulose, the soups require none of the thickening agents used with other vegetable purées *(pages 28-29);* all that need be added is an enrichment such as butter or cream. The starchy purées may, however, be enhanced by the addition of herbs and aromatic vegetables if they are used in small quantities that will not interfere with the sweetness and intensity of these soups *(recipes, pages 91-105).*

As indicated by the two demonstrations on these pages, different vegetables may call for slightly different cooking and puréeing techniques. For example, carrots, which are strong tasting, can be given a preliminary stewing with aromatics, such as the onions used at right; the carrots' flavor is enhanced but not overwhelmed by that of the onions. A mild broth, such as veal, chicken or vegetable, can be used as a cooking liquid to add still another flavor element.

By contrast, fresh peas are delicate in taste. In a pea purée *(right, below),* plain water is used as the cooking liquid to preserve the purity of the peas' flavor. Any flavoring ingredients should be as mild as the lettuce and leeks shown here.

No matter what vegetable you use, it should be cooked long enough to be tender, but not so long that its flavor dissipates into the liquid; the cooked vegetable should retain some firmness. The next step—puréeing—will vary, however, according to the vegetable. One that is soft throughout after cooking—such as carrots or celeriac—may be puréed by a single pounding with a masher or one passage through a food mill, strainer or sieve. Peas or beans, on the other hand, must be sieved twice: first to purée them, then to remove their fibrous skins.

In either instance, sieving is easier when you purée the vegetables in small batches and moisten them with a little cooking liquid as you proceed: this keeps them from clogging the holes or mesh. Then stir more liquid into the puréed vegetables to give the soup the consistency of heavy cream: a common proportion is one part purée to two parts liquid.

Exploiting the Character of Carrots

1 **Combining carrots with aromatics.** Melt a layer of butter ¼ inch [6 mm.] deep in a heavy pan over low heat, then add a thick layer of chopped onions and a few herb sprigs—tarragon is used here, but mint or parsley could be substituted. Cover and simmer gently until the onions are soft but not brown—about 10 minutes—then add peeled, sliced raw carrots *(left).* Cover the pan and let the carrots cook undisturbed for 15 minutes or so. The moisture from the aromatics will soften and perfume the carrots.

Fine Texture for Peas Sieved Twice

1 **Preparing the flavoring base.** Cut lettuce leaves and leeks in fine slices. Add chopped herbs—in this case, mint and savory leaves. Stew in butter over low heat for 10 minutes, until the leaves wilt and begin to exude their juices. Then add freshly shelled peas.

2 **Cooking in water.** To shorten cooking time and to help the peas retain color, bring the water to a boil before adding it to the pot. Add water to cover the peas *(above)* and simmer them until tender. Timing will vary with the peas' age and size: test for doneness by biting into a pea after 5 minutes.

2 **Adding liquid.** Add enough hot liquid—in this case chicken broth—to cover the pieces of carrot. Simmer them in the liquid, uncovered, for about 20 minutes, until they are just tender. Then pick out and discard the herbs.

3 **Puréeing the carrots.** Remove small batches of carrots from the broth with a wire skimmer or perforated spoon, and press each batch through a food mill, ladling a little broth over the carrots to speed the puréeing. If the resulting purée is too thick to stir easily, dilute it with more cooking liquid or with milk or heavy cream.

4 **Finishing.** Taste for seasoning and add a spoonful of dry white wine or lemon juice if the carrots are too sweet—or a pinch of sugar if they are not sweet enough. Pour in enough heavy cream to give the soup the desired consistency, then return the soup to low heat, bring it to a simmer and serve.

3 **Pulping the peas.** Using a skimmer or perforated spoon, transfer batches of peas to a coarse strainer or food mill (above, left) and pass them through it to separate the flesh from the skins; add a little of the cooking liquid to the whole peas to moisten them. Then force the roughly pulped flesh through a fine-meshed sieve (right). With some of the cooking liquid, dilute the resulting thick purée to the desired consistency. Season to taste.

4 **Finishing with butter.** Warm the purée over a low heat before serving it, stirring regularly to prevent sticking. Remove the soup from the heat as soon as it reaches a simmer. Stir in chunks of butter to enrich the soup without dimming its emerald color.

Extra Starch for Added Body

When a puréed soup is based on a non-starchy ingredient such as meat or shell-fish, very young peas, mushrooms, onions or leaf vegetables, the purée will need a supplementary thickener to give it body and a smooth consistency. Among the thickeners that are used for purées, only bread and bread crumbs are added to the soup when it is nearly finished. Raw thickening agents—potatoes, flour, dried beans, dried lentils, pasta and rice —all require cooking in the soup.

Potatoes have an exceptionally broad range of applications in heavy-textured purées because they serve simultaneously as a thickener and a main ingredient—as in the leek and potato soup demonstrated at right, top *(recipe, page 110)*. For any potato-thickened purée, choose baking, not boiling, potatoes. As they simmer in the cooking liquid, mealy baking potatoes will break up more readily than waxy boiling types, and when puréed afterward, baking potatoes will disperse more evenly in the soup. Cut up the potatoes beforehand so that they will be done at the same time as the other ingredients. Here, both potatoes and leeks are sliced thinly to cook in just 15 minutes.

For lighter-textured purées, flour can provide an unobtrusive support to the main ingredient. Because flour requires long cooking to eliminate its raw taste, a soup based on delicate, quick-cooking ingredients such as mushrooms and sorrel is endowed with the requisite body by means of a separately prepared velouté sauce *(pages 28-29)*. However, flour can be added directly to the soup if the other ingredients can withstand a lengthy simmer—as with the onion soup shown at right, bottom *(recipe, page 94)*.

When using flour in this way, add it before you pour in the cooking liquid. Stir well to coat the basic ingredient thoroughly and ensure that the flour will be completely incorporated in the soup as the simmering proceeds.

A Leek Soup Thickened with Potato

1 **Cutting up the vegetables.** Trim away the roots and coarse, dark green leaves of each leek. Slit the tender green leaves lengthwise, rinse them, then cut the leek crosswise into thin slices. (For vichyssoise, use the white parts only, to ensure a pale soup.) Peel and quarter potatoes and cut them into thin slices.

2 **Cooking the vegetables.** Melt butter in a saucepan over low heat. Add the sliced leeks, cover the pan and cook for 4 to 5 minutes, until the leeks are soft but not colored. Add the sliced potatoes *(above)* and stir them in with the leeks.

An Onion Soup Thickened with Flour

1 **Preparing the onions.** Peel the onions and halve them vertically. Cut the halves lengthwise into thin slices of equal size that will cook evenly. Melt butter in a saucepan small enough so that the onions will fill it about halfway. Add the onions *(above)*, cover the pan and set it on a fireproof pad over low heat. Stir the mixture occasionally.

2 **Adding flour.** After about 30 minutes, the onions will be soft but still pale, and reduced to less than a third of their volume. Sprinkle flour over the onions *(above)* and, with the pan still over low heat, stir to combine the onions and flour into a smooth mixture.

3 **Adding liquid.** Pour hot water, milk, or chicken broth, as shown above, into the pan. Salt lightly. Simmer gently, uncovered, skimming off any scum that rises to the surface. Cook for 15 minutes, or until the potatoes are soft enough to crush easily when pressed against the side of the pan.

4 **Puréeing.** Pour the soup into a strainer set over a bowl. Then hold the strainer, filled with potatoes and leeks, over the pan in which the vegetables were cooked. With a wooden pestle, press the vegetables through the strainer. When they become too dry to purée easily, moisten them with the cooking liquid (above).

5 **Finishing the purée.** Gradually add the cooking liquid to the pan, stirring, until the soup reaches the desired consistency. Enrich the soup with cream if you wish, then reheat it gently. (For vichyssoise, thoroughly chill the soup without enriching it, then add cream at serving time.)

3 **Adding liquid.** In a separate saucepan, warm some water, broth or, as here, milk. Add the liquid all at once to the onion, butter and flour mixture (above). Remove the fireproof pad, raise the heat and stir the soup until it comes to a boil, then replace the fireproof pad and reduce the heat. Season the soup with grated nutmeg.

4 **Sieving and serving.** Gently simmer, uncovered, for about 30 minutes, occasionally stirring so that the soup thickens gradually without sticking. Pour the soup through a strainer into a bowl and push the onions through with a pestle (above). Reheat the soup, stirring well. Add cream, if you like, and serve in warmed plates (right).

Eggs and Cream for a Velvet Finish

Purées based on a fragile, nonstarchy vegetable such as mushrooms or asparagus require thickening but cannot withstand long cooking. These soups—and any other purée, for that matter—may be endowed with extra body by either of the two strategies demonstrated here.

The first technique produces a velvety soup called a velouté, based—like the sauce of the same name—on a broth thickened with a flour-and-butter roux. An hour or so of simmering kills the flour taste and yields a thick base for a cooked, puréed vegetable. The soup may be enriched with butter, cream or the egg yolks and cream used in the mushroom velouté at right *(recipe, page 95)*.

Egg yolks and cream may also serve as thickeners on their own, as in the sorrel purée below *(recipe, page 96)*. If you choose this tactic you must use 4 or 5 yolks and ½ cup [125 ml.] of heavy cream for 1 quart [1 liter] of soup. For the same amount of velouté, in contrast, you need only 2 or 3 egg yolks and ½ cup of cream.

Preparing the Versatile Velouté

1 **Making a velouté base.** Melt butter in a saucepan over low heat; stir in flour *(above, left)* and cook, stirring, for about 3 minutes, until the roux turns golden. Add hot broth *(center)* — chicken broth is used here — raise the heat and whisk until the mixture boils. Move the pan half off the burner and gently simmer the velouté for 40 minutes to 1 hour, until it is the consistency of light cream. Regularly remove the skin that forms on the soup's cooler side *(right)*.

Blending Egg Yolks into a Sorrel Mixture

1 **Cooking.** Remove the stems from sorrel leaves, then rinse and drain them well. Mass the leaves into a compact bunch and slice into coarse shreds. Melt butter in a pot and toss in the leaves *(above)*. Cook over low heat, stirring occasionally, until the sorrel is very soft — about 15 minutes.

2 **Sieving the sorrel.** To extract any fibrous sorrel ribs, pass the cooked leaves through a sturdy, fine-meshed sieve set over a bowl *(above)*. Discard the fibers that remain in the sieve.

3 **Adding liquid.** Return the puréed sorrel to the pot and moisten it with broth; chicken broth is used above. Stir the mixture to combine the sorrel and broth thoroughly; adjust the heat to maintain the soup at a bare simmer.

2 **Mixing in the mushrooms.** Purée raw, trimmed mushrooms in a food mill or food processor; add a little lemon juice to preserve their color. Cook the mushrooms in butter over high heat, stirring and tossing until their liquid evaporates. Add them to the velouté.

3 **Adding yolks and cream.** In a bowl, blend egg yolks with heavy cream; season lightly with grated nutmeg. Be sure this mixture is at room temperature to prevent curdling, then stir it into the soup. Immediately remove the pan from the heat and whisk the velouté so that the yolks will thicken the soup evenly.

4 **Finishing the soup.** Still off the heat, enrich the soup further, if you like, by whisking in chunks of butter. Ladle the velouté into warmed soup plates (above) and garnish with slices of raw mushroom that have been drenched in lemon juice, which adds a refreshing acid note to the rich soup.

4 **Thickening the soup.** Blend 4 egg yolks with ½ cup [125 ml.] of heavy cream. Stir a ladleful of the warm soup into the bowl (left) to heat the mixture gently and to prevent curdling. Add the warmed and diluted egg-and-cream mixture to the soup (right), whisking continuously as you pour.

5 **Serving the soup.** Continue whisking the soup as it thickens, taking care to keep the heat low so that the liquid does not approach a simmer. Cook and whisk for 2 to 3 minutes, until the soup is creamy, with sufficient body to just coat a spoon. Remove the soup from the heat and, if you like, whisk in small pieces of butter. Serve garnished with a sprinkling of chervil leaves (above).

Improvising with a Collection of Leftovers

Puréeing techniques, which are designed to amalgamate flavors and textures, can turn a collection of leftover vegetables into a fresh-tasting soup that quite belies its humble beginnings. Since most vegetables combine well, the contents of your refrigerator can determine the recipe; the soup demonstrated here is made from both cooked and raw leftovers.

The tough outer leaves of lettuce or cabbage—which are usually sound but not quite tender enough for a salad—make good raw ingredients for such a soup; so do such quick-cooking raw vegetables as large, starchy peas. Do not use overage or discolored vegetables, however, or any salad ingredients that already have dressing on them.

Two essential ingredients are raw aromatic vegetables, which help to unify the flavors, and a starchy element to stabilize the purée and keep it from separating into solids and liquid. Onions, celery, garlic, leek greens or scallions in any combination will provide a strong aromatic flavor base. The starchy element may be leftover cooked potatoes, beans, rice or macaroni; if none of these is available, thicken the soup with a handful of fresh bread crumbs or some croutons.

The raw vegetables you choose for this soup should be washed and trimmed. If the cooked vegetables you include were buttered for their first appearance at the table, scrape off as much of the butter as possible before adding them to the soup. Any remaining butter will rise to the surface of the liquid during cooking and should then be skimmed off.

Do not overcook the soup. Start by simmering the raw aromatic and leaf vegetables, cooking them the longest to extract the maximum flavor. Next, add ingredients that need a somewhat briefer simmer—raw peas and cooked asparagus in the case of the leftover soup made here. Finally, add any already puréed vegetables—mashed potatoes or spinach, for example—at the last minute, just before puréeing the entire mixture.

After puréeing the soup, you can add an enrichment of either fresh butter or cream, according to your taste.

1 Gathering the ingredients. Assemble the leftovers. This selection includes boiled carrots, turnips and snow peas; boiled asparagus; chopped, sautéed mushrooms; mashed potatoes; macaroni with tomato sauce; and spinach purée. Supplement leftovers with quick-cooking raw vegetables—peas, in this case—and with raw aromatic and leaf vegetables.

5 Adding purées. Simmer the soup for 15 minutes, until the vegetables are tender. Add any puréed leftovers—potatoes and spinach, in this instance—and heat them through.

6 Puréeing the soup. Press the soup through a strainer or a food mill. Here the soup is puréed with the coarse disk of the mill so that the vegetables retain some of their original textures.

2 **Starting the soup.** Put the raw, trimmed leaves and aromatics—here leek, onion, scallion, garlic, fennel, cabbage and lettuce—in boiling water. Simmer uncovered for 15 minutes.

3 **Adding leftovers.** Stir in any quick-cooking raw vegetables, such as the peas used in this soup. After 5 minutes or so, add the macaroni and the cut-up, cooked vegetables.

4 **Cleansing the soup.** Both scum from raw vegetables and any butter present in cooked vegetables will rise to the surface. Spoon off the impurities as the soup returns to a boil.

7 **Seasoning and enriching.** Add salt with care: many of the soup ingredients will have been salted during their first cooking. Reheat gently, then grind in some pepper and enrich the soup with butter chunks *(left)* or with a little cream before serving it in warmed soup plates *(above)*.

A Seafood Bisque Enhanced with Shells

A purée based on shellfish—which may be anything from oysters to lobster—is generally known by its French name, *bisque,* a term that probably derives from the word for the bread crumbs that are used to give the soup its velvety body.

If the basis of the soup is a heavy-shelled mollusk such as an oyster or clam, only the meat is used. However, if the purée is made of such thin-shelled crustaceans as crab, shrimp, crayfish or lobster, the shells and other parts of the body are cooked in the soup with the meat. During the cooking, every tiny crevice offers up its meat and juices, and the shells provide extra flavor and color.

Use the freshest possible mollusks or crustaceans for a bisque; usually, this means live ones. Kill a lobster just before cooking by inserting a knife between the eyes; divide the body, shell and all, into manageable sections. (Save the red coral—the roe—and the green liver to enrich the soup.) Keep headless shrimp in their shells; leave crabs and crayfish live. Simply drop the crustaceans into a shallow, simmering bath of fish or chicken broth or one of white wine and brandy, flavored with herbs and diced aromatic vegetables. (Onions, carrots, thyme, bay leaf and parsley are used here.) The heat of the liquid kills crustaceans swiftly and cooks them in less than 10 minutes.

After cooking, most of the shellfish meat is reserved as a garnish—the crayfish tail meat is used in this demonstration *(recipe, page 105)*. The intestines of all crustaceans should be discarded—they can give the meat a bitter flavor.

Use a mortar and pestle to break up shells; mechanical devices cannot cope with these large, brittle pieces. After the initial pounding, use the coarse disk of a food mill, as here, or a food processor to grind the shells finer. Just before serving a shell-enriched bisque, push it through a strainer or sieve. This combines the ingredients and filters out the shell bits, leaving a satiny, luxurious soup.

1 **Cooking the crayfish.** Melt butter in a skillet and add chopped aromatic vegetables and herbs. Cook over low heat, stirring often *(top),* for about 15 minutes, until the vegetables are soft but not colored. Add brandy and white wine, then bring the mixture to a boil. Add the crayfish and stir *(above)* until they turn red. Cover the pan, reduce the heat and simmer for 7 to 8 minutes; put the pan contents in a colander set in a bowl.

2 **Shelling the tails.** When the crayfish cool, twist each tail from the head *(above),* and put the head in a mortar. Split the underside of the tail to remove the meat *(left)*; put the shell in the mortar. Draw out and discard the intestine from the meat by twisting and pulling the middle tail fin, and remove the other fins. Reserve the meat. Put the vegetables and liquid into a saucepan.

3 **Pounding the crayfish.** With a pestle, pound the shells into fragments and add them to the saucepan with the vegetables and cooking liquid *(above)*. Add more liquid — here, fish broth — and a pinch of cayenne pepper.

4 **Extracting more flavor.** Simmer, uncovered, for 2 to 3 minutes. Add more broth if the mixture seems too thick, then pour the mixture into a food mill set over a bowl and grind it finer.

5 **Thickening the bisque.** Return the milled pulp and its liquid to the saucepan, and set the pan over moderate heat. Add white bread crumbs *(above)* and cook, stirring, until the bisque comes to a simmer.

6 **Straining the bisque.** Pour the soup mixture into a strainer set over a large bowl. Press the mixture through the strainer with a broad, heavy pestle *(above)*. Discard the shell fragments that remain in the strainer.

7 **Serving.** Return the soup to the pan, set it over moderate heat, and stir in heavy cream as you bring the bisque back to a simmer. Combine the reserved crayfish tail meat with the soup, and serve from a warmed tureen *(left)*.

Pulverizing for a Sumptuous Result

It takes time to transform poultry flesh into a smooth purée, but generations of cooks have found that *potage à la reine* (recipes, page 103) amply rewards their efforts. The classic purée shown here blends chicken breast with almonds and lemon peel for flavor, hard-boiled egg yolks and cream for richness, and broth-soaked bread for body. Turkey could replace the chicken; quail, squab or guinea hen would contribute a different flavor. Duck or goose, however, are too rich and strong for this subtle soup.

Whatever bird you choose, use only the fine-grained breast meat. You can buy and roast separate breasts, but maximum flavor and juiciness come from a whole, slightly under-roasted bird. Either way, the puréeing will be much easi-er if the meat is still warm from the oven

You may purée the meat and other in gredients in a food processor or a foo mill, but a mortar and pestle produce th best consistency. The pestle gives th cook the close control essential in pu réeing ingredients with varied textures Steady pounding, with attention paid t each element, yields a uniform purée.

1 **Puréeing the solids.** Assemble the more resistant ingredients in a mortar: blanched almonds, strips of lemon peel, and the chicken breast, torn into small pieces and stripped of any skin or connective tissue. (If you like, cut some breast meat into julienne and reserve to garnish the soup.) Pound the ingredients with the pestle to merge them into a fine purée; the almonds will require the greatest effort. Pound in hard-boiled egg yolks when the other ingredients are reduced almost to a paste.

2 **Adding bread.** Trim the crust from a chunk of coarse white bread and drop the chunk into simmering chicken broth *(top)*. After a minute or so, the bread will soften and crumble; transfer it, a spoonful at a time, to the mortar *(above)* and thoroughly pound each spoonful into the chicken mixture.

3 **Incorporating liquid.** Transfer the purée from the mortar to a large mixing bowl. Pour in heavy cream *(above)* — the main liquid of this rich soup — and stir well to mix it in. Carefully add chicken broth, a little at a time, to dilute the soup to the desired consistency: it should be almost as thick as pancake batter.

4 **Sieving the purée.** Ladle the diluted purée into a fine-meshed nylon or stainless-steel strainer placed over a pan. (An aluminum strainer could discolor the yolks.) Use a broad pestle to force the purée through the strainer. If any solid residue remains, return it to the mortar for additional pounding, mix it with a little soup and strain again.

5 **Serving the soup.** Stir well, and taste the purée for seasoning. Before serving, gently heat it just to the simmering point. Ladle the soup into warmed bowls and garnish it with chopped fresh parsley *(left)*, which adds color and a contrasting flavor, or with strips of reserved breast meat.

A Complete Guide to Puréeing Opportunities

Almost any food can become the base for a purée soup, providing it is cooked with a complementary liquid and—if necessary—thickened with a suitable starchy element, then puréed with appropriate equipment and, finally, enriched.

The chart on these pages is a guide to the wide range of purée-making options. For each of the 53 types of foods that may serve as the main ingredient of a soup, the chart shows what puréeing equipment, basic liquids, thickeners and last-minute enrichments are appropriate.

The equipment needed for puréeing should be your first concern, even though puréeing is almost the final step in the process. Many ingredients can be puréed with just one device, but others require two or three, used in specific succession, to achieve the right texture. The chart tells you which devices to use at each stage of puréeing.

Choices of liquids, thickeners and enrichments appear under each main ingredient listed at the top of the chart. Which you choose is primarily a matter of availability and personal preference. However, you should bear a few points in mind. If you use flour as your thickener, for instance, remember that it will give the soup a sticky texture and starchy taste unless it is thoroughly cooked. You should, therefore, make a roux from flour and butter, mix it with the soup liquid and simmer it for at least 40 minutes.

If the main ingredient requires extended cooking, it can be done in this roux-thickened liquid *(pages 26-27);* otherwise, the main ingredient should simmer separately. Among the thickeners, potatoes, lentils, rice and pasta can be simmered to tenderness with the main ingredient. Dried beans, however, take so long to soften that they should first be precooked, then simmered and puréed with the main ingredient.

Butter, cream and a combination of egg yolks with cream are the most often-used enrichments. If you like, add more than one enrichment; velouté soups, for example, often include butter as well as egg yolks and cream *(pages 28-29).*

Puréeing equipment. The numbers in the column under each main ingredient indicate what equipment to use at each stage of puréeing: (1) indicates devices suitable for the first or the only puréeing; (2) and (3) list in order the equipment to be used to eliminate skins, fibers or shells. Crustaceans, for example, must be puréed first in a mortar, then in a food mill or processor, and last through a strainer or sieve.

Liquids, thickeners and enrichments. From the column beneath each main ingredient, choose the complementary ingredients specified by black dots. To make a spinach soup, for example, you could cook the leaves in water or in a broth. The mixture could be thickened with flour or bread, then puréed and enriched with butter, cream or egg yolks and cream combined.

		Artichoke	Asparagus	Avocado	Beans: Broad/Lima	Beans: Green/Wax	Beet	Belgian Endive	Broccoli	Brussels Sprouts	Cabbage	Carrot	Cauliflower
Puréeing Equipment	Masher	1		1			1					1	1
	Food Mill		1		1	1	1	1	1	1	1	1	1
	Mortar and Pestle	1		1									
	Strainer	2	2		2	2	2	2	2	2	2	1	2
	Fine-meshed Sieve	2	2									2	
	Blender	1	1	1	1	1	1	1	1	1	1	1	1
	Food Processor	1	1	1	1	1	1	1	1	1	1	1	1
Liquids	Water	●	●	●	●	●		●	●	●	●	●	●
	Milk												●
	Meat or Chicken Broth	●	●				●	●	●	●	●		
	Vegetable Broth	●	●	●	●		●	●	●	●	●	●	●
	Fish Broth												
Thickeners	Flour	●	●		●			●	●	●	●		●
	Bread or Bread Crumbs	●	●		●			●	●	●	●	●	●
	Pasta								●	●	●		●
	Rice	●		●	●		●	●	●	●	●	●	●
	Potatoes	●						●	●	●	●	●	●
	Dried Beans									●	●		
	Lentils												
Enrichments	Butter	●	●	●	●	●	●	●	●	●	●	●	●
	Cream	●	●	●	●	●	●	●	●	●	●	●	●
	Egg Yolks and Cream	●	●	●	●		●	●	●	●	●	●	●

	Fresh Vegetables																														Dried Beans and Peas					Fish and Shellfish			Poultry and Game		
	Celeriac	Celery	Chestnut	Corn	Cucumber	Eggplant	Fennel	Greens: Beet/Collard/Mustard/Turnip	Jerusalem Artichoke	Kale	Kohlrabi	Leek	Lettuce	Mushroom	Onion	Parsnip	Peas	Pepper	Potato	Rutabaga	Snow Peas	Sorrel	Spinach	Summer Squash	Winter Squash	Sweet Potato	Swiss Chard	Tomato	Turnip	Watercress	Beans: Black/Kidney	Beans: White	Chick-peas	Lentils	Split Peas	Crustaceans	Fish	Mollusks	Chicken	Game Birds	Rabbit
	1		1			1			1		1				1			1	1				1	1					1							2	1		1	1	1
	1	1	1	1	1	1	1	1	1	1	1	1	1	1	1	1	1	1	1	1	1	1	1	1	1	1	1	1	1	1	1	1	1	1	1	1	1		1	1	1
	2	2	2	2	2	2	2	2	2	2	2	2	2		1	2	2	2	1	2	2		2	2	2	2	2	2	1	2	2	2	2	2	2	3			2	2	2
						2									2	2			2	1																3	2		2	2	2
	1	1	1	1	1	1	1	1	1	1	1	1	1	1	1	1	1	1	1	1	1	1	1	1	1	1	1	1	1	1						2		1	1	1	
	1	1	1	1	1	1	1	1	1	1	1	1	1	1	1	1	1	1	1	1	1	1	1	1	1	1	1	1	1	1											

Compound Broths
Hearty Combinations with Meats and Vegetables

The first soup ever cooked was almost certainly a compound broth—that is, a soup made with chopped ingredients that are eaten with the liquid they have flavored. Most compound broths include a large number of different ingredients, each of which contributes its characteristic flavor and texture. In Mediterranean mixed-vegetable soups *(page 41),* for example, up to a dozen soft, crisp and starchy vegetables are cooked together; in Scotch broth *(pages 42-43),* lamb and turnips are set off by nutty kernels of barley and sweet-tasting peas; and a whole range of leftover meats can be combined with fresh vegetables to make a rustic broth *(opposite, and pages 46-47).*

In fact, many compound broths are bulky, nourishing dishes that resemble main-course stews in their chief components, in the herbs and aromatic vegetables that flavor them, and in the poaching method by which they are cooked. But unlike stews, compound broths require that you cut up the ingredients—usually at the start of cooking, but sometimes at the end—into pieces that are small enough to be spooned up. In addition, broths contain a higher proportion of liquid than stews do. Water is the customary starting point, since it will gain plenty of flavor from the solid ingredients that cook in it. For a highly flavored soup, however, you can substitute a clear broth *(pages 10-11)* or a velouté base, which is a broth cooked with a flour-and-butter roux *(demonstration, pages 28-29).* A velouté enriched with egg yolks and cream makes a smooth, rich liquid for the mussel soup demonstrated on page 52.

There are many classic compound broths that call for more or less fixed combinations of foodstuffs. In hearty chowders, for example, fish or shellfish are combined with such New England winter staples as salt pork, potatoes and onions; fowl and leeks are constant elements in Scottish cock-a-leekie *(recipe, page 121),* to which prunes are frequently added. But these compound broths also offer the imaginative cook an opportunity to experiment with different flavors and textures: any cuisine you draw upon will give you fresh ideas for embellishing basic ingredients. In Mexico, for instance, tripe is enlivened by fresh coriander to produce the *menudo* demonstrated on pages 48-49; in Philadelphia, whole peppercorns turn tripe soup into pepper pot; and in Italy, the tripe soup often is finished with garlic and fat cut from a ham *(all recipes, pages 124-125).*

Shredded cabbage is dropped into a casserole containing a chicken carcass and giblets, sliced aromatic vegetables, a bouquet garni and water. After simmering, the bones and the bouquet garni will be discarded, whereas the vegetables and meat will be served in the rich broth that all these elements have flavored.

The Importance of Balancing Cooking Times

Even Cooking after Careful Cutting

When a soup includes several different vegetables—as compound broths usually do—you must take into account that vegetables need different cooking times to reach the desired degree of doneness at the same moment. To control results you can, of course, add vegetables to the cooking liquid in stages, according to their timing requirements. But for closer control, you should change the vegetables' cooking times by the way you prepare them: the smaller the vegetable piece and the larger the surface area exposed to the heat, the more quickly it will cook.

A case in point is the leek and potato soup demonstrated at right. Both of the vegetables are cut small for the soup so that they will cook through in 15 minutes; if you prefer soup vegetables in larger pieces, you may have to cook them as long as 30 minutes to make them tender. In addition, to make sure that the potatoes will be ready in the same time as the faster-cooking leeks, the potatoes are cut into relatively large but very thin slices to expose as much surface area as possible to the cooking liquid.

Adding vegetables in stages, beginning with those that take the longest to cook, is an easier stratagem when you are dealing with many different vegetables whose cooking times vary widely. In the soup demonstrated opposite, for example *(recipe, page 114)*, sliced onions, leeks, carrots, very thinly sliced potatoes and fresh white beans are added to the cooking water first: they take longest to cook. (If you have only dried beans, soak them in water overnight and precook them before adding them to the liquid.) Quick-cooking winter squash also is added at the beginning so that it will partly disintegrate, adding body to the broth.

When the soup has simmered about 30 minutes, quick-cooking ingredients that should emerge tender, but slightly firm, are added. Here, sliced green beans and zucchini, and elbow macaroni are used; when they are ready—a matter of only 10 to 15 minutes—the soup is done.

A mixed-vegetable soup such as this can be simply garnished with freshly grated Parmesan cheese. Or, for a silky finish, ladle on *pistou (box, opposite; recipe, page 114)*, a Provençal sauce fragrant with garlic, basil and olive oil.

1 Preparing the vegetables. Wash the leeks well and trim off the roots and the tough, dark green leaves. Slice the leeks ½ inch [1 cm.] thick. Peel the potatoes, quarter them lengthwise and cut the quarters into the thinnest possible slices. Add the vegetables to a pan of boiling salted water *(above)*.

2 Removing the scum. Spoon off the frothy scum that will gather on the surface of the liquid *(above)* as the soup returns to the boiling point. Adjust the heat to keep the liquid at a steady simmer. Then cover the pan.

3 Serving the soup. After about 15 to 20 minutes, both the leeks and the potatoes should be tender but still intact. Ladle the soup into warmed plates *(above)* and add a chunk of butter to each serving. Season with freshly ground black pepper and garnish with a sprinkling of chopped fresh parsley or chives.

Adding Vegetables in Sequence

1 **Starting slow-cooking vegetables.** Cut up trimmed carrots, potatoes, leeks, onions and squash. Bring salted water to a boil in a large pan and add the vegetables, white beans and a bouquet garni. Spoon off any scum that forms as the liquid returns to a boil, then reduce the heat, cover and simmer for 30 minutes.

2 **Adding quick-cooking vegetables.** Add sliced zucchini *(above, left)*, green beans cut into ½-inch [1-cm.] lengths and elbow macaroni *(right)*. Stir it all together well and simmer, uncovered, for about 15 minutes, or until the macaroni is soft but still slightly chewy and the vegetables are tender.

Pistou: A Basil Sauce

Pounding the sauce. In a mortar, pound some peeled garlic cloves and fresh basil leaves with salt and pepper. Add grated Parmesan and stir the mixture to make a stiff paste. Pounding continuously, gradually add peeled, seeded, chopped tomatoes, more cheese and some olive oil, until the mixture becomes somewhat fluid. Slowly incorporate more oil until the sauce is thick and creamy. Stir the *pistou* well before serving.

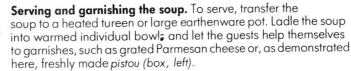

3 **Serving and garnishing the soup.** To serve, transfer the soup to a heated tureen or large earthenware pot. Ladle the soup into warmed individual bowls and let the guests help themselves to garnishes, such as grated Parmesan cheese or, as demonstrated here, freshly made *pistou (box, left)*.

A Substantial Blend of Lamb and Barley

Nourishing broths made with vegetables and less expensive cuts of meat are cherished wherever good cooking accompanies thrifty housekeeping. The French, for example, poach tough, flavorful beef with aromatic vegetables for pot-au-feu; the Scots fortify themselves with Scotch broth *(recipe, page 129)* — a combination of mutton, barley and vegetables.

Mutton is not widely available nowadays, but winter lamb, which is older and stronger in taste than the lamb available in spring and summer, makes a good substitute in Scotch broth. For the best flavor, choose an inexpensive, bony cut, such as neck (used here) or shoulder. If you wish, add a veal shank for extra gelatin. The bones are not left in the soup: after they have rendered their flavor, the meat is removed from them, cut into small pieces and returned to the broth.

Start the meat for Scotch and other meat broths in cold water: this helps the meat to render its juices, intensifying the flavor of the broth. Heat the water gently, and spoon off the albumin scum that forms. If you use fatty meat, you will also have to skim off the fat at intervals while the broth is cooking. Better still, make the soup a day in advance, chill it, then spoon off the congealed fat.

After skimming, add the aromatic enrichments. In a Scotch broth, the bouquet garni *(Step 2)* is traditionally supplemented with marigold petals, which are available dried at shops specializing in herbs. Barley, softened by soaking in cold water, is another addition: during the cooking the grains swell, distributing much of their starch through the liquid to thicken it. Thickeners for other meat soups include potatoes and rice. Suitable vegetables include onions, carrots, leeks, turnips or rutabagas and dried beans or split peas. The latter, like the barley, are more tender if soaked before cooking.

The long cooking time that all meat-based soups require exhausts the flavor of the bouquet garni and the aromatic vegetables; discard them, except for the onions and turnips or rutabagas, which can be puréed and returned to the broth to give it more body. Garnish vegetables—carrots, tomatoes, kale, cabbage or fresh peas instead of split peas—may be added toward the end of cooking.

1 **Cleansing the broth.** Cut the meat—in this case, lamb—into even-sized pieces and trim away the fat. Put the lamb—with a veal shank, if you like—into a large pan. Cover with cold water and bring it slowly to a boil. Skim *(above)*, add a cup of cold water and skim again as the water returns to a boil. Repeat until no more scum forms.

2 **Preparing the aromatics.** Quarter onions, and slice carrots and leeks. Wrap the flavorings—here, parsley, thyme, celery leaves and crumbled, dried marigold petals—to prevent them from dispersing. Place them on a square of muslin or cheesecloth, draw the edges together to make a sack and tie it with string.

5 **Puréeing the reserved vegetables.** If you like, add shelled fresh peas to the soup at this stage. Bring the soup back to a boil. Purée the reserved vegetables into the soup *(above)*. Return the meat to the soup, simmer briefly, until the peas are tender, then transfer the soup to a warmed tureen.

3 **Adding vegetables and barley.** Add the aromatic vegetables and the bouquet garni to the liquid. Strain the barley from the water in which it has been soaking and add it to the soup. (If you are using soaked split peas, drain and add them, too.) Bring the soup back to a simmer, remove any scum from its surface, and cook for 1¼ hours or until the meat is nearly tender when tested with a fork. Spoon off the fat occasionally.

4 **Separating meat from bones.** Add quartered turnips or rutabagas and simmer the soup for about 30 minutes more. When the meat and barley are tender, remove all the solid ingredients except the barley (and split peas, if you have included them). Cut the meat from the bones *(above)* and chop it into small pieces. Discard the bones, the bouquet garni, the carrots and leeks. Reserve the meat, onions, and turnips or rutabagas.

6 **Garnishing.** Cut fresh carrots and turnips into julienne *(page 13)*. Pour a ladleful of the broth into a small saucepan and simmer the julienne in it for 5 to 6 minutes until tender. Add them to the soup in the tureen. You may also add a little lemon juice, or a few capers preserved in vinegar, to counteract the barley. Serve the broth in warmed soup plates *(left)*.

Secrets of a Creole Gumbo

A pungent Creole gumbo can include almost any combination of meat and shellfish, from the crab, shrimp and ham on these pages to chicken, turkey, game and oysters. What makes a soup a gumbo is two key ingredients that thicken and flavor the broth: a roux of flour and oil cooked so long it develops a distinctive, brown color and nutty taste; and cooked okra, which secretes a substance that adds body and flavor to the soup. It is okra, in fact, that gives the dish its name: okra was called gumbo by the African slaves who brought it to America.

Making a gumbo is a 4-hour process, and the secret of success is careful timing: the soup incorporates a variety of separately cooked ingredients. The broth —water flavored with aromatics, crustacean shells and bones from any poultry or meat used—must simmer for 2 hours. During this time you must pan fry the okra to make its glutinous, ropy threads dissolve into a tangy glaze *(Step 2, below)*. This takes about 30 to 45 minutes, as does the preparation of the brown roux *(Step 3, below)*. The okra and the roux— enriched with tomatoes, meat and sautéed aromatic vegetables—must simmer an hour and a half longer in the strained broth. Shellfish meat is added only during the last minutes of cooking, since long simmering would toughen it.

Disjointing a Steamed Crab

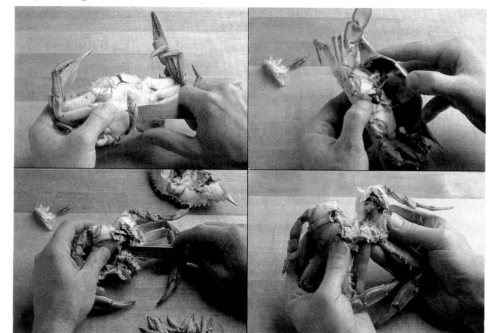

Separating shell and flesh. With your fingers or a knife, pry back the apron flap on the underside of each crab shell *(top left)* until you can snap off the flap. Pull off the top shell in one piece *(top right)*; most of the crab's intestines will come with it. With a knife, cut out the inedible white gills ("dead men's fingers") that line each side of the bottom shell *(lower right in picture at bottom left)*, and scrape out any soft intestinal matter that remains in the center. Then snap the cleaned crabs in half *(bottom right)*, cover them with plastic wrap and refrigerate them.

1 Making the stock. Put sliced carrots, onions, celery and water in a large pot. Add the shells from peeled shrimp and the top shells from the crabs *(box, above)*. Simmer, covered, for 2 hours; strain the stock, discard the solids and return the liquid to the pot.

2 Cooking okra. Cut rinsed okra into slices ½ inch [1 cm.] thick. In a skillet, heat a layer of oil ¼ inch [6 mm.] deep. Fry the okra gently for 30 to 45 minutes. At first the okra will exude glutinous threads *(above)*; as it browns, the dissolving threads will form a glaze.

3 Making the roux. In a skillet, stir together flour and oil to make a paste. Cook the paste over very low heat, stirring continuously. The mixture will foam, subside and darken. Continue cooking and stirring until the roux is dark brown *(above)* — about 45 minutes.

4 **Flavoring the roux.** Add peeled, seeded and chopped tomatoes to the roux *(above, left)* and simmer, uncovered, until the mixture is reduced to a thick paste, about 10 to 15 minutes. Then stir in chopped ham *(above, right)* and herbs: in this demonstration, thyme, bay leaf and basil are used.

5 **Simmering the soup.** To the strained stock add a combination of chopped onion, celery, green pepper and garlic that has been stewed in oil until soft. Then add the okra and stir in the roux mixture *(above)*.

6 **Cooking the shellfish.** Cover the pot and simmer the soup gently for 1 hour. Then add the cleaned crab in the shells and cook for 10 minutes more. Add the peeled shrimp. Season with salt, pepper, Tabasco and Worcestershire sauce to taste. Simmer for a final 10 minutes.

7 **Serving the gumbo.** Pour the gumbo into a heated tureen and garnish it with chopped fresh parsley. Place a few spoonfuls of boiled rice — the traditional accompaniment to gumbo — in the bottom of each heated soup plate and ladle the gumbo over the rice.

The Advantages of Using Precooked Meat

When making a meat-based soup, either choice or circumstance may lead you to vary the customary process of starting a stock by poaching raw ingredients. To intensify the flavor and color, for example, you can give the meat and aromatic vegetables an initial browning in an oven, as demonstrated at right, top, with oxtail soup *(recipe, page 129)*. Or you can improvise an original, quickly made soup with leftover cooked meats *(recipe, page 114)*. Both of these variations can be applied to almost every cut of meat and every kind of poultry or game. However, do not use any liver; it would turn dry and bitter with long cooking.

When producing a browned-meat soup, the first step is to roast the meat with the aromatics for about 30 minutes in a hot oven. The meat will brown and its juices will form rich drippings while the natural sugar in the vegetables caramelizes their cut surfaces.

When the meat and vegetables are transferred to a soup pot for poaching—a 4-hour process in the case of fibrous but rich oxtail—the drippings and caramel will dissolve into the broth, surrendering extra flavor to the liquid and turning it a rich, brown color. Both effects are intensified by adding chopped tomatoes for the last few minutes of cooking. After cooking, the oxtail meat is removed from the bones, cut into bite-sized pieces and returned to the broth. The bones are discarded, as are the aromatics.

When making a soup from leftover meats, the cook has a free hand to use them singly or in almost any combination. The cooked meats—including any bones and juices—are put to simmer in water, along with raw aromatic and leaf vegetables. By the time the vegetables are cooked, the meat will be dissolving into the soup. Tender garnish vegetables—such as peas, beans or zucchini—can be added near the end of cooking. If leftover cooked vegetables are also to be included, they should be reheated in the soup for only a brief time.

Browning Oxtails for Richness and Color

1 Preparing the meat. Choose a pan that can be used both in the oven and on top of the stove. Line it with chopped vegetables—carrots, onions and celery are used here. Lay oxtail pieces on the vegetables. For extra body, add a veal shank. Put the pan, uncovered, in a preheated 475° F. [250° C.] oven.

2 Starting the broth. Roast the meat and vegetables for 30 minutes, turning them to brown them evenly. Transfer the meat to a large pan *(above)*; cover the meat with water and bring it slowly to a boil. Skim off the scum that rises. Add cold water and continue heating and skimming until the liquid is clear.

Extracting Fresh Goodness from Leftovers

1 Assembling the meats. Cut up leftover cooked meats; omit the livers. Beef, a goose carcass, beef and goose roasting juices, goose giblets and pork chop bones are shown here. Half-fill a large cooking pot with water.

2 Filling the soup pot. Thickly slice fresh aromatics—in this case, onions, carrots and a turnip. Cut leaf vegetables—here, cabbage, lettuce and sorrel—into a chiffonade *(page 13)*. Put the meats, bones and vegetables in the pot; add salt and a bouquet garni.

3 **Deglazing the pan.** Leave the vegetables in the pan in which they were browned, add a cup of cold water and bring it to a boil, scraping the pan until the coagulated juices dissolve. Add the vegetables and liquid to the oxtails. Bring the soup back to a boil, spooning off any scum or fat.

4 **Removing the bones.** Simmer the soup, partially covered, for 4 hours, or until the meat is tender. Add peeled, seeded and chopped tomatoes 15 minutes before the end of cooking. Lift out the meats, cool them, then remove the bones. Trim off the fibrous ligaments and cut up the meats. Strain the broth and discard the vegetables.

5 **Thickening the broth.** Skim any fat from the broth. In a small pan, simmer a carrot and turnip *brunoise (page 13)* in a little broth for 5 minutes. Return the remaining broth to the saucepan, add the meat and simmer the soup for 1 minute. Combine the soup and *brunoise* in a warmed tureen, and serve.

3 **Adding garnish vegetables.** Bring the liquid to a boil and skim off any scum. Simmer, uncovered, for about 45 minutes, then add garnish vegetables — peas and cut-up green beans are shown. Simmer for 5 to 10 minutes until all the ingredients are tender.

4 **Serving the soup.** Carefully remove and discard all the poultry and meat bones *(above)* and the bouquet garni. Put a slice of dry bread in the bottom of each warmed bowl and ladle out the finished soup *(right)*.

The Several Advantages of Tripe

The delicate flavor and slightly chewy texture of tripe are celebrated in a number of famous soups, from Philadelphia pepper pot *(recipe, page 125)* to *menudo,* the Mexican tripe soup that is shown here. These soups are characterized by a velvety broth—usually enriched with gelatinous veal cuts—and assertive seasonings that provide a contrast to the mellow flavors of the meat and broth.

Each of the three kinds of beef tripe—blanket, thick-seam and honeycomb—comes from a different part of the animal's stomach, provides different texture and calls for slightly different preparation *(Step 1, right).* Honeycomb tripe is by far the most readily available, but it is well worth visiting ethnic markets for thick-seam and blanket tripe: a soup that includes all three types is distinguished by its complex range of textures.

Before it is offered for sale, tripe is parboiled. The preliminary boiling time varies, however, so ask the butcher how long the tripe must cook. It may be as little as 1 hour or as much as 5 hours.

Many tripe soups are cooked in two stages. First, the parboiled tripe is simmered to tenderness in water enriched with aromatic vegetables, a veal shank and, for extra gelatin, some calf's or pig's feet. Next, the bones and spent vegetables are discarded and new flavorings are added. The cooking should proceed at a leisurely simmer: boiling would make the tripe stringy.

Menudo is given extra body by the processed dried corn kernels known as hominy; if they are not available, use chick-peas (garbanzos). Dried hominy or chick-peas should be soaked in water overnight and cooked with the tripe from the start. Canned chick-peas or hominy need only be drained and rinsed; they can be added during the last half hour.

Serve the *menudo* with bowls of dried oregano or chopped coriander leaves; and with chopped raw onion; pounded, dried red chilies; and stemmed, seeded and chopped fresh green chilies—sometimes known as Jalapeño peppers. These head-clearing accompaniments—all available where Latin American foods are sold—have earned the soup a reputation as a sure-fire cure for hangovers.

1 **Cutting up the tripe.** To make the helmet-shaped honeycomb tripe *(above, top left)* lie flat, halve it symmetrically and cut short nicks around the edges. To prepare thick-seam tripe, cut between the two layers right through to the soft center. Scrape away the fat and the lymph nodes on the inner surfaces, as shown above at left. Blanket tripe requires no special trimming; cut it—and the other two types—into rectangles *(above, right).*

5 **Introducing fresh flavorings.** Pour a ladleful of the broth into the pot. Drop in a finely chopped onion, some chopped fresh coriander leaves and a little dried oregano. Bring the mixture to a simmer over medium heat and cook, stirring occasionally, for 5 to 6 minutes. Add the chopped meats and the remaining strained broth to the pot.

6 **Adding hominy.** If you are using canned hominy—as shown in this demonstration—add it at this stage, drained, rinsed in cold water and thoroughly drained again to remove all traces of its canning liquid. Simmer the *menudo* for about 30 minutes longer.

2 **Preparing the meat.** Sever two or three calf's feet at the joint above the foot, and halve the feet lengthwise. Pry out the marrow from the veal shank with a knife and reserve it. Put the tripe, shank and calf's feet in a large pot, cover with cold water and add a little salt.

3 **Adding vegetables.** Bring the water to a boil; spoon off the scum. Add cold water and skim again as the liquid returns to a boil. Skim until the liquid is clear. Add a bouquet garni and aromatic vegetables—in this case, unpeeled garlic cloves, sliced onions, carrots, celery and leeks.

4 **Straining the broth.** Cover the pot, leaving the lid slightly ajar. Simmer for at least 1 hour, or until the tripe is just tender. Strain the liquid into a bowl. Take the veal meat off the bones. Cut the veal and tripe into bite-sized pieces *(above)*; discard the bones, herbs and vegetables. Rinse the pot.

7 **Garnishing and serving.** With a pestle and mortar, pound whole, dried red chilies to coarse flakes. Stem, seed and dice fresh green chilies. Offer the chilies, finely chopped onions and either dried oregano—as shown here—or chopped coriander leaves for guests to sprinkle on their soup.

Starting with Fish

Because fish have little connective tissue, fast boiling breaks up their flesh. Such fragility can be a great asset in soup making: just a few minutes' vigorous cooking melts the flesh into the liquid, yielding a broth rich in body and flavor that can be combined with other, separately cooked ingredients to produce a soup as hearty as the *soupe de poisson (recipe, page 130)* demonstrated here.

Any lean fish is suitable for the soup—among the many possibilities are bass, cod, flounder, haddock and whiting. For the best flavor include several varieties, and always use whole fish—gutted and scaled but not skinned—or include carcasses and heads with cut-up fish.

The fish, together with aromatic vegetables and seasonings, should first be boiled to strip the flesh from the bones, then simmered more gently lest any solids stick to the pan. After about 30 minutes, the soup is strained to produce a shimmering fish essence—thinner than a purée, but with substance lent by the minuscule particles of fish that pass freely through the strainer. The vegetables and the remains of the fish are discarded.

There are as many ways to enhance *soupe de poisson* as there are fish. The Provençal dish shown at right is distinguished by the addition of garlic, saffron, fennel and dried orange peel; other versions include such diverse ingredients as celery, white wine and anchovies.

A wide range of precooked foods may be added to the finished broth: in this demonstration, separately boiled noodles enrich the soup. Croutons, cooked potatoes or cooked rice would perform the same function. To accentuate the flavor, you may wish to poach shellfish or fresh fish pieces briefly in the broth. For contrast, you could add steamed vegetables such as green beans or peas.

Because this version is Provençal, its final garnish is *rouille (box, far right; recipe, page 165):* olive oil, garlic, sweet red pepper and hot chilies blended together into a thick, spicy sauce.

1 Stewing the vegetables. Cover the bottom of a large saucepan with a thin film of olive oil. Over medium heat, stew sliced leeks and onions, whole unpeeled garlic cloves and chopped tomatoes. Season with salt, a bay leaf, savory, dried orange peel and fennel. You can reinforce the fennel's flavor with a splash of anise-flavored liqueur.

2 Adding the fish. After about 10 minutes, when the tomatoes have softened, add the cleaned fish—whiting, bass and two sole carcasses are used here. Pour in boiling water to cover the fish. Boil vigorously for a few minutes, stirring to break up the fish.

4 Cooking the pasta. Homemade noodles *(page 16)*—in this case, flavored with saffron—must first be parboiled in water so that any loose flour left clinging to them will not cloud the soup. Bring the pan of water to a rolling boil, and add salt and a spoonful of olive oil to prevent the pasta ribbons from sticking together. Drop in the noodles *(above, left)*, boil for 1 to 2 minutes, then drain them in a colander. Slide the pasta into the soup *(above, right)*.

3 **Straining the broth.** Simmer the broth uncovered for 30 minutes, stirring occasionally. Ladle some of the broth and fish into a strainer set over a bowl *(above, left)*. Press hard with a pestle to squeeze out all the fish juices *(right)*, but do not grind the solids through the strainer. Discard the solids before ladling more broth and fish into the strainer. After straining all the soup, return it to the rinsed-out pan and bring it to a boil. Stir in saffron threads, crumbled and dissolved in a little hot water.

Pounding the rouille. In a mortar, pound the dry ingredients —coarse salt, dried red hot chilies and peppercorns —to a powder. Pound in basil leaves and garlic cloves. Next, add crustless bread that has been soaked in warm water and squeezed dry. Add sweet peppers that have been broiled, peeled, sliced and seeded. When the mixture is homogeneous, add olive oil drop by drop, while stirring continuously, until the sauce has the consistency of mayonnaise. To control its flow, decant the olive oil into a bottle that has a cork and cut a narrow V-shaped groove in the cork for dispensing the oil.

5 **Stirring the sauce.** Bring the soup to a boil. Taste to see if the pasta is done: it should offer some resistance to the bite. If it is not tender, simmer it for a minute more. Ladle the soup and noodles into plates. Offer *rouille (box, above)* for guests to stir into their soup *(left)*.

Capitalizing on Bivalves and Their Juices

The hinged shells of clams, mussels and oysters enclose sweet flesh and salty liquor. When you steam the shellfish briefly in water or wine, they open and release enough liquor to serve as the basis of a soup. The liquor and flesh of any species of clams may be combined with milk, potatoes, onions and lean salt pork for a New England chowder (*demonstration, right; recipe, page 135*) or with water, tomatoes and aromatic vegetables for a Manhattan chowder. Mussels or other bivalves and their liquor may be incorporated into a velouté to make a rich soup (*box, below; recipe, page 137*).

Bivalves must be bought live; discard any that have open or damaged shells. The rest can be stored for up to 24 hours in a plastic bag in the refrigerator. They require soaking in cold water to flush out grit before cooking (*Step 1, right*).

The steaming that opens bivalves is usually enough to cook their flesh; only the necks of some clam species need extra cooking to tenderize them. The softer meat is simply reheated in the soup.

1 **Cleaning the clams.** Soak the clams in cold, salted water for several hours. Change the water at intervals; it will become cloudy from grit expelled by the clams. Scrub the shells clean (*above*) and rinse them under the tap.

2 **Steaming the clams.** Put the clams in a large pan with enough water to cover them. Cover with a tight-fitting lid and bring the water to a vigorous boil. Shake the pan occasionally to redistribute the clams so that they cook evenly. Remove them from the heat when they have opened — after about 10 minutes. Discard any that stay closed.

Incorporating Mussel Broth in a Velouté

The simplest mussel soup is prepared by steaming the bivalves with wine, herbs and aromatic vegetables. The liquor released by the mussels merges with these flavorings to become a fragrant broth. This dish, in which the unshelled mussels are served in the broth, is known as *moules à la marinière*.

For the richer soup shown here, the mussel broth is combined with a fish velouté sauce and thickened with egg yolks and cream to yield a classic velouté soup (*page 28; recipe, page 137*). The shelled mussels are added to the soup at the last moment.

1 **Steaming the mussels.** Prepare the mussels as for clams (*Step 1, top*), detach the beards and steam them open — about 5 minutes. Drain the broth (*above*) and strain it through cheesecloth (*Step 3, top*). Shell the mussels.

2 **Preparing the soup.** Add the liquid to a roux-thickened fish broth cooked over low heat. Bring slowly to a boil and skim. Add a little saffron, dissolved in hot water. Whisk egg yolks with cream; dilute them with warm soup.

3 **Adding the mussels.** Remove the soup from the heat and stir in the egg-and-cream mixture. Return the soup to low heat and add the shelled mussels. Cook the soup for a minute, but do not simmer, lest the egg yolks curdle.

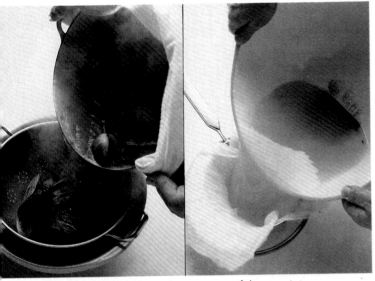

3 **Straining the broth.** Pour the contents of the pan into a colander set in a bowl *(above, left)*. Pull the clams from their shells and dip them in the broth to wash away any remaining grit. Decant the broth carefully into a second bowl through a fine sieve lined with a double layer of dampened muslin or cheesecloth *(right)*. The heavy particles of grit will settle in the first bowl and the finer particles will be caught in the layers of muslin.

4 **Preparing the clam meat.** If you are using long-neck clams, as here, pull off and discard the black skin that covers the necks *(above, left)*. Cut off the necks *(right)* and chop the tough meat fine. Chop the body meat coarse, cover it with a clean, damp cloth and refrigerate the meat until it is needed.

5 **Cooking the vegetables.** Cut a thick slab of salt pork into ½-inch [1-cm.] cubes. Heat oil in a fireproof casserole and fry the cubes lightly. Add thinly sliced onions and cook gently until soft. Stir in sliced potatoes and cook for 2 to 3 minutes. Add the neck meat *(above)* and the strained broth, cover and simmer for 30 minutes.

6 **Completing the soup.** In a separate pan, heat some milk just to boiling. Add this scalded milk to the soup and spoon off any scum that rises to the surface. Add the remaining clam meat *(above)*, some butter and plenty of chopped parsley and thyme. Season with pepper and cayenne pepper. Ladle the chowder into serving bowls *(right)*.

3
Panades
A Time-honored Marriage of Bread and Broth

Slices of rough-textured white bread, turned golden by a saffron broth, are ladled from a fragrant *mourtairol*. The bread was layered in the casserole with pieces of cooked chicken and sliced carrot, then moistened with broth. Baking has colored the bread and produced an amalgam of flavors.

Every diner has succumbed to the urge to soak up the last drops of soup with a scrap of bread. Indeed, bread and soup seem destined for each other. How logical it is, then, to combine them and make the bread an integral part of the soup. This alliance is usually referred to by its French name, *panade,* but it is celebrated in the cooking traditions of many countries *(recipes, pages 138-142).*

Probably the most radically simple panade is the Provençal version, made by steeping bread—preferably sourdough bread—in boiling water or broth, whisking the mixture to a purée and then enriching it with egg yolks and butter *(pages 56-57).* In the Périgord region of southwestern France, layered slices of coarse country bread are moistened with a saffron-flavored chicken broth to produce *mourtairol (opposite);* the name—"death" in the dialect of Périgord—refers to the tradition of serving this soup after funerals.

More elaborate and substantial panades can be created by adding cooked meats and vegetables—poached chicken or beef, sautéed squash or caramelized onions, for example. In Italy, rounds of thinly sliced bread are sandwiched with chopped chicken, prosciutto and marrow to provide the base for *zuppa di pane farcito.* A popular German interpretation is *brotsuppe,* created by simmering dark, coarse bread—made from whole-grain rye flour—in broth with sour cream or sliced bratwurst.

No matter what ingredients are incorporated into a panade, the taste and texture of the finished soup depend primarily on the quality of the bread itself. The soft-textured commercial breads found in most supermarkets will disintegrate to an undistinguished mush in hot soup liquid. The ideal base for a bread soup is a firm, coarse-textured loaf with a thick crust—the kind of bread found at good bakeries and many ethnic markets. Such a loaf, composed of flour, yeast leavening, water and a little salt, can also be made at home *(recipe, page 165);* you can vary it, if you like, by experimenting with different kinds or combinations of flours. For soup making, the loaf should be stale; it should be kept for several days before it is used, so that it will develop a pronounced flavor and dry out enough to soak up liquid readily. If you must make a panade with fresh bread, slice the loaf thinly and dry the slices for 5 to 7 minutes in a 325° F. [160° C.] oven.

Variations on the Simplest Bread Soup

A Vegetable-accented Purée

A soup of bread and broth, excellent in its own right, readily lends itself to elaboration. The ingredients may simply be simmered together, then whisked to form a purée, or the bread can be arranged in layers and baked in the broth so that its surface forms a crisp gratin. Furthermore, as shown here, the addition of commonly available ingredients can give the basic bread-and-broth mixture a wide range of flavors and textures.

The puréed panade at right (recipe, page 138) gains a sweet, oniony aroma from leeks that have first been stewed in butter. Sautéed garlic, sorrel or spinach could replace the leeks; so could parboiled celery or aromatic root vegetables.

A layered *mourtairol* baked in a casserole offers even wider scope for improvisation (recipe, page 139). Here, poached chicken and sliced carrots left over from a *poule au pot* (page 155) are interspersed with bread and bathed with saffron broth to make a substantial soup. You might substitute cooked lamb or rabbit for the chicken, and other root or aromatic vegetables for the carrots.

1 **Cooking the leeks.** Melt butter in an earthenware casserole set on a fireproof mat over low heat. Add thin slices cut from only the white parts of leeks. Simmer until the leeks soften but do not color—about 10 minutes. Half-fill the casserole with hot chicken or veal broth, water mixed with milk, even plain water; chicken broth is used here.

2 **Adding the bread.** Remove the casserole from the heat. Break a generous quantity of stale bread, crust included, into rough chunks. Add bread chunks to the casserole *(above)* until they come up to the surface of the broth. Cover and leave the casserole in a warm place for at least 10 minutes to allow the bread to soak up the broth.

A Baked Assembly Enriched with Meat

1 **Layering the ingredients.** Cut stale bread into thin slices, halving them if the slices are large. In a deep casserole, arrange a layer of cooked meat and vegetables—in this case, pieces of poached chicken and slices of carrots. Top with a layer of bread. Continue to alternate the layers until the casserole is three quarters full, ending with a layer of the bread.

2 **Infusing the saffron.** Heat chicken broth in a separate pot. Place a little ground saffron, or saffron threads pulverized in a mortar, in a large serving spoon and add to it several small spoonfuls of the broth *(above, left)*. When the mixture in the spoon is a deep red-orange, stir it into the broth *(right)*.

3 **Puréeing the bread.** Whisk the mixture to break the bread into small pieces *(above)*. Set the casserole on the fireproof mat over medium heat and bring the soup to a boil, then reduce the heat to maintain a steady simmer. Cook, uncovered, for 30 minutes, whisking once or twice.

4 **Finishing the soup.** At the end of the cooking time, whisk briskly to disperse the bread evenly through the soup. Remove the casserole from the heat. Add a chunk of butter and the yolks of 4 large eggs, then whisk again to amalgamate them *(above)*. Serve the soup in warmed bowls *(right)*.

3 **Moistening the soup.** Preheat the oven to 400° F. [200° C.]. Ladle the saffron-flavored chicken broth over the layered ingredients in the casserole *(above)*. When the topmost layer of bread slices begins to float, add another cup or so [about ¼ liter] of the liquid. Then put the uncovered casserole in the oven.

4 **Cooking and serving.** Let the casserole bake for about an hour: much of the liquid will be absorbed by the bread and a light gratin will form on the surface of the soup. Serve the *mourtairol* heaped onto shallow soup plates *(above)*.

Two Ways to Feature Onions

Onion slices or bits, caramelized to replace their pungency with sweetness, are the hallmark of the most famous of all panades: the bistro-style French onion soup shown opposite, below *(recipe, page 142)*. Divided among individual ovenproof bowls or casseroles, each portion of the onion and broth is crowned with a thick bread slice and heaped with a handful of cheese that is then gratinéed under a broiler until it melts and bubbles. Strictly speaking, the bread and cheese topping is merely a garnish, but it is such an invariable one that the dish would be unrecognizable without it.

Less renowned, but unmistakably a panade, is the thick onion soup shown opposite, top *(recipe, page 141)*, composed mostly of coarse bread slices coated with onions. An old-fashioned recipe, which may well be the ancestor of all onion soups, this panade is made by sprinkling the coated slices with cheese and stacking them in layers in a broad casserole, then pouring in water enough to moisten the bread and make it float.

Both soups require large, sweet, yellow or Spanish onions prepared in the same way *(box, below)*. To rid them of any raw, hot taste, cook the onions for about an hour in two stages: first, stew them gently in butter to soften them and help them render their juices. Then fry them briefly over slightly higher heat so that the sugar they exude will caramelize, giving the onions—and the soups to come—a rich, sweet flavor and fine, brown color.

Whether part of the soup or part of the topping, the traditional cheeses that are used for onion panades are freshly grated or shredded Gruyère and Parmesan. If you must substitute Cheddar, Romano or another sharp-flavored cheese, be sure to pick one that is relatively dry so that it will grate or shred easily and melt without turning stringy.

Any firm-textured bread can be used for the layered soup; dark breads such as rye or whole wheat are as suitable as crusty white loaves and they contribute a sweet taste of their own to intensify the caramel flavor of the onions. Such breads may also serve for onion soup bistro-style, but tradition calls for slices of stale *baguette*—the long, narrow French loaf.

The Gentle Process of Caramelizing

Browning without burning. In a sauté pan or skillet, melt butter over very low heat. Fill the pan with thinly sliced onions. Add salt, cover *(left)* and cook, stirring occasionally, until the onions are very soft but not colored—about 40 minutes. Uncover the pan, increase the heat slightly and stir the onions regularly *(center)*, adjusting the heat as needed, until the onions turn a rich caramel color *(right)*—after 30 minutes or so.

A Layered Casserole with a Crisp Crust

1 Layering the bread. Spread dry bread slices with caramelized onions *(box, opposite)*. Put a layer of bread in a heavy casserole; sprinkle it with grated Parmesan. Repeat until the casserole is two thirds full. To avoid disturbing layers, add boiling water through a funnel *(inset)* until the bread floats.

2 Cooking the soup. With a fireproof pad over the burner, simmer the soup, uncovered, for 30 minutes. Add boiling water if the liquid evaporates to below the bread, then sprinkle the top with cheese and thin shavings of butter. Bake, still uncovered, in a preheated 325° F. [160° C.] oven for about 1 hour.

A Bistro-Style Gratin

1 Preparing the onion broth. Pour boiling liquid — here, beef broth — into a pan containing caramelized onions *(box, opposite)*. Bring the liquid to a boil again, then reduce the heat to maintain a simmer without covering the pan.

2 Ladling into bowls. Simmer the mixture for 10 minutes to allow the onions' flavor to permeate the liquid. Skim off any butter that rises to the surface. Ladle the broth and the onions into individual, heatproof bowls.

3 Finishing the soup. Top each bowl with a slice of dry French bread, and cover the bread and soup with shredded Gruyère cheese. Put the bowls under a hot broiler. As soon as the cheese begins to bubble, serve the soup.

Squash Shells: Choice Containers

The dense flesh of a round winter squash such as acorn, pumpkin or turban makes a rich basis for a panade, and the shell can provide a special fillip: when the flesh is removed for cooking, the empty squash serves as a natural and picturesque—although inedible—soup tureen or bowl. Acorn squashes, used in this demonstration, are just the right size containers to hold individual servings. A large pumpkin will hold enough soup for a dinner party (*recipe, page 138*).

Winter squash rind is tough, so choose a stout, sharp knife for opening the vegetable. Stand the squash upright on the working surface; with an acorn squash, pull off the stem and stand it on its rounded stem end. Cut a thick slice off the top to form an opening broad enough for easy cleaning of the squash. After scraping out all the seeds and fiber, carve away the flesh. A melon baller is an efficient tool for removing flesh from inside the base of the squash; a sharp spoon or small knife with a curved blade—if you have it—works well on the sides.

The squash flesh is cooked by stages. First, soften and flavor it by stewing the chopped-up pieces in butter and aromatic onions, as in this demonstration, although garlic, leeks or celery could be used instead. When the squash begins to exude its moisture, add a little water and simmer the flesh until it becomes a purée. Next, the soup—enriched with cream, if you like—is transferred to its shell container, along with alternate layers of bread and cheese. Gruyère cheese is used here, but you can substitute any fairly dry cheese, such as Parmesan and aged Cheddar, which is easily grated and does not become stringy when cooked.

When the assembly is baked in a hot oven for about 10 to 15 minutes, the soup will be thick, the cheese richly colored, and the uniquely self-contained panade ready for the table.

Preparing the squash. Slice across each acorn squash about one quarter down from its pointed end and discard the slice. Clean out the seeds and fibers, then scoop out the flesh *(left)*, leaving a wall of flesh ¼ inch [6 mm.] thick to prevent the shell from leaking. Reserve the shell and coarsely chop the scooped-out flesh *(above)*.

2 **Preliminary cooking.** Melt butter in a heavy saucepan, drop in finely chopped onions and sauté the onions gently in the butter until they are soft but not brown. Stir in the cut-up squash, a handful or two at a time.

3 **Breaking up the squash.** Cook the squash over low heat, stirring continuously to break up the flesh and prevent it from sticking to the bottom of the pan. After about 10 minutes, the squash flesh will begin to exude moisture. At this stage, stir in enough hot water to just cover the squash.

4 **Enriching the soup.** Season the squash with salt, pepper and nutmeg to taste. Simmer the soup uncovered over low heat for 30 minutes, stirring occasionally, until it is a smooth purée. Pour in heavy cream to enrich the mixture, and recheck the seasoning.

5 **Cooking in the shell.** Ladle soup into each shell and add bread cubes and grated Gruyère. Repeat until the layers almost fill each shell, finishing with cheese. Place the squash on a baking sheet and cook it in a preheated 425° F. [220° C.] oven until the cheese forms a golden crust. Serve immediately *(below)*.

4
Cold Soups
Appealing Creations for Summer

When hot weather parches throats and dulls appetites, cold soups—either chilled versions of soups usually served hot, or soups specially designed to be served on ice—make a refreshing start to a meal.

Among hot soups, the best for chilling are vegetable purées *(pages 24-29)*, which remain both light and rich, and clear meat broths such as consommé *(pages 64-65)*, which set into glittering jellies. Both types, however, require slightly different preparations if they are to be chilled. A consommé, for example, should be reinforced during cooking by adding gelatinous cuts of meat to ensure that the cooled broth gels properly. Purées to be served cold should be made with a minimum of butter or none at all, and every particle of fat they contain must be skimmed off after cooking: fat becomes an unappetizing scum when chilled. A chilled purée should be enriched with cream or sour cream instead of butter—as in the famous vichyssoise *(recipe, page 144)*, a modern American version of an ancient European leek and potato soup. Cream also dilutes purées—a helpful function, since these soups thicken as they chill.

Cold soups frequently depend on ingredients that act as a tonic to the palate: summer fruits, crisp vegetables and acidic flavorings. Many of these ingredients are used raw so that their fresh flavors remain unaltered. Soft fruits such as berries and pears, for example, often go uncooked into fruit soups. And gazpacho *(pages 66-67)* is an invigorating mixture of uncooked peppers, tomatoes, cucumbers, onions and other vegetables floating in an icy liquid such as tomato juice, each vegetable adding a clear, individual note of flavor and texture to the liquid base.

Similar refreshing contrasts of flavor are characteristic of many cold soups. In a Senegalese soup *(pages 70-71)*, the mild, milky liquid extracted from coconuts balances the pungency of hot curry spices. In the cherry soup at left *(recipe, page 148)*, white wine and sour cream provide a foil for the sweetness of the fruit. And in the Russian *botvinya (pages 68-69)*, a pleasantly acidic sauce made from fermented rye bread sets off the milder flavors of poached fish, cooked leaves and crisp salad vegetables.

No matter how a soup is flavored or prepared, chilling will mute the tastes, particularly that of salt. Even if you adjust the seasoning after cooking, taste the soup after it has been chilled and just before you serve it: extra seasoning may be needed to give the dish the perfect finish.

A chilled cherry soup, thickened with sour cream and garnished with cherries, is ladled from a glass bowl that reveals the soup's bright color. The cherries were soaked in warm wine ahead of time to soften them and release some of their juices into the soup.

Clarifying Broth for a Jellied Consommé

Attractively garnished, a basic chicken or meat broth *(pages 8-9; recipes, pages 88-91)* is an excellent soup by itself. The soup can be endowed with a greater subtlety and complexity of flavor, however, if the broth is cooked a second time with fresh meat and vegetables. The result is what the French call a consommé: a consummate broth.

If the consommé is to be served cold and jellied, one of the enriching ingredients of the second cooking must be high in natural gelatin. In the demonstration here, a consommé *à la Madrilène (recipe, page 151)* based on chicken broth receives its secondary infusion from lean beef, chicken parts, aromatic vegetables and tomatoes, which add a rosy color as well as flavor. The chicken parts, particularly the feet (obtainable at ethnic markets), provide enough gelatin to set the broth—when chilled—to a light jelly that liquefies in the mouth.

The mark of a successful consommé, whether it is jellied or not, is perfect clarity. Prepare the basic broth by the slow-cooking method demonstrated on pages 10-11, making sure that you skim and strain it meticulously. Chill it, then remove every speck of fat on the surface.

Combine the cold broth with the enriching ingredients and simmer them gently for about an hour. During the cooking, the fresh ingredients release small particles of fat and bits of food into the soup. Some of these particles are too fine to be strained out, but they can be trapped by molecules of the protein albumin, supplied in nearly undiluted form by the addition of raw egg whites.

While the soup is heating, the albumin in the whites will coagulate and attract the particles of fat and food. But the cooking must by very gentle or the albumin will solidify before it has done its job. The white, along with the trapped particles, is filtered out when the consommé is strained after cooking.

A jellied consommé merits an elaborate presentation to display its clarity and jewel-like color: put the soup in a clear glass bowl nested in a larger container partly filled with cubes of ice. This will keep the consommé chilled and enhance its shimmering.

1 **Preparing the ingredients.** Trim all the fat from a piece of lean beef—chuck is used here—and chop it to a fine consistency. Trim and clean the carrots and leeks, then chop them equally fine. Cut unpeeled tomatoes into coarse pieces. Chop the chicken parts into chunks *(above)* to expose their gelatin-rich tissues.

2 **Enriching the broth.** Put the beef, chicken and vegetables into a heavy pan. Add 1 or 2 egg whites *(left)* — and, if you like, the finely crumbled eggshells — and stir them well into the mixture. Ladle in cold chicken broth *(right)* and stir to combine it with the other ingredients. Heat the cold broth very slowly and gently so that the egg-white albumin does not solidify too soon.

3 **Simmering the broth.** Stir occasionally as the liquid slowly comes to a boil. Skimming is not necessary, since the impurities will be removed later. Partially cover the pan, then adjust the heat and let the soup barely simmer for an hour to extract all the flavor from the solid ingredients.

4 **Straining out the solids.** Line a strainer with several layers of muslin or cheesecloth wrung out in cold water, and set the strainer over a bowl. Pour the warm broth into the lined strainer and let it drain through. To keep the broth absolutely clear, do not press the solids to extract extra drops of liquid.

5 **Serving the consommé.** Chill the consommé until it sets to a light jelly. To serve, put the bowl of consommé inside a larger bowl containing ice cubes. Ladle the soup into chilled consommé cups *(left)*. Garnish *(below)* with sweet red pepper, broiled to loosen its skin, then peeled and diced.

Mixtures That Need No Cooking

In the hot summer months when cold soups are appropriate, dozens of vegetables ripen. Chopped or puréed and authoritatively seasoned, this bounty from the garden makes what many cooks consider the finest chilled soups of all.

All such soups invite improvisation, but one rule must be observed: because the soups are uncooked, the vegetables in them should be of the very best texture and flavor. For example, the avocado soup demonstrated at right, top *(recipe, page 143)*, depends on avocado flesh that is soft, creamy and perfectly ripe. If possible, choose the pebbly-skinned, dark green California avocados that are plentiful in summer; they have the richest flesh. Buy the avocados when they are hard and unripe—avocados bought ripe are often bruised—and put them in a warm, dark place for a few days until the skins yield slightly to gentle pressure.

To make soup from the ripe avocados, purée their flesh—to either a rough or smooth texture, as you wish—and add liquid. Chicken stock, veal stock or white wine are all good choices, and the blend may be enriched with heavy cream, sour cream or yogurt.

Since avocados are bland tasting, judicious seasoning is in order. Garlic and lemon or lime juice brighten the flavor. Some soups are garnished with parsley or chives, and some with fresh dill.

The same freedom applies to gazpacho *(bottom right)*, a favorite raw-vegetable soup of Spain and Latin America. Gazpacho demands crisp garnishes: chopped peppers, celery, cucumber and scallions as well as croutons are traditional. But the soup itself can be made any number of ways. Its base is a mixture of tomatoes, cucumber, green pepper, onion and garlic—all moistened with olive oil, wine vinegar and either water, stock or the tomato juice used here *(recipe, page 146)*.

The vegetables may be puréed in a blender or food processor to produce a thick, smooth soup. Or for a crunchier texture, they may be chopped and the chunks stirred into the desired liquid, thickened perhaps with bread crumbs. As for seasonings, fresh basil is especially appropriate with this tomato-based soup, but you can also use cumin, chili, thyme, parsley, dill, and even mint.

A Cool Blend of Avocado and Cream

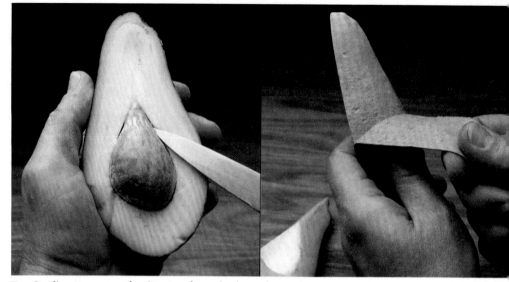

Peeling an avocado. Starting from the broader end, cut through the flesh to the pit. Rotate the knife around the pit to halve the avocado lengthwise. Pull the halves apart and pry out the pit with the knife tip *(above, left)*. Slice each half in two and, starting at the stem end, peel off the skin *(right)*. Place the peeled pieces in a large bowl, then scrape off the dark green flesh that clings to the inside of the skins and add it to the bowl. Drench all the flesh with lemon juice to prevent discoloration and to add a slight tartness.

Tomatoes: The Heart of a Liquid Salad

Preparing the soup base. Core fresh tomatoes, immerse them for 10 seconds in boiling water to loosen the skins, then drain and peel them *(above, left)*. Halve the tomatoes horizontally, squeeze out the seeds and chop the pulp. Add the tomatoes to a paste *(right)* made by pounding fresh bread crumbs, garlic cloves, cumin seeds, wine vinegar and olive oil together in a mortar.

2 **Puréeing.** Mash the avocado flesh with a fork to make a rough purée. If you want a smooth-textured soup, pass this purée through a food mill or press it through a strainer. For a varied texture, try mixing a very smooth purée with some of the flesh that has been only roughly mashed.

3 **Combining ingredients.** Stir into the purée enough liquid—chicken broth is used here—to make it easy to pour. Add salt, white pepper and cayenne pepper to taste; enrich the soup with heavy cream or well-beaten sour cream. Pour the soup into a tureen, and cover and refrigerate it.

4 **Serving the soup.** Let the soup chill at least 3 hours to blend the flavors. Just before serving, garnish it with fresh chives or dill, chopped fine. Ladle the soup into well-chilled soup plates.

2 **Adding raw vegetables.** Chop up the other raw vegetables—in this case, sweet Spanish onions, pitted ripe olives and seeded red and green sweet peppers. Add them to the tomato mixture, together with a sprinkling of chopped fresh marjoram and mint.

3 **Stirring in liquids.** Pour chilled tomato juice into the bowl and stir to combine it with the other ingredients. Add ice water (above) to dilute the gazpacho to the desired consistency. In a mortar, pound black pepper, coarse salt and dried chilies, and stir them in. Cover and refrigerate for 1 to 2 hours.

4 **Presenting the soup.** Put the gazpacho in a serving bowl and add a chunk of ice. Sprinkle on some chopped scallions. Accompany the soup with bowls of small croutons (page 21) and chopped fresh vegetables—here, celery, peeled and seeded cucumber, sweet pepper and onion.

A Unique Pairing of Fish and Vegetables

Most soups are a fusion of flavors, created by cooking an array of foods together. Some soups, however, depend for effect on counterbalancing sharply contrasted tastes. Fruit soups *(pages 72-73)* belong in this category. So do cold soups such as *botvinya (recipe, page 150)*, the Russian fish soup demonstrated here, whose components are prepared separately and assembled just before serving so that each retains its own flavor.

Botvinya takes its name from *botva*, the Russian word for the beet greens that traditionally are puréed to form part of the soup. When beet greens are unavailable, spinach or sorrel (or both) can be used as a substitute. As a contrast to the soft, strongly flavored green purée, the soup also includes crisp, raw vegetables such as cucumbers and scallions, and it is accompanied by peppery radishes and grated horseradish.

The central element of *botvinya*, however, is its fish, poached separately in an aromatic broth, then cut up and chilled. Any firm-fleshed, full-flavored variety is suitable: salmon is used here, but mackerel or trout could be chosen instead. To support the fish flavor, the soup may feature a separately cooked garnish of shellfish—either shrimp or crayfish may be used—whose shells can be transformed into a flavoring for the soup liquid by a technique similar to that used for a shellfish bisque *(pages 32-33)*.

The soup liquid itself gives the final assembly its distinctive character: it is a slightly bitter, beerlike concoction called *kvas (botvinya recipe, page 150)*, made by fermenting rye bread with water, yeast and molasses. Preparing *kvas* takes at least three days; if time is short, a strong, dark beer or ale may be substituted to give the soup a similarly tart taste.

1 **Poaching the fish.** Combine water with onion, fennel, thyme and a bay leaf in a pot large enough to hold the fish flat, and drape foil across the pot to support the fish; lay the fish—here, salmon—on the foil so that the liquid covers it. Bring the water to a simmer, cover the pot and poach the fish until the flesh flakes when probed. This will take about 10 minutes for each inch [2½ cm.] of the fish's thickness. Grasp the foil and lift the fish out.

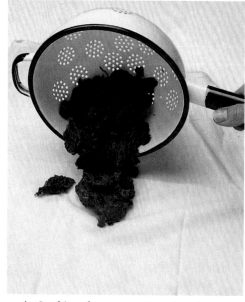

4 **Cooking the greens.** Trim the ribs from spinach—used here—or young beet leaves. Cook the leaves for 1 minute in boiling salted water, drain, squeeze the leaves dry with a cloth *(above)*, then chop them into coarse pieces. Parboil sorrel, then purée it through a fine-meshed nylon sieve *(page 28)*.

5 **Cutting raw vegetables.** Peel a cucumber and cut it lengthwise into five or six slices. Cut each slice into long strips, then cut the strips into small dice *(above)*. Trim off the roots and tips of scallions and chop them fine. Mince some fresh parsley and dill.

2 **Skinning and carving.** Set the fish on a work surface. While it is still warm, peel off the skin. Cut down to the backbone along the length of the fish, then slice across the base of the tail. Using the knife, ease the two sections of flesh off the backbone *(above, left)*. Pry out the backbone *(right)*. Divide the other half of the fish lengthwise into two sections and lift them up from the skin. Cut each section of flesh into three or four pieces. Chill the fish.

3 **Preparing the shrimp.** Simmer the shrimp in water for 5 minutes, then shell and devein them, leaving on the tail fins for decoration. Chill the shrimp. In a mortar, pound the shells to fragments, adding a little *kvas;* strain and reserve the flavored *kvas.*

6 **Combining the kvas and the vegetables.** Put the spinach, sorrel and chopped raw vegetables in a chilled tureen and pour in the *kvas (above)*. Add finely chopped fresh parsley and finely cut fresh dill. Pour in the liquor flavored with shrimp shells. To offset the sourness of the *kvas,* add 1 to 2 teaspoons [5 to 10 ml.] of molasses or brown sugar. Stir the mixture well. Season to taste with salt.

7 **Presenting the accompaniments.** Trim the ends from a horseradish, peel it with a sharp knife and grate it. Put it in a serving dish and sprinkle on lemon juice to prevent discoloring. On a separate plate, arrange radishes around a mound of coarse salt. Add the salmon pieces and the shrimp to the soup, then serve it over ice with the horseradish and radish accompaniments *(above)*.

Hot Spices in a Bland Liquid

As long as all its fat is removed, a velouté *(pages 28-29)* makes an excellent cold soup and a perfect vehicle for imaginative flavoring. Since chilling mutes seasonings, the flavors should be authoritative: a case in point is the Senegalese soup demonstrated here.

A Senegalese soup made with chicken, meat or vegetable stock, draws its piquancy from curry spices. Whereas a commercial curry powder may be used for this soup *(recipe, page 149)*, the results will be far tastier if you blend your own aromatics and spices *(box, opposite, bottom)*, then stew the spices in the velouté butter *(Step 1, right)* to release their flavors.

Many curry spices are fiery, and although chilling diminishes the effect, the soup benefits from the tempering of a mildly sweet ingredient. In this demonstration, the soup is enriched with the liquid of a fresh coconut—one in which you can hear the liquid splash when you shake the shell—and is then garnished with the grated flesh *(box, below)*.

1 **Preparing the flavorings.** In a mortar, crush about 1 tablespoon [15 ml.] each of coriander, cumin, fenugreek and black mustard seeds into coarse pieces. Melt a little butter in a sauté pan or skillet, and stew the spices over low heat for a minute or so. Add peeled, sliced garlic cloves, chopped onions and celery *(above, left)*, and cook them until the onions are translucent. Add flour *(center)*, warmed broth — chicken broth, in this case — a bay leaf and some turmeric root pounded to powder *(right)*; if the root is unavailable, substitute ground turmeric.

The Goodness in a Coconut

Opening the shell. To tap the liquid of a coconut, drive an ice pick or a screwdriver blade into two of the dark "eyes" at the nut's pointed end and pour out the fluid. Break the shell with a mallet and cut the flesh from the husk. Pare off the skin and grate the flesh. Taste the coconut liquid; if it is sweet, you may add it to any curry just before serving: long simmering lessens its flavor.

2 **Simmering the soup.** Bring the broth rapidly to a boil. Reduce the heat to a simmer and skim off the film that collects on the surface. When the soup is clear, cover the pan and continue to simmer gently for at least 40 minutes.

3 **Straining the liquid.** Add coconut liquid *(box, left)* and a few crushed dried chilies. Since the chilies would impart too much of their fieriness to the soup if cooked in it for long, bring the soup back to a simmer, then pour it through a strainer into a bowl *(above)*.

4 **Enriching with cream.** Cover the strained soup and chill it. Before serving, stir in heavy cream to thicken the liquid and mellow its flavor. The turmeric will give the soup a striking yellow hue.

5 **Garnishing and serving.** Serve the soup in chilled soup plates *(right)*. To balance the pungency of the spices, offer a dish of freshly grated coconut for guests to sprinkle on their soup.

Blending Your Own Spices

The spices that flavor the Senegalese soup are common constituents of commercial curry powders—but in these powders, the spices are too frequently inferior and old. To avoid disappointment, make your own curry flavorings. To do this, buy whole spices; they will keep their flavor longer than preground spices do. With a mortar and pestle you can crush spices into fragments large enough to be strained off when cooking is completed. If you want to reduce the spices to powder, use an electric food processor or small electric coffee grinder reserved just for this purpose.

You can vary the basic curry mixture *(Step 1, opposite)* in many ways. Among the milder spices that you can add in liberal amounts are coriander, cardamom and cinnamon. Turmeric and fenugreek are always added to curries, use them sparingly, however: large quantities can make a dish bitter. Use restraint also with strong-tasting saffron, cumin, cloves and mustard seeds. For extra bite, add peppercorns, fresh or dried chilies, and fresh or dried ginger root. (Wear rubber gloves when handling chilies: their volatile oils can irritate the skin. And keep them—and their oils—away from the eyes. To remove the bitter seeds, pull out the stem, then slice the chili lengthwise and pick out any seeds that remain inside.)

Heat brings out flavor in cumin, saffron, coriander, fenugreek, cinnamon and cloves. Toast whole spices individually before you grind them: put them in a dry, heavy pan over medium heat until their aromas become pronounced. Or fry the spices *(Step 1, opposite)* in the same pan you use for your curried dish. Cook cinnamon and cloves for 5 to 7 minutes, the other spices more briefly. Cumin should be heated for only a minute; otherwise it will become too strong.

Many spices can be added to the soup either early or late, but turmeric is one that profits from lengthy cooking to mellow its flavor. It should therefore be included at the beginning of the cooking process—after you have added liquid to the mixture. Turmeric burns easily and should never be fried or toasted.

By contrast, peppercorns should be added only when the cooking is finished: long cooking turns them bitter. Chilies can overwhelm all other flavors if they are cooked a long time; add them when the soup is nearly ready.

Fruit: An Unexpected Resource

When married to ingredients that set off its sweetness, almost any fruit—from melon to berries—can serve as the basis for a refreshing and unusual soup. Only citrus fruits and watermelon are too acid, watery or fibrous to produce the creamy blend of savory, acerbic and sweet flavors characteristic of fruit soups.

For the freshest flavor, fruit for soup is left raw or, if it is very crisp, cooked only long enough to soften it. To intensify the taste, the soup liquid may be flavored by steeping in it the aromatic seeds or pits, stems and skins of the fruit.

The liquid itself may add a savory note—a role played by the chicken broth used in the pear soup demonstrated below *(recipe, page 149)*. Or the liquid may be sharper-tasting red or white wine, as in the cherry soup opposite. A very tart flavoring such as lemon or lime juice is almost always included, giving a clear contrast to the sweetness. Still other flavorings can add subtle but distinctive touches: in the pear soup, for example, watercress provides a peppery taste; cinnamon enlivens the cherry soup.

The final touch—enriching or thickening—should bring all the flavors into harmony. In the pear soup, for instance, the liquid is thickened by puréeing the pears. The soup can be thickened further with arrowroot, cornstarch or tapioca, but the heavy-cream enrichment used here blends the flavors to perfection. In the cherry soup, the fruit is left whole; the sour-cream thickener adds yet another element to a complex mixture.

To protect the flavor and color of the soup, use nylon or stainless-steel strainers and sieves, and enameled or tin-lined pots: acid in most fruits interacts with such metals as aluminum and cast iron.

A Pear Purée Sharpened with Watercress

1 **Puréeing the pears.** Immerse quartered, cored and peeled pears in hot, fat-free chicken broth *(recipe, page 164)*, cover with foil and let them soften for 20 minutes. Purée the mixture in a food mill, using the fine blade.

2 **Adding flavors.** Simmer the pear skins and cores in broth. Strain the broth, add chopped watercress, boil the broth and stir it into the pear purée.

3 **Finishing the soup.** Add lemon juice, salt and white pepper, then cover and chill the soup. Before serving, stir in heavy cream. For a garnish, drop watercress sprigs in boiling water, then drain and rinse them in cold water: this brightens and softens the sprigs.

Capturing the Tang of Sour Cherries

1 **Preparing the cherries.** Pit the cherries with a cherry pitter *(left)*, or halve them with a knife and pick out the pits. Fold half of the pits in a cloth and crack them with a mallet to expose the kernels, which have an agreeably bitter flavor. Cherry pits and stems may be unsafe to eat if not cooked promptly. Put the crushed pits, stems and whole pits into a nonreactive pan *(right)*, add wine, and proceed immediately to Step 2.

2 **Flavoring the liquid.** Add sugar, a piece of cinnamon stick and some grated lemon peel. Bring the mixture to a boil, reduce the heat and simmer for 5 to 10 minutes. Strain the liquid through a nylon or stainless-steel sieve, then pour it back into the pan.

3 **Assembling.** Halve and reserve a few cherries. Put the rest in the wine and cool until tepid. Whisk sour cream until it is smooth, then stir in the cherry mixture. Add lemon juice and salt until the liquid is slightly more tart than the fruit.

4 **Serving.** Cover the soup and refrigerate it for at least 3 hours. Transfer the soup to a chilled bowl and garnish with the reserved cherry halves. Serve in chilled plates, accompanied by toasted brioche *(right)* or other slightly sweet bread.

5
Full-Meal Soups
Two Courses from a Single Pot

Generous servings with chicken and beef
Varied roles for cabbage
Tenderizing dried beans
Dealing with cured meats
A piquant sauce for fish
The key to a zesty borscht

Many soups are substantial enough to qualify as light meals in themselves. A generous serving of Scotch broth, for example, will assuage all but the heartiest of appetites; a bowl of thick onion soup is a customary late-night meal for revelers in Paris. The soups that are demonstrated in this chapter are prepared on an even more ample scale. All of them provide two courses from a single pot.

The first course is a rich broth; the second is the meat, poultry or fish that has been cooked with vegetables in the broth. When the broth has been drunk, soupspoons are exchanged for knives and forks, and the platter of carved meat and vegetable accompaniments is presented. This arrangement is flexible, however: if you prefer, you can bring both broth and meat to the table at the same time.

Full-meal soups often include a varied selection of meats or fish that will give the broth a great depth of flavor and make a splendid array for the second course. The dish shown opposite, for example—an especially generous version of *poule au pot (pages 76-77)*—features not only a whole, stuffed chicken, but also two cuts of beef. And it is garnished with stuffed cabbage leaves in addition to the usual aromatic vegetables. On a less lavish scale, the bean and ham soup demonstrated on pages 78-79 is supplemented with pork sausage and pig's ears; and the traditional Provençal *bourride (pages 80-81)*—distinguished by its garlic-flavored mayonnaise garnish—is made from a variety of firm, white-fleshed fish.

In spite of their generous proportions, full-meal soups originated as thrifty peasant dishes that could be prepared with a minimum of fuel and cooking utensils. Many of them have since been elevated to the status of classic dishes worthy of the most discriminating table. The borschts of Eastern Europe, for example, can be simple soups made with beets and other vegetables; however, an elaborate Ukrainian version *(pages 84-85)* also includes lean salt pork and beef, and is garnished with small savory pastries. And the borscht served at the court of Czar Nicholas II included a whole duck *(recipe, page 152)*.

Borscht in any version is so ample that it is unlikely to be consumed at a single sitting, thus giving you plenty for another full hot meal. Or you can serve the strained liquid, iced and garnished, for a light luncheon the following day *(page 86)*.

The amber broth from the gentle poaching of stuffed chicken, beef and aromatic vegetables for *poule au pot* is ladled into plates. Toasted bread stuffed with puréed vegetables *(page 21)* garnishes the broth, while carved meats, vegetables and stuffed cabbage await service as the second course.

Beef and Stuffed Chicken Poached in a Pot

Preparing a soup and a meat course in a single pot has been a rustic tradition since the days when broth was kept simmering permanently on the hearth, occasionally supplemented with meat or fowl. The everlasting pot of broth is gone, but in rural France a Sunday meal of soup and poached beef *(pot-au-feu)* or chicken *(poule au pot)* is still customary. In the bounteous holiday version of *poule au pot* shown here *(recipe, page 155),* beef or veal and a stuffed chicken are cooked with vegetables to make a fragrant broth and a substantial main course.

The important difference between the preparation of this dish and that of a basic broth *(page 10)* is that the cooking times for the meat and chicken must be carefully gauged so that the meats enrich the poaching liquid without themselves becoming tasteless and stringy. For a balanced dish, choose an older stewing chicken and two cuts of meat—here, beef short ribs and a piece of shank. The shank, like the chicken, contains gelatin that not only keeps the flesh succulent, but also gives body to the broth; the short ribs contain layers of fat that help keep their meat moist during cooking.

Since the meat requires longer cooking than the chicken, poach it on its own for about an hour. In the meantime, stuff and truss the chicken. The moist bread stuffing used in this demonstration is in keeping with the economical character of the dish, but you can use any stuffing suitable for a roast bird. If you prefer, make more stuffing than you need and wrap the surplus in parboiled cabbage leaves *(box, right).* Since the flavor of cabbage is enhanced by fat, but would overpower the other vegetables in the broth, cook the stuffed leaves separately in a mixture of broth and liquid chicken fat spooned from the surface of the soup.

Aromatic vegetables are added to the broth with the chicken. In the two or more hours required to cook the chicken, the vegetables will be drained of flavor: replace them with fresh garnish vegetables—you could use carrots, small boiling onions, leeks, turnips or potatoes—about 30 minutes before serving. You can mash the spent vegetables with a fork and spread them on toasted crusts of bread to make a garnish *(page 21).*

1 Preparing the meat. Using cotton string, tie the cuts of meat into compact bundles *(above)* so that they will cook evenly and be easy to carve. Place the trussed meat in a pot large enough to hold the chicken and vegetables as well. Cover the meat with cold water and set the pot over medium heat.

2 Skimming. As the water comes to a boil, spoon off the gray scum from the surface. To encourage the scum to form, add cold water and skim again as the liquid returns to a boil. Repeat until the scum is gone. Reduce the heat, partly cover the pot and barely simmer the meat; meanwhile, prepare the chicken.

Filled Cabbage Leaves as Garnish

1 Stuffing the leaves. Cut off the tough stems of cabbage leaves and parboil the leaves for 5 minutes; drain well. Place stuffing at the base of each leaf, fold over the base, then the sides, and roll up the leaf to make a neat package.

2 Cooking the leaves. Place the leaves, seam down, in a pan. Half-submerge them with fatty broth spooned from the surface of the soup, cover and simmer for 30 minutes. Remove the leaves with a slotted spoon.

3 **Stuffing and trussing the chicken.** To make the bird easier to carve, remove its wishbone: pull back the neck skin to expose the arch of flesh that covers the wishbone — the first bone in the cavity. Locate it with your fingers, and with a small knife cut it free. Then pull it out. Stuff the chicken loosely through the tail vent. The stuffing shown is made of eggs, chopped and sautéed chicken liver, and salt pork. Use a trussing needle and string to sew up the tail vent. Tie the bird securely or truss it.

4 **Cooking the chicken.** When the meat has cooked for about 1 hour, ladle out and reserve enough liquid to allow room for the chicken and vegetables. Add the bird, a peeled onion stuck with cloves, an unpeeled garlic bulb, carrots and a bouquet garni (above). Remove any scum formed as the broth returns to a boil. Simmer, partly covered, for 2 hours, adding reserved broth, if necessary, to keep the meat covered with liquid. Spoon off the fat that collects on the surface and reserve it.

5 **Serving.** Half an hour before serving, remove the vegetables, mash and spread them on bread. Add garnish vegetables (carrots, leeks and turnips are used here) and cook until tender. Remove the meat and fowl, strain the broth and ladle it over the bread; then serve the meat, fowl and vegetables.

Cured Pork with Beans: Warming Winter Staples

Among the soups that provide hearty, warming meals on cold nights, the most substantial are those that are made of old-fashioned winter staples: smoked or salted pork and dried beans or peas. Versions of these soups range from the yellow pea and pork soup of Sweden *(recipe, page 154)* to the Italian *zuppa di fagioli* (bean soup) that is demonstrated here *(recipe, page 154)*.

The pork for the soup may be any strong-flavored cut: a picnic ham is used in this demonstration. For the richest flavor and tenderest meat, buy a cut surrounded by fat and rind: these are rarely available except in ethnic markets but you can ask a butcher to tie fat and rind around the meat for you.

To make the soup meatier, you can add other inexpensive pork products: pig's feet, for example, or the sausages used here. Pig's ears, available at ethnic markets, are a particularly good addition because the gelatin they contain will give the soup a rich body.

The cook has a similar latitude in choosing beans for the soup. The earthy flavor of almost any dried bean or pod—white or kidney beans, peas or lentils, for example—combines equally well with the assertive flavor of the meat. The beans themselves require the greatest amount of time for preliminary preparation: most types must be soaked in cold water overnight to restore their moisture and reduce their cooking times; split peas and lentils require no soaking.

The beans, pork and pig's ears are simmered together for 1½ to 3 hours, depending on the tenderness of the beans. If sausages are included, they should be added about 40 minutes before the soup is ready: they cook quickly, since ground meat is readily penetrated by heat. If you are using split peas or lentils, boil them separately first and add them about 15 minutes before serving.

When both the meats and beans are tender, you can thicken the soup, if you like, by puréeing some of the beans. And you can garnish the soup with *sofrito*—a thick, sautéed mixture of onions, tomatoes and, sometimes, garlic. Do not add salt until the soup is ready for the table; the cured meats may provide all the necessary seasoning.

1 Soaking the beans. Pick over the dried beans—in this case, white beans—and remove the blemished specimens and any stones and fibers. Put the beans in a large bowl and cover them with cold water *(above)*. Leave the beans to soak overnight.

2 Starting the soup. Put the slow-cooking meats—in this case, a picnic ham and a pig's ear that has been singed to remove hairs—in a pot with aromatic vegetables and a bouquet garni that includes savory. Add cold water. Drain the beans and add them.

6 Frying the sofrito. In a sauté pan over medium heat, cook chopped onions in olive oil until they begin to color. Add peeled, seeded and coarsely chopped tomatoes *(above)* and cook, stirring occasionally, until most of the liquid evaporates. Stir in some chopped, fresh parsley.

7 Finishing the broth. Increase the heat under the pot containing the broth and beans. As the liquid returns to a simmer, add the *sofrito* and stir well. Taste the soup for seasoning; reduce the heat and continue to cook for 2 to 3 minutes to amalgamate the flavors.

3 **Cleansing the soup.** Put the pot over medium heat and bring the liquid to a boil, occasionally spooning off the surface scum. Adjust the heat to a simmer and partially cover the pot. Cook the soup for 1½ to 3 hours, or until the beans are tender when tested with a fork.

4 **Adding quick-cooking meat.** Prick fresh or cured pork sausages to prevent their skins from splitting and add them to the pot 30 to 40 minutes before the end of cooking. From time to time, skim off any sausage fat that rises to the surface of the soup.

5 **Thickening the broth.** Lift out the cooked meats and keep them warm. Discard the vegetables and the bouquet garni. Scoop out some beans; purée them through a wire strainer into the soup, moistening them with broth to facilitate the puréeing.

8 **Presenting the soup.** Slice up the ham, pig's ears and sausages, and arrange them on a heated platter. Transfer the soup to a heated tureen, then ladle it into warmed soup plates *(left)* and serve before, or with, the meats.

Fish Steaks and a Creamy Broth

Because even a large piece of fish will cook in less than 30 minutes, you can prepare a soup containing enough fish to make a meal in under an hour. Cooking is simply a matter of poaching any lean species—flounder or rockfish, for example—in water or fish stock with aromatic flavorings. Timing is easy: allow 10 minutes' simmering for each inch [2½ cm.] of the fish's thickness.

To give the soup body, the cooking liquid may be thickened after the fish has been poached: slices of bread are frequently used for this purpose (recipes, pages 159 and 160). The bourride shown on these pages is the traditional soup of Provence and its stock is thickened with aioli, a pungent, garlic-flavored mayonnaise (box, below; recipe, page 159).

Serve the fish portions separately or, as here, in the thickened liquid. When the thickener is aioli, extra sauce is offered as a garnish.

1 **Preparing the fish.** Cut up the fish; in this instance, angler tail and conger eel have been skinned and sliced into cross sections. Briefly stew aromatic vegetables, such as the chopped leeks, peeled garlic cloves and chopped parsley shown, in olive oil to soften them. Arrange the fish pieces on the vegetables (above).

Aioli: Garlic Mayonnaise

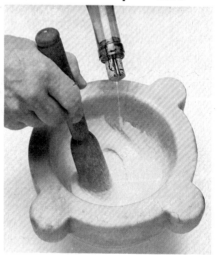

A garlicky emulsion. In a mortar, pound peeled garlic and coarse salt to a smooth paste, then incorporate room-temperature egg yolks. Stirring briskly, add drops of oil from a spoon or from a bottle with a grooved cork (page 51). As the aioli thickens, increase the flow of oil (above). When the sauce is stiff, thin it with lemon juice and add a little warm water to stabilize the emulsion. Stir in oil until the sauce is the consistency of mayonnaise.

4 **Thickening the soup.** Put half of the aioli in a saucepan, reserving the rest as a garnish for the soup. Over very low heat, whisk in the broth, a ladleful at a time (above). Cook, stirring, until the soup thickens just enough to coat the whisk. Do not allow the soup to boil, lest it curdle.

2 **Adding liquid.** Distribute more flavorings—parsley, bay leaves, thyme, fennel and dried orange peel are used here—around the fish. Pour in hot liquid—water or, as here, fish broth—to cover the fish. Bring the liquid to a boil; reduce the heat so the liquid barely simmers. Partly cover the pan.

3 **Straining the broth.** While the fish cooks, make the aioli *(box, opposite page)*. When the fish is opaque—after 15 minutes, in this case—gently lift the pieces from the broth with a slotted spoon. Bone them, if you like. Place the fish in a heated tureen and keep warm in a slow oven. Strain the broth into a bowl *(above)*.

5 **Serving the bourride.** Pour the soup over the fish in the tureen *(above)*. Garnish with finely cut chives. Serve pieces of fish and the thickened broth together, as shown, or separately. Allow the diners to garnish their own portions with the reserved aioli *(right)*.

Garbure: A Display of Seasonal Vegetables

There is no fixed formula for a peasant vegetable soup; what goes into the pot depends largely on the season and on the contents of the vegetable patch. The garbure of southwestern France, for example, is made with cabbage, which is available in some variety the year round, and with whatever other vegetables come to hand *(recipe, page 157)*. In fact, the soup takes its name from *garbe*, French for "sheaf," or "bunch," an apt description of the miscellany of vegetables and meat that results in the soup.

The garbure is started by sautéing coarsely chopped potatoes, for body, and such aromatic vegetables as leeks, carrots, onions and turnips. At the same time that the vegetables are put into a pot with water, any smoked or salted meat that profits from slow cooking—a ham bone, salt pork or a slab of bacon—can be added to the soup. After the vegetables and meat flavor the liquid, the shredded cabbage goes in. Tender green or Savoy cabbages may be used raw; older, tougher cabbages should first be parboiled so that their strong flavor does not dominate the soup.

Sausages as well as fully cooked preserved meats that need only to be heated through can also be added along with the cabbage. In the Béarn region of France, a farmer's wife will probably include some *confit d'oie,* or salted goose preserved in its own fat: its pungent, briny taste gives the garbure a particularly interesting flavor. Preserved goose—if you wish to use it—is available in America at specialty markets.

More tender fresh vegetables—such as peas or green, fava or lima beans—may follow the cabbage into the soup. If fresh peas or beans are not available, you can substitute dried lima beans, white beans or lentils that have been soaked in water overnight and then simmered until they are tender.

Whatever ingredients you decide on, make generous use of them. According to tradition, a garbure should be so thick that a wooden spoon thrust into the soup will stand upright.

1 **Preparing aromatics.** Peel and chop the root and aromatic vegetables—here, potatoes, turnips, leeks, carrots and onions. Select a whole, unpeeled garlic bulb and assemble a bouquet garni of parsley, thyme, bay leaf, lovage, marjoram, savory and a dried red chili.

2 **Precooking vegetables.** Using rendered goose, salt-pork or bacon fat, stew the chopped vegetables over low heat for about 15 minutes, until they are tender but not browned. Half-fill a fireproof pot with hot water and bring it to a boil. Add the garlic bulb, bouquet garni and the softened vegetables.

6 **Presenting the garbure.** Cook the soup, still partially covered, for a further 20 minutes, until the vegetables and the meat are tender. Lift out all of the meat; drain, then slice it into serving portions. Scoop out most of the vegetables with a perforated spoon, letting them drain into the pot, and arrange them on a heated platter along with the meat slices. Discard the bouquet garni and the garlic. Put pieces of stale rye or whole-wheat bread in a heated tureen and pour the garbure broth over them.

3 **Adding the meats.** Trim excess fat from preserved meat — salt pork *(above)*, bacon and a smoked ham hock are used here — and put the meat in the pot. Bring the water back to a boil. Then cover the pot and reduce the heat. Simmer the soup for an hour to tenderize the meat and flavor the liquid.

4 **Preparing cabbage.** Separate cabbage leaves and cut out their tough stems. A few at a time, stack the leaves, roll them tightly and slice them to make a chiffonade. Add them to the pot along with any cooked preserved meat. With the lid ajar, simmer the soup gently for about 10 minutes.

5 **Shelling the beans.** Slit fava-bean pods down their seams with your thumb and remove the beans. Using your fingernails, pierce the opaque skin that covers each bean and peel off the skin. Stir the beans into the pot.

7 **Serving the soup.** Ladle the bread-thickened broth into individual soup bowls and top each serving with vegetables and meat. Serve the soup with glasses of a hearty red wine; traditionally, each guest empties his glass into the last few spoonfuls of soup at the bottom of his bowl.

Borscht on a Grand Scale

Beet soups are traditional stand-bys in the kitchens of Russia, Poland and the Ukraine. Known in the West by their Russian name, borscht *(recipes, pages 151-152)*, they may be simple beet-and-sour-cream purées that serve as a first course or they may be as lavish as the Ukrainian speciality—a meal in itself—demonstrated here. This bountiful offering, which includes several kinds of meat as well as shredded cabbage, is served with a medley of traditional garnishes.

The first step in making this or any borscht takes place several days in advance of actual cooking, when beets are prepared for fermentation *(box, below, right)*. The fermented liquid gives the soup its characteristic sour tang and deep ruby color. Passably tangy borscht can also be made by substituting *kvas (botvinya recipe, page 150)* for the fermented beets, or by using beets macerated in vinegar in place of freshly cooked ones and adding a little of the vinegar to the broth.

The cooking gets under way at least four hours before the soup is to be served. Fresh and salted meat is simmered to make a broth: for flavor and body, both pork and beef are used; some cuts should have bones and some should be fairly fatty. Beets—left whole and unpeeled to preserve their juices—are baked in the oven. After baking, the beets are cut up and simmered, along with shredded cabbage, in broth mixed with the fermented beet liquid. The meats themselves are served separately.

The lengthy cooking process allows you adequate time to prepare a selection of accompaniments for the borscht. Piroshki *(recipe, page 163)*, little crescent-shaped meat pies, are a traditional garnish for the soup. In addition, buckwheat groats, known as kasha, are baked with water and butter *(recipe, page 162)* and spooned into each soup plate to add substance to the broth.

Since a lot of time and effort go into making borscht, it is sensible to make a large quantity. What is left over will keep well in the refrigerator for three or four days, and can be served again, either reheated or chilled *(page 86)*.

1 **Preparing the meats.** In a large pan, assemble an assortment of meats—beef shank and chuck, a smoked ham hock and a slab of lean salt pork are used here. Add several whole, peeled onions and one or two bay leaves. Cover with cold water.

2 **Cooking the meats.** Bring the water to a boil and remove the scum until no more appears. Partially cover the pot and simmer for about 3 hours. Transfer the meats to a casserole, cover and set in a 225° F. [110° C.] oven. Strain and reserve the meat broth.

Making a Beet Liquor

Fermenting the vegetables. Grate peeled, raw beets into a pot. For 5 or 6 beets, add 2 quarts [2 liters] of warm water, a chunk of rye bread and a teaspoon [5 ml.] of sugar. Cover, leave in a cool room for 3 to 4 days, then strain: the liquid will keep, refrigerated, in a tightly closed bottle for several weeks.

5 **Assembling the borscht.** Bring the soup to a simmer over medium heat and cook the cabbage until it is just tender—about 10 minutes. Add the baked beet julienne *(above)* and reduce the heat to the barest simmer so that the ingredients warm through.

3 **Baking the beets.** While the meats simmer, lightly scrub and then rinse the beets; do not peel or pierce them. Put the beets in a baking dish, cover it and place it in an oven, preheated to 300° F. [150° C.]. Bake for 3 to 3½ hours, until the beets are tender when pierced with a fork. Cool the beets, then peel them with a small, sharp knife *(above)* and cut them into thick julienne.

4 **Preparing the cabbage.** Pull off the leaves of a green cabbage. Cut out the tough stems, then roll up and slice the leaves into narrow strips *(page 83)* and put them in a large pan. Cover the cabbage with the strained meat broth *(above, left)* and then a similar quantity of the strained, fermented beet liquid *(right)*.

5 **Serving.** Cut the meats into slices, removing any bones *(above)*. Arrange the slices on a large, warmed platter. Serve the borscht from a warmed tureen, accompanied by the meats and other side dishes — here, piroshki and kasha. Place a spoonful of kasha in each soup plate and ladle the borscht over it *(right)*. Garnish the soup with a dollop of sour cream and a sprinkling of fresh chopped dill or parsley.

A Fitting Encore for Borscht

Strained, thoroughly degreased and then chilled, a meat-based borscht *(pages 84-85)* yields an extra dividend: it becomes a refreshing summer dish. For an elaborate presentation, you can pour the soup over a cluster of ice cubes, made by freezing a handful of individual cubes inside a plastic bag. Surround the ice with an array of mixed, chopped vegetables: raw peppers, onions, scallions, cucumbers or celery, or freshly cooked, chilled beets all make good garnishes. Scatter cut fresh herbs, such as parsley, chives or dill, over each bowl of soup.

Sour cream is a traditional enrichment for borscht. For a marbled effect, gently stir a little cream into each person's bowl. If you prefer a uniform rose color, whisk the cream and the soup together before serving, as shown at right.

1 **Chilling the borscht.** Strain the borscht and chill it for at least 4 hours. As the soup cools, it will develop a film of surface fat. Spoon off the fat, then blot the surface of the soup with a paper towel to remove every trace of it.

2 **Mixing in sour cream.** Spoon sour cream into a chilled tureen. Whisk the cream to thin it slightly. Add the borscht, a ladleful at a time, stirring with the whisk as you pour to blend it thoroughly with the cream *(above)*.

3 **Serving the borscht.** In the soup plates, arrange the vegetables — in this case, chopped red and green pepper, scallion and cucumber. At the center of each plate, put a cluster of ice cubes, frozen together. Pour the borscht over the ice *(left)* and sprinkle with fresh dill or another herb, cut fine.

Anthology of Recipes

Drawing upon the cooking traditions and literature of more than 25 countries, the editors and consultants for this volume have selected 212 published soup recipes for the Anthology that follows. The selections range from the simple to the unusual—from fresh vegetable soups to a luxurious crayfish bisque.

Many of the recipes were written by world-renowned exponents of the culinary art, but the Anthology, spanning more than 300 years, also includes selections from now-rare and out-of-print books and from works that have never been published in English. Whatever the sources, the emphasis is always on authentic dishes meticulously prepared with fresh, natural ingredients that blend harmoniously.

Since many early recipe writers did not specify amounts of ingredients, the missing information has been judiciously added. Where appropriate, clarifying introductory notes have also been supplied; they are printed in italics. Modern terms have been substituted for archaic language, but to preserve the character of the original recipes, and to create a true anthology, the authors' texts have been changed as little as possible. Some instructions have necessarily been expanded, but in any circumstance where the cooking directions still seem somewhat abrupt, the reader need only refer to the appropriate demonstrations in the front of the book to find the technique explained.

For ease of use, the soup recipes are organized by types. Garnishes and accompaniments are grouped separately. Recipes for standard preparations—basic broths and garnishing elements, bread and pasta dough—appear at the end of the Anthology. Cooking terms and ingredients that may be unfamiliar are explained in the combined General Index and Glossary at the end of the book.

Apart from the primary components, all of the recipe ingredients have been listed in order of use, with both the customary U.S. measurements and the new metric measurements provided in separate columns. The metric quantities supplied here reflect the American practice of measuring such solid ingredients as flour or sugar by volume rather than by weighing them, as European cooks do.

To make the quantities simpler to measure, many of the figures have been rounded off to correspond to the gradations that are now standard on metric spoons and cups. (One cup, for example, equals precisely 240 milliliters; wherever practicable in these recipes, however, a cup appears as a more readily measurable 250 milliliters.) Similarly, weight, temperature and linear metric equivalents are rounded off slightly. For these reasons, the American and metric figures are not equivalent, but using one set or the other will produce equally good results.

Simple Broths

Recipes for basic broths appear in Standard Preparations, pages 163-167.

Soup with Dumplings

Potage de Poireaux aux Kliotzki

To serve 6

4 or 5	leeks	4 or 5
1½ quarts	salted water	1½ liters
1 tbsp.	finely chopped fresh parsley	15 ml.
	Butter-and-egg dumplings	
2 tbsp.	butter	30 ml.
1	egg, lightly beaten	1
2 tbsp.	boiling water	30 ml.
1 tbsp.	semolina or farina	15 ml.
	salt	
3 to 4 tbsp.	flour	45 to 60 ml.

To make the dumplings, place the butter in a bowl and pour in the boiling water. When the butter is melted, stir in the egg, semolina or farina, salt and enough of the flour to make a fairly stiff dough. Mix well, knead for a few minutes, cover the bowl loosely with foil or a kitchen towel and let the dough rest at room temperature for several hours.

Cook the leeks in the salted water for about 30 minutes. Remove the leeks and reserve them to eat at another meal with a vinaigrette sauce.

Bring the leek broth back to a boil. To shape each dumpling, dip a teaspoon in cold water and then use it to scoop up a small spoonful of the dumpling dough; push the dough into the broth with another spoon. Alternatively, the spoon may be dipped in oil and the dough dropped into the broth by tapping the spoon against the rim of the pan.

Cook for 8 to 10 minutes over low heat, until all the dumplings rise to the surface. Serve with the parsley.

H. WITWICKA AND S. SOSKINE
LA CUISINE RUSSE CLASSIQUE

Chicken Soup with Flakes of Egg and Cheese

Stracciatella

To serve 4 to 6

1 quart	chicken broth	1 liter
2	eggs	2
2 tbsp.	freshly grated Parmesan cheese	30 ml.
2 tsp.	finely chopped fresh parsley	10 ml.
	grated nutmeg	
	salt	

In a small bowl, beat the eggs until they are just blended; then mix in the cheese, parsley, nutmeg and salt. Bring the chicken broth to a bubbling boil in a heavy 2- to 3-quart [2- to 3-liter] saucepan over high heat. Pour in the egg mixture, stirring gently and constantly with a whisk, and simmer, still stirring, for 2 to 3 minutes. The egg mixture will form tiny flakes. Taste for seasoning, then ladle the soup into a heated tureen or individual soup bowls and serve at once.

FOODS OF THE WORLD/THE COOKING OF ITALY

Broth with Omelet Bits

Mariola

To serve 6

5 cups	chicken broth	1¼ liters
4	large eggs	4
6 tbsp.	fine bread crumbs	90 ml.
	salt	
	freshly ground pepper	
¼ tsp.	marjoram	1 ml.
2 tbsp.	chopped fresh parsley	30 ml.
3 tbsp.	freshly grated Parmesan cheese	45 ml.

Beat the eggs well. Sift the bread crumbs and add them to the eggs, along with the salt, pepper, marjoram and parsley.

Melt a bit of butter in a heavy skillet over medium-high heat and pour in just enough egg mixture to make a very thin omelet. As soon as the omelet is solid on the underside, turn it, and as soon as the second side is cooked, remove the omelet to a plate. Keep on making thin omelets until you have used up everything.

When the omelets are cool, cut them into squares of about ½ inch [1 cm.]. Bring the broth to a boil, drop in the omelet squares, and serve after the broth has come back to a boil. Sprinkle with the Parmesan cheese.

MARGARET AND G. FRANCO ROMAGNOLI
THE ROMAGNOLIS' TABLE

Chicken and Avocado Soup

	To serve 6	
1	whole chicken breast	1
1	ripe avocado	1
6 cups	chicken broth	1½ liters
2	onions, sliced	2
½ tsp.	ground coriander	2 ml.
½ tsp.	oregano	2 ml.
¼ tsp.	freshly ground black pepper	1 ml.

Pour the chicken broth into a large saucepan. Add the chicken breast, onions and seasonings. Bring to a boil, reduce the heat, cover and poach the chicken breast in the simmering broth for 20 minutes. Remove the chicken breast and let it cool. Strain the stock into another saucepan and set it aside. Discard the cooked onions.

When the chicken is cold and firm to the touch, peel off the skin. Then, using a sharp knife, cut the chicken into small julienne. Just before serving, stir the strips into the stock and heat. Peel the avocado, cut it into thin slices and add them to the soup. The slices will float on top.

ELEANOR GRAVES
GREAT DINNERS FROM LIFE

Japanese Soup Broth

Dashi

The so-called *dashi* broth is the basis of almost all Japanese soups, as well as of most casseroles, stews, sauces and so forth. Although its preparation is unfamiliar to Western housewives, *dashi* is easy and quick to make once the ingredients are purchased. They can be bought at any shop dealing in Japanese foodstuffs. You will probably be shown two types of bonito fillet *(katsuobushi):* one resembling a block of dried wood, the other ready-shaved and packaged, called *hanagatsuo.* By all means use the *hanagatsuo* — shaving a dried bonito fillet is a lengthy job requiring a special tool.

	To serve 6	
7½ cups	water	1¾ liters
½ oz.	kelp seaweed (kombu)	15 g.
½ oz.	dried bonito fillet (katsuobushi), shaved	15 g.

Bring the water to a boil and add the seaweed. Stir it around in the water for 3 to 4 minutes in order to release its flavor. Remove the seaweed and add the bonito shavings. Bring the water to a boil again, then immediately remove the pan from the heat. Allow the shavings to settle to the bottom of the pan; this will take only 2 or 3 minutes. Strain, and the broth is ready to use.

PETER AND JOAN MARTIN
JAPANESE COOKING

Rapid Broth

Bouillon d'une Heure

This is a good stand-by recipe for occasions when you need broth but do not have time to make the classic version. The broth is colored with caramel syrup, which does not affect the taste or consistency. To make 1 cup [¼ liter] caramel syrup, melt 1 cup of sugar slowly in a saucepan until it is amber-colored. Pour in 1 cup of water and boil for several minutes to dissolve the caramelized sugar in the water. The caramel syrup can be kept for several months in a small bottle, with a channel cut in the side of the cork so that the syrup can be poured out drop by drop.

	To serve 4	
1 lb.	lean boneless beef, fat and connective tissue removed, chopped	½ kg.
1	carrot, chopped	1
1	leek, white part only, chopped	1
1	rib celery, chopped	1
	salt	
1 quart	water	1 liter
	caramel syrup	

Put the meat, vegetables and seasoning in a saucepan, add the water and bring to a boil, stirring continuously. Cover the pan, setting the lid ajar, and then cook very slowly for 1 hour, over a fireproof pad if possible. Strain the broth through a fine sieve lined with dampened muslin or several layers of dampened cheesecloth. Add a few drops of caramel syrup to give the broth the color of a pale gold coin.

ÉDOUARD NIGNON
LES PLAISIRS DE LA TABLE

Consommé with Threads of Egg

Consommé aux Oeufs Filés

	To serve 8	
2 quarts	consommé	2 liters
3	eggs	3
1 tbsp.	flour	15 ml.
	salt and grated nutmeg	

Bring the consommé to a boil in a saucepan. Beat the eggs with the flour, and season with pinches of salt and nutmeg; roll strong paper into a cone and cut off the end, then pour the egg mixture into the cone. Dribble the egg mixture from the cone into the boiling consommé. The egg will set as soon as it is immersed in the consommé, and the soup should be served immediately.

LÉON ISNARD
LA CUISINE FRANÇAISE ET AFRICAINE

Consommé

Consommé is a particularly important part of the cook's repertoire, as it is used in so many other culinary preparations.

To make about 4 quarts [4 liters] consommé		
5 quarts	water	5 liters
5 lb.	beef (short ribs, plate or shank), chicken carcasses and giblets (but not livers), as available	2½ kg.
	salt	
5	carrots	5
2 or 3	turnips	2 or 3
1	parsnip	1
5	leeks	5
1	onion, stuck with a whole clove	1
1	rib celery	1
1	sprig parsley	1

Put the water, meat and salt into a deep pot. Bring to a boil and skim, then add the vegetables and parsley. Cover, with the lid ajar, and cook over low heat for 5 to 6 hours. When the consommé is done, strain it through a colander lined with dampened cheesecloth.

LÉON ISNARD
LA CUISINE FRANÇAISE ET AFRICAINE

Marrow Dumpling Soup

Markklösschensuppe

For instructions on extracting beef marrow from a marrowbone, see page 18. If you do not have enough marrow to make the quantity of dumplings you wish, the marrow may be stretched by the addition of a little butter. The dumplings may be either cooked directly in the broth, or poached in salted water, drained and added to the soup at serving time.

To serve 6		
about ¼ lb.	beef marrow	about 125 g.
	salt	
	grated nutmeg	
1	egg, lightly beaten in a warmed bowl	1
1 tbsp.	chopped fresh parsley	15 ml.
2 to 3 tbsp.	dry bread crumbs	30 to 45 ml.
1½ quarts	beef broth, heated to simmering	1½ liters

Chop the marrow finely, and sieve it, if necessary, to remove any bone fragments. In a bowl, stir the marrow with a little salt and nutmeg until the marrow is light and creamy. Stirring constantly, add the warmed egg, the parsley and, final-

ly, enough bread crumbs to make a firm dough that is neither dry nor sticky. Cover the bowl and allow the mixture to stand for a few minutes to blend the flavors.

Form small dumplings by shaping pieces of the dough between two teaspoons that have been dipped in cold water. Place the dumplings on a plate that has been rinsed in cold water. When all the dumplings are formed, drop them one by one into the simmering broth. Cook for 10 to 12 minutes.

GRETE WILLINSKY
KOCHBUCH DER BÜCHERGILDE

"Boiled Water"

L'Aïgo Boulido

In addition to its reputed medicinal virtues, this amusingly titled soup is delicious and tangy.

This Provençal infusion is said to have extraordinary virtues. Nothing can resist it: hangover, illness, childbirth—there can be no convalescence without "boiled water." The old proverb says, *Aïgo boulido sauova la vida* ("boiled water" saves your life).

To serve 4		
1 quart	water	1 liter
	salt	
12 to 15	garlic cloves	12 to 15
1 or 2	bay leaves	1 or 2
1 or 2	sprigs sage	1 or 2
¼ cup	olive oil	50 ml.
	slices of day-old firm-textured white bread	
	freshly grated Gruyère or Parmesan cheese	

In a saucepan, salt the water, add the garlic and bring to a boil. After 10 minutes, add the bay leaves, sage and a dash of oil. Let cook a few minutes more, then take the pan off the heat, cover, and allow the soup to stand for about 10 minutes to infuse the water with the seasonings. Strain.

Put the bread into a warmed soup tureen, cover with grated cheese, sprinkle with the remaining oil and pour in the strained infusion.

JOSÉPHINE BESSON
LA MÈRE BESSON "MA CUISINE PROVENÇALE"

Brown Rabbit Soup

This clear broth was no doubt originally intended to be made with wild rabbits. With domesticated rabbits, you can reduce the cooking time to 1 to 1 ½ hours. Either way you can serve the boned, cut-up meat in the soup or save it for a salad.

	To serve 10 to 12	
2	large (or 3 small) rabbits (about 6 lb. [3 kg.] in all), skinned, cleaned and cut into sections	2
7 tbsp.	butter	105 ml.
3	medium-sized onions	3
¾ cup	flour	175 ml.
4 quarts	water	4 liters
1½ tsp.	salt	7 ml.
1	bunch parsley, tied together	1
4	small carrots	4
½ tsp.	peppercorns	2 ml.
	croutons (recipe, page 166)	

Melt the butter in a large saucepan. Add the onions and fry them to a clear brown. Remove the onions from the pan. Toss the rabbit sections in the flour, and lightly fry them in the butter. Return the onions to the pan. Bring the water to a boil and gradually pour it into the pan, throw in the salt, and clear off all the scum with care as it rises. Then put into the soup the parsley, carrots and peppercorns. Cover and simmer very gently for 5 to 5½ hours. Add more salt if needed, strain the soup and let it cool sufficiently for the fat to be skimmed clean from it. Heat it afresh, and send it to the table with the croutons.

ELIZA ACTON
MODERN COOKERY

Chicken Mousse in Broth

Budino di Pollo in Brodo

	To serve 6	
6 oz.	raw chicken white meat, finely chopped	175 g.
7½ cups	chicken broth	2 liters
4	eggs	4
½ cup	freshly grated Parmesan cheese	125 ml.
	salt and pepper	
	grated nutmeg	

Pound the chicken meat in a mortar, adding from time to time a little of the broth (about ⅓ cup [75 ml.] in all); it must now be put through a sieve or puréed in an electric blender, so that a fine cream is obtained. Beat the eggs, pour them

through a strainer into the chicken mixture and mix them thoroughly. Add the grated cheese and season with salt, pepper and nutmeg.

Put the chicken cream, which should be very smooth, into six small buttered molds or china ramekins, of the kind in which eggs are baked. Put the ramekins in a pan containing hot water about halfway up the little pots; cover and cook gently for 15 minutes, until the chicken mixture is firm. Turn each one out onto a soup plate and pour over them the hot chicken broth.

ELIZABETH DAVID
ITALIAN FOOD

Purées

Corn Chowder

	To serve 6	
4 cups	corn kernels, cut from 8 large ears	1 liter
2	medium-sized potatoes, cut into ½-inch [1-cm.] cubes	2
1	small Bermuda onion, finely chopped (1 cup [¼ liter])	1
2½ cups	water	625 ml.
2 cups	chicken broth	½ liter
5 tbsp.	butter	75 ml.
2 cups	hot milk	½ liter
	salt and coarsely ground pepper	
	cayenne pepper	
1 cup	heavy cream	¼ liter

Place the corn in a large (4-quart [4-liter]) pan. Pour in 1 cup [¼ liter] of the water, and the chicken broth. Place on low heat, bring to a boil and simmer for 15 minutes. Stir occasionally to prevent scorching.

In the meantime, boil the potatoes in the remaining 1½ cups [375 ml.] of water until tender, or for about 15 minutes. Drain. Gently cook the chopped Bermuda onion in 4 tablespoons [60 ml.] of the butter, without browning, until soft (about 10 minutes). Add the onion, well-drained potatoes and hot milk to the corn. Purée this mixture in a blender, a cup or two [½ liter] at a time, running for 1 minute at low speed and another minute at high speed. Place the purée in the top of a very large double boiler. Season to taste with salt and pepper and a dash of cayenne.

Place the pot over boiling water and heat the soup thoroughly. When the mixture is scalding hot, stir in the heavy cream. Place the remaining tablespoon [15 ml.] of butter in a soup tureen, pour in the corn chowder and serve at once.

JUNE PLATT
JUNE PLATT'S NEW ENGLAND COOK BOOK

Broad Bean Soup

Potage aux Fèves de Marais

To serve 6

3 lb.	broad beans, shelled and skinned	1½ kg.
2 quarts	water	2 liters
2 tsp.	salt	10 ml.
	sliced bread	
¼ cup	finely shredded sorrel	50 ml.
¼ cup	finely shredded chervil leaves	50 ml.
4 tbsp.	butter	60 ml.

In a large saucepan, bring the water to a boil. Toss in the beans and salt, and boil for 10 minutes only. Place the bread in a warmed soup tureen; sprinkle the shredded sorrel and chervil over the bread; add the butter. Strain the bean cooking liquid into the tureen through a sieve, and press the beans through the sieve with a wooden pestle. Check the seasoning and serve immediately.

MME. JEANNE SAVARIN (EDITOR)
LA CUISINE DES FAMILLES

Green Bean Soup with Swirled Pesto

To serve 4

1½ lb.	tender green beans	¾ kg.
1	small onion, chopped	1
2 tbsp.	olive oil	30 ml.
2 cups	chicken broth	½ liter
1 cup	heavy cream	¼ liter
	Pesto sauce	
3	large garlic cloves	3
2 tbsp.	pine nuts	30 ml.
1 cup	packed basil leaves	¼ liter
2 or 3	sprigs summer savory (optional)	2 or 3
½ cup	freshly grated Parmesan cheese	125 ml.
	olive oil	
	salt	

Cook the onion in the olive oil and 2 tablespoons [30 ml.] of the stock until the onion is just tender. Bring a pot of salted water to a boil and throw in the beans. Cover the pot and boil the beans rapidly until they are almost fork-tender. Drain the beans. Bring the broth to a simmer; add the beans and

onions. Simmer gently for 5 minutes, then purée the mixture in a blender or food processor. Add the cream, taste for seasoning and set the soup aside. It should be quite thick.

To make the pesto sauce, pound the garlic into a smooth purée in a mortar or heavy bowl. Add the pine nuts and continue pounding to make an even paste. Add the herbs and mash to a purée. Mix in the cheese by the spoonful and add enough oil to make the sauce the same density as the soup.

Reheat the soup until it is warm but not hot. Ladle the soup into four bowls and spoon pesto into the middle of each serving. Using a spoon handle, lightly stir the pesto into feathery swirls, dark green against the paler beans.

JUDITH OLNEY
SUMMER FOOD

Cream of Asparagus Soup

Crème d'Émeraude

The asparagus in this recipe should be peeled and thinly sliced, then parboiled for no more than 2 to 3 minutes. To blanch and skin the pistachios, place them in a bowl and pour boiling water over them. Then drain the nuts and rub their skins off. If any skins resist, reheat the nut briefly.

To serve 4 to 6

1 lb.	asparagus, parboiled and drained	½ kg.
20 tbsp.	butter	300 ml.
3 tbsp.	flour	45 ml.
1 quart	chicken broth	1 liter
1	rib celery	1
1	sprig basil	1
	salt	
	cayenne pepper	
¾ cup	shelled green pistachios, blanched, skinned and pounded in a mortar	175 ml.
5	egg yolks	5
1 tbsp.	fresh lemon juice	15 ml.

Melt 14 tablespoons [210 ml.] of the butter in a large saucepan, add the flour to make a smooth roux and whisk in the broth. Add the celery, basil, salt and cayenne pepper. Simmer slowly for 1 hour, skimming occasionally; a few minutes before the end of the cooking period, add the asparagus and the pistachios.

Purée the soup in a blender, then strain the soup through a fine sieve into a clean pan. Beat a few tablespoons of the soup into the egg yolks, then stir the yolk mixture back into the soup. Reheat without allowing the soup to boil. Remove the soup from the heat and add the remaining butter and the lemon juice. Serve very hot.

LÉON ISNARD
LA CUISINE FRANÇAISE ET AFRICAINE

Asparagus Soup

To serve 8

3 lb.	asparagus, cut into 2-inch [5-cm.] pieces	1½ kg.
12 tbsp.	butter	180 ml.
4 cups	finely chopped onions	1 liter
6	medium-sized potatoes, diced	6
1 quart	chicken broth	1 liter
	water	
2 tsp.	salt	10 ml.
1 tsp.	freshly ground white pepper	5 ml.
2 cups	light cream	½ liter
¼ tsp.	grated nutmeg	1 ml.

Heat 8 tablespoons [120 ml.] of the butter in a large saucepan and cook the onions over high heat—stirring constantly—until they are wilted, about 5 minutes. Stir in the potatoes and asparagus, reserving the asparagus tips. Pour in the chicken broth and enough water, if needed, to cover the vegetables. Season with salt and pepper, bring to a boil, cover, reduce the heat to simmer and cook until the vegetables are tender, about 20 minutes. Put the mixture through a food mill, using the finest disk. Add the cream, nutmeg and asparagus tips and bring the soup to a boil. Pour the soup into a warmed tureen, and float the remaining 4 tablespoons [60 ml.] of butter, cut into chips, on the top.

JULIE DANNENBAUM
MENUS FOR ALL OCCASIONS

Carrot and Orange Soup

To serve 3

6 to 8	carrots (about ¾ lb. [⅓ kg.]), sliced	6 to 8
2	large oranges, 1 peeled and the peel reserved, both squeezed and the juice strained	2
3 tbsp.	butter	45 ml.
2	medium-sized onions, sliced	2
1 quart	stock	1 liter
¼ cup	heavy cream	60 ml.
	salt and pepper	

Melt the butter in a saucepan over low heat and stir in the carrots and onions. Cover the pan and let the vegetables sweat for 5 minutes. Pour in the stock, bring to a boil over high heat, reduce the heat to low again and simmer, covered, for 15 minutes. Remove the pan from the stove, allow the soup to cool slightly and then purée the vegetables and stock in a blender. Pour in the orange juice and blend for a few seconds more. Put the soup back into the saucepan and stir in the cream. Season and reheat gently without boiling.

Cut the orange peel into thin slivers. Simmer the slivers in water for 5 minutes, then drain them well. Float them on top of the soup just before serving.

GAIL DUFF
FRESH ALL THE YEAR

Carrot Soup

To serve 4

1 lb.	carrots, thinly sliced	500 g.
3 tbsp.	butter	45 ml.
2 tbsp.	chopped onion	30 ml.
1 quart	stock or water	1¼ liters
3 tbsp.	raw unprocessed rice or 2 slices stale white bread with the crusts removed, broken up	45 ml.
	salt	
1 tsp.	sugar	5 ml.
	croutons (recipe, page 166)	

Gently cook the carrots, together with the onion, in half of the butter. When they are tender, add the stock or water and the rice or bread. Season with a pinch of salt and the sugar. Simmer for 20 minutes, then pass the soup through a sieve, adding more stock or water if the purée is too stiff. Reheat the soup with the rest of the butter and serve with croutons.

TERENCE CONRAN AND MARIA KROLL
THE VEGETABLE BOOK

Lettuce Purée

Soupe du Père Tranquille

To serve 2

1	head Boston lettuce, halved, cored and shredded	1
about 3 cups	broth	about ¾ liter
1 tbsp.	butter	15 ml.
	very thinly sliced stale bread	

Over low heat, simmer the lettuce in a little of the broth, adding more broth several times to replace the liquid that cooks away. When the lettuce is almost completely reduced, after 45 minutes to 1 hour, add enough broth to bring the soup to the desired consistency. Simmer the soup for 8 to 10 minutes more. Take out any bits of lettuce that are not completely melted, and add the butter. Put the bread into a warmed tureen, pour in the soup and cover the tureen. The soup will be ready to serve in 3 minutes.

B. RENAUDET
LES SECRETS DE LA BONNE TABLE

White Soubise

To serve 3 or 4

4	medium-sized onions (about 1 lb. [½ kg.]), chopped	4
4 tbsp.	butter	60 ml.
1¼ cups	light stock or water	300 ml.
1¼ cups	milk	300 ml.
1 cup	fresh white bread crumbs	¼ liter
	salt and pepper	
	croutons (recipe, page 166)	

Stew the onions in the butter in a covered pan, without browning them, for an hour. Keep the heat really low, or use a fireproof pad. The idea is that the onions should gently dissolve into a purée.

Mix in the stock or water, the milk and the bread crumbs. Increase the heat and bring the soup just to the boiling point. Sieve through the medium blade of a food mill (a blender would make the purée too smooth). Season.

Return the soup to the heat to simmer for a further hour; again, keep the mixture barely at the simmering point. Check from time to time and give the soup a stir-up. Add more water if the mixture becomes too thick.

Serve with croutons.

JANE GRIGSON
JANE GRIGSON'S VEGETABLE BOOK

Jerusalem Artichoke Soup

Minestra di Carciofi di Giudea

To serve 4

6	large Jerusalem artichokes, peeled and sliced into a bowl of water acidulated with 1 tbsp. [15 ml.] fresh lemon juice	6
4 tbsp.	butter	60 ml.
1	onion, chopped	1
	salt and pepper	
5 cups	milk	1¼ liters
	light cream	
	chopped chervil	
	fried bread croutons (recipe, page 166)	

Melt the butter in a saucepan, put in the drained Jerusalem artichokes and the onion, and season lightly with salt and pepper. Cover and simmer gently for 10 minutes. Add the milk and bring to a boil. Simmer gently for a further 10 minutes and pass the soup through the fine blade of a vegetable mill. Return the soup to the saucepan, boil again and correct the seasoning. Before serving, add a little cream and chervil and the croutons.

JANET ROSS AND MICHAEL WATERFIELD
LEAVES FROM OUR TUSCAN KITCHEN

Thick Cream Soup

Potage Velouté

This kind of soup can include a wide variety of additions. Vegetables such as carrots, celery, cauliflower, pumpkin, beans, mushrooms, or Jerusalem artichokes can be puréed and added, and the soup may be garnished with quenelles or with diced cooked chicken, game or fish. The cooking liquid from vegetables should always be saved for the soup pot, and, if possible, a few of the vegetables themselves should be kept for garnish.

To serve 6

4 tbsp.	butter	60 ml.
½ cup	flour	125 ml.
1½ quarts	broth, degreased and heated	1½ liters
3	egg yolks	3
½ cup	heavy cream	125 ml.
	salt and pepper (optional)	
1 tbsp.	butter (optional)	15 ml.

In a large saucepan, make a lightly colored roux with the butter and flour. Remove the pan from the heat and dilute the roux with the warmed broth. Return the pan to the heat and bring the soup to a boil, stirring constantly. Then let the soup simmer over low heat for at least 20 minutes, and preferably double that time, skimming occasionally.

At serving time, remove the soup from the heat. Beat the egg yolks with the cream, then beat them into the soup. The heat of the soup will cook the egg yolks. Check the seasoning and pour the soup through a strainer into a tureen. Serve with whatever garnish you wish, and, if you like, swirl in a bit of additional butter.

MADAME SAINT-ANGE
LA CUISINE DE MADAME SAINT-ANGE

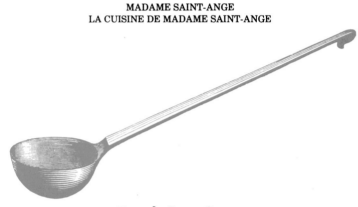

Fresh Pea Soup

If the peas are particularly young and fresh, water may be substituted for chicken broth as a cooking liquid. If the peas are mature, they will be starchy enough to thicken the soup: flour will not be necessary. The heart of a small lettuce, finely sliced, may replace the onion for added freshness of flavor.

To serve 6

2 cups	freshly shelled peas (about 2 lb. [½ kg.] unshelled)	½ liter
3	leeks, finely chopped	3
1	onion, finely chopped	1
4 tbsp.	butter	60 ml.
2 tbsp.	flour	30 ml.
6 cups	chicken broth	1½ liters
1	sprig mint	1
	salt and freshly ground black pepper	
1 cup	heavy or light cream	¼ liter

Sauté the leeks and onion in the butter in a heavy saucepan until tender. Sprinkle with the flour and stir to mix.

Stir in the broth, bring to a boil and add the mint and peas. Cook, covered, until the peas are tender, about 15 minutes. Remove the mint.

Purée the mixture through a food mill or in batches in a blender. Return to the clean pan. Bring to a boil and add salt and pepper to taste and the cream. Reheat. If too thick, add a little milk. This soup is also delicious chilled.

JEAN HEWITT
THE NEW YORK TIMES NEW ENGLAND HERITAGE COOKBOOK

Cucumber Soup

This purée can be served either hot or cold.

To serve 6

2	8-inch [20-cm.] cucumbers, peeled, halved, seeded and chopped	2
2 tbsp.	chopped scallions	30 ml.
2 tbsp.	butter	30 ml.
1 tbsp.	wine vinegar	15 ml.
1 quart	chicken broth	1 liter
1 tbsp.	farina	15 ml.
	salt	
	fresh or dried tarragon or dill	
½ cup	sour cream or fresh cream	125 ml.
	cucumber slices	
	chopped fresh parsley	

Cook the chopped scallions in the butter until soft. Add the chopped cucumbers and the wine vinegar. Add the broth, farina and salt to taste; then add a pinch of tarragon or dill. Let the soup simmer for 20 minutes until the cucumbers are soft. Put the soup into a blender and purée it. Pour the purée into a bowl, add the sour cream, beat well with a whisk, and taste the soup for seasoning. Pour the soup into bowls and garnish with cucumber slices and chopped parsley.

THE WOMEN'S COMMITTEE OF THE WALTERS ART GALLERY
PRIVATE COLLECTIONS: A CULINARY TREASURE

Cream of Mushroom Soup

To serve 4

2½ cups	fresh chopped mushrooms (about ½ lb. [¼ kg.])	625 ml.
¼ cup	chopped onion	50 ml.
5 cups	chicken stock	1¼ liters
4 tbsp.	butter	60 ml.
¼ cup	flour	50 ml.
1 cup	light cream	¼ liter
	salt and pepper	
¼ cup	Sauternes or other sweet white wine	50 ml.

Put the mushrooms and onion into the stock and simmer for 20 minutes; pass the vegetables and stock through a sieve. Put the purée back on the stove. Work the butter and flour together to make a paste, and whisk this into the soup to thicken it. Stir in the cream, season with pepper and salt, and add the wine at the last moment.

MRS. C. F. LEYEL AND MISS OLGA HARTLEY
THE GENTLE ART OF COOKERY

Pea Pod Soup

If the peas in your market are not fresh, don't make this soup. Fresh pods make a deliciously unusual soup, totally different from dried-pea soup.

	To serve 8	
2 quarts	pea pods (not snow peas)	2 liters
6 cups	strong chicken broth	1½ liters
1 cup	shredded lettuce, well packed	¼ liter
1 cup	chopped onions	¼ liter
1 quart	light cream	1 liter
1	bay leaf	1
4	sprigs parsley	4
2 tsp.	salt	10 ml.
½ tsp.	freshly ground white pepper	2 ml.
¼ tsp.	grated nutmeg	1 ml.
2	egg yolks	2
4 tsp.	butter	20 ml.
4 tsp.	finely chopped fresh parsley	20 ml.

In a large saucepan, combine the pea pods, chicken broth, lettuce and onions. Bring to a boil, reduce the heat, cover and simmer until the pea pods are barely tender, about 20 to 30 minutes. Purée this mixture through a food mill, using the fine disk, or in a blender. Return the purée to high heat and stir in the cream, bay leaf and parsley sprigs. Bring the soup to a boil. Season with the salt, pepper and nutmeg.

Beat the egg yolks, warm them with a little of the hot soup and stir them into the soup. Heat the soup just to boiling, but do not let it boil. Remove the bay leaf and serve the soup in individual bowls, garnished with butter and finely chopped parsley.

JULIE DANNENBAUM
MENUS FOR ALL OCCASIONS

Sorrel and Cream Soup

Potage Germiny

	To serve 4	
2 cups	sorrel leaves, stems and center ribs removed	½ liter
1 cup	cream	¼ liter
3 tbsp.	butter	45 ml.
about 1 quart	consommé	about 1 liter
4	egg yolks	4
2 tbsp.	chervil leaves	30 ml.
	salt and pepper	
	croutons (recipe, page 166)	

In a large saucepan, sauté the sorrel in 1 tablespoon [15 ml.] of the butter until it is very soft and limp. Add the consommé, bring the soup to a boil and simmer for 8 to 10 minutes.

Beat the egg yolks in a bowl with the cream. Two minutes before serving, remove the soup from the heat and add two large spoonfuls of the hot soup to the egg-yolk mixture to warm it. Then pour the mixture into the saucepan and put the soup over very low heat; stir well with a ladle. It soon thickens, but you must be careful that the soup does not reach the boiling point.

Finish, away from the heat, by adding the remaining butter. Shake the saucepan gently till the butter has disappeared, add the chervil, see that the soup is well seasoned, and serve with very small croutons.

X. MARCEL BOULESTIN
RECIPES OF BOULESTIN

Pumpkin Purée

Soupe au Potiron

This soup can be turned into a panade by simply omitting the potatoes and filling the shell with alternate layers of sliced bread and pumpkin purée.

	To serve 10	
1	whole pumpkin (6 to 7 lb. [3 kg.])	1
2 quarts	water	2 liters
4	medium-sized potatoes (about 1 lb. [½ kg.]), thickly sliced	4
	salt and pepper	
½ cup	cream	125 ml.
	fried croutons, made from 3 slices of bread (recipe, page 165)	
½ cup	grated Gruyère cheese	125 ml.

Cut out a lid from the top of the pumpkin and discard it. Scoop out the seeds and fibers with a spoon. Remove the flesh from the interior, using a knife and a spoon; leave a shell at least ½ inch [1 cm.] thick and be careful not to pierce it. Put the shell on a heavy baking sheet and set it aside.

Cut enough pumpkin flesh into pieces to yield about 3 to 4 cups [¾ to 1 liter]. (You can use the rest of the flesh for a tart or gratin.) Put the pieces in a saucepan with the water and the potatoes. Season with pinches of salt and pepper, bring to a boil, cover and cook over low heat for 45 minutes.

Put the soup through a strainer or food mill. Add the cream. Pour the soup into the hollowed-out pumpkin shell and sprinkle the surface of the soup with the croutons and the Gruyère. Set the shell on its baking sheet into a preheated 425° F. [220° C.] oven, and bake for 15 minutes. To serve, bring the soup-filled pumpkin to the table.

ODETTE KAHN (EDITOR)
CUISINE ET VINS DE FRANCE

Cream of Pumpkin and Shrimp Soup

Potage Crème de Potiron aux Crevettes

To serve 6

2 to 2½ lb.	pumpkin, peeled, seeded and diced	1 kg.
¼ lb.	peeled raw shrimp	125 g.
	salt and pepper	
1	rib celery, cut in pieces	1
1 quart	boiled milk	1 liter
2 cups	mild stock or water	½ liter
1 tsp.	fresh lemon juice	5 ml.
2 tbsp.	butter	30 ml.

Season the pumpkin pieces with salt and pepper and put them into a heavy saucepan with the celery. Cover them with the boiled milk and the stock or water, and simmer until the pumpkin is quite soft, about 30 minutes. Sieve the mixture; return the purée to a clean pan.

Mash or pound the shrimps in a mortar, adding the lemon juice and diluting with a little of the pumpkin purée. Add this mixture to the purée, simmer gently for 10 minutes or so, and strain the soup again through a very fine sieve. Taste for seasoning. When reheating, thin with a little hot milk or stock if necessary. Immediately before serving stir in the butter. Cooked pumpkin is a vegetable that tends to go sour very quickly, so this soup should be used up on the day, or day after, it is made.

ELIZABETH DAVID
FRENCH PROVINCIAL COOKING

Pumpkin Soup

Soupe des Maures

To serve 6 to 8

½ lb.	pumpkin, peeled, seeded and diced	¼ kg.
2 tbsp.	butter	30 ml.
1	large onion, finely chopped	1
2 quarts	beef broth, pot-au-feu bouillon or bean cooking liquid	2 liters
¾ cup	soaked and cooked dried white beans	175 ml.
3½ oz.	thick vermicelli pasta	100 g.

Melt the butter in a large pan and lightly brown the onion. Pour in half of the broth and add the pumpkin and the beans. Simmer, covered, for about 25 minutes or until the pumpkin is tender. Put the soup through a fine sieve, and thin down the resulting purée with the rest of the broth. Bring to a boil. Add the vermicelli and cook at a light boil for 12 minutes or until the pasta is *al dente*. Serve.

70 MÉDECINS DE FRANCE
LE TRÉSOR DE LA CUISINE DU BASSIN MÉDITERRANÉEN

Tomato Soup

Tomatensuppe

This soup can be served with toasted bread crumbs and with eggs boiled for 5 to 6 minutes and shelled. If you choose this garnish, the rice should be omitted.

To serve 4 to 6

8	medium-sized ripe tomatoes (about 2 lb. [1 kg.]), cut up	8
1	onion, sliced	1
2 tbsp.	butter or oil	30 ml.
1 quart	boiling water	1 liter
	salt and pepper	
½ tsp.	thyme	2 ml.
3 tbsp.	raw unprocessed rice	45 ml.
2 tbsp.	butter (optional)	30 ml.
	finely chopped fresh parsley (optional)	

Cook the tomatoes and onion in the butter or oil until soft, purée them through a fine-meshed sieve into another saucepan and add the boiling water. Season with a little salt and pepper and the thyme, add the rice, and simmer for 20 minutes. The soup is made even better by the addition of the extra butter and the parsley just before serving.

GRETE WILLINSKY
KOCHBUCH DER BÜCHERGILDE

Cream of Tomato Soup

Crème de Tomate

To serve 4 to 6

6	medium-sized ripe tomatoes, roughly chopped	6
1 cup	canned tomatoes	¼ liter
2 tbsp.	butter	30 ml.
1	onion, chopped	1
1	carrot, chopped	1
3 tbsp.	flour	45 ml.
1 quart	chicken stock or water	1 liter
1	small garlic clove	1
2	leeks, thinly sliced (optional)	2
4	white peppercorns	4
1 tsp.	salt	5 ml.
1 tbsp.	sugar	15 ml.
	chicken carcass (optional)	
1 cup	light cream	¼ liter

Melt the butter in a deep saucepan, add the onion and carrot, and cook slowly until golden brown. Add the flour and mix. Add the stock or water, the garlic, leeks, white peppercorns, salt, sugar, tomatoes and chicken carcass (if using). Cover and cook over low heat for 1 to 1½ hours, skimming as needed. Remove the chicken carcass and rub the soup through a fine strainer. Combine the cream with the strained soup and correct the seasoning. If the soup is too thick, add a little more cream or stock to obtain the desired consistency. Serve with croutons or with rice.

LOUIS DIAT
FRENCH COOKING FOR AMERICANS

Spinach Soup

To serve 4 to 6

1 lb.	spinach, stems removed, washed and chopped	½ kg.
2 tbsp.	butter	30 ml.
1	small onion or shallot, finely chopped	1
1 quart	chicken stock	1 liter
3	egg yolks	3
2 tbsp.	fresh lemon juice	30 ml.
	salt and pepper	
4 to 6	strips of lemon peel	4 to 6

Melt the butter in a large pan, add the onion and sweat very gently until it is tender, then add the spinach and let it sweat until it has wilted down. Bring the stock to a boil and pour it over the spinach. Allow to simmer for about 7 to 8 minutes until the spinach is completely tender but still green. Pass the spinach and the stock through the finest blade of a food mill or purée it in an electric blender.

Beat the egg yolks in a separate bowl with the lemon juice, and gradually add 1 cup [¼ liter] of the hot purée, beating all the time. Return this liquid to the soup and heat very gently, stirring all the time until very slightly thickened. Do not let the soup boil after the eggs have been added. Season, and serve with a strip of lemon peel in each bowl. This soup is delicious when it is chilled and served with a whirl of sour cream.

TERENCE CONRAN AND MARIA KROLL
THE VEGETABLE BOOK

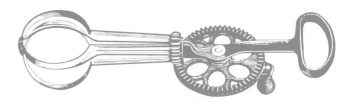

Cream of Turnips

Crème à la Vierge

This soup is at its best made with new turnips in the spring.

To serve 6

12	turnips, peeled and thickly sliced	12
8 tbsp.	butter	120 ml.
1½ quarts	milk	1½ liters
	salt	
	mixed spices	
	white pepper	
	dry bread sliced as thinly as possible	

Bring a large pot of water to a boil. Throw in the turnips, cover the pot, and remove from the heat; the water should not boil again. After 5 minutes, drain the turnips and plunge them into cold water, then drain them on a cloth.

Melt half of the butter in a saucepan and sauté the turnips without letting them brown; add the milk and simmer over low heat, covered, seasoning the mixture with salt, mixed spices and white pepper.

When the turnips are cooked, after about 20 minutes, purée the soup through a fine sieve, working the turnips through with a wooden pestle. If the purée is too thick, dilute it with a little additional milk, heated to boiling. Incorporate the remaining butter. From this moment, the soup should be kept very hot, but not allowed to boil. Put the bread in a warmed tureen, and pour in the soup.

B. RENAUDET
LES SECRETS DE LA BONNE TABLE

Watercress Cream Soup

To serve 8 to 10

2 cups	watercress leaves	½ liter
2 cups	light cream	½ liter
4 tbsp.	unsalted butter	60 ml.
6	white boiling onions, sliced	6
1	large onion, sliced	1
2	ribs celery, thinly sliced	2
4	potatoes, diced	4
6 cups	chicken broth	1½ liters
	salt and pepper	

Melt the butter in a deep saucepan. Add the onions and celery. Cook them over low heat until they are soft, then add the potatoes and chicken broth. Simmer until the potatoes are completely soft. Add the watercress and continue cooking for only a minute or two, or until the watercress wilts. Cool the soup slightly.

Purée the entire mixture in a blender or food mill to make a smooth cream. Season with salt and pepper. Chill if desired. Just before serving, stir in the cream.

PAULA PECK
PAULA PECK'S ART OF GOOD COOKING

Spring Vegetable Soup

Potage Printannié en Maigre

To serve 4

1 lb.	peas, shelled (about 1 cup [¼ liter])	½ kg.
2 cups	chopped chervil (about 2 oz. [75 g.])	½ liter
1 cup	chopped purslane (or substitute beet greens or lamb's-ear lettuce)	¼ liter
1	head Boston or romaine lettuce, halved, cored and shredded	1
2 cups	sorrel (about ½ lb. [¼ kg.]), shredded	½ liter
3 or 4	onions, thinly sliced	3 or 4
1 tbsp.	chopped fresh parsley	15 ml.
1 quart	water	1 liter
2 tbsp.	butter	30 ml.
	salt	
6	egg yolks	6

Put everything except the egg yolks together in a pot and simmer, covered, over medium heat until the vegetables are cooked—about 15 minutes. Press through a fine sieve into a bowl. Pour three quarters of the purée back into the pot and simmer over very low heat for another 10 minutes or so.

In a small pan combine the remainder of the purée with the egg yolks. Stir the yolk mixture over low heat until thickened, being careful not to let the mixture boil. At the last moment, stir the yolk mixture into the soup, check for salt, and serve.

MENON
LA CUISINIÈRE BOURGEOISE

Mixed Vegetable Purée

Purée Léontine

To serve 6

10 to 12	leeks (about 2 lb. [1 kg.]), cut into chunks	10 to 12
1 cup	spinach leaves with stems removed (about 2 oz. [60 g.])	300 ml.
1 cup	freshly shelled peas	¼ liter
1 cup	lettuce leaves, preferably romaine (2 oz. [60 g.]), shredded	¼ liter
½ cup	olive oil	125 ml.
	salt and pepper	
2 tbsp.	fresh lemon juice	30 ml.
1 quart	water	1 liter
	milk (optional)	
1 tbsp.	chopped fresh parsley	15 ml.
1 tbsp.	chopped fresh mint	15 ml.
1 tbsp.	chopped celery	15 ml.

Into a thick marmite or other fireproof casserole, put the olive oil and, when it is warm, put in the leeks, seasoned with salt, pepper and the lemon juice. Simmer slowly for about 20 minutes. Now add the spinach, the peas and the lettuce, stir for a minute or two and add the water. Cook until all the vegetables are soft—after about 10 minutes—then press the whole mixture through a sieve. If the purée is too thick, add a little milk. Before serving, stir in the chopped parsley, mint and celery.

This soup turns out an appetizing pale green.

ELIZABETH DAVID
A BOOK OF MEDITERRANEAN FOOD

Vegetable and Barley Soup
Bouillon de Légumes

To serve 6 to 8

4	medium-sized carrots	4
½	small turnip or rutabaga	½
¼ cup	pearl barley	50 ml.
⅓ cup	white beans, soaked in water overnight if dried	75 ml.
	salt	
3	leeks	3
1	onion, stuck with a whole clove	1
1	bouquet garni	1
1	rib celery	1
1	potato	1
3 quarts	water	3 liters
4 tbsp.	butter	60 ml.

Put all the vegetables, the barley and the seasonings into the water, and simmer very slowly for several hours. At serving time, remove the bouquet garni, purée the vegetables and barley through a strainer and add the butter.

SUZANNE ROBAGLIA
MARGARIDOU

Chestnut Soup

To prepare the chestnuts called for in this recipe, first slash a cross in the flat end of each one with a sharp knife. Parboil the chestnuts for 10 minutes and drain them. When they are cool enough to handle, the outer and inner skins will slip off; if any skins resist, briefly reheat the chestnut.

To serve 12 to 16

2 to 2½ lb.	chestnuts, slit, parboiled, peeled and skinned	1 kg.
3 quarts	stock	3 liters
2 cups	heavy cream	½ liter
	salt	
	cayenne pepper	
4	lumps sugar	4

Put the chestnuts into a soup pot, cover them with stock, and let them simmer slowly until quite soft, about 40 minutes. Then pound them smooth in a mortar and press through a fine sieve into the soup pot; add to them very gradually, and stirring all the time, the remaining stock, the cream, a little salt and cayenne, and the sugar. Boil the soup once, constantly stirring it, and serve it up very hot.

MARY JEWRY (EDITOR)
WARNE'S MODEL COOKERY AND HOUSEKEEPING BOOK

Pea Soup
Potage St. Germain

You will find the flavor and color of this soup made of dried peas greatly improved if a cup of fresh green peas (or the pods of very young tender peas), which have been cooked until soft and then rubbed through a sieve, are added to the soup after it has been strained. We would have this soup the day before or after we had leek and potato soup because it uses up the green part of the leeks that are left.

To serve 6

2 cups	dried split peas, soaked for 1 hour in water and drained	½ liter
5 cups	water, or 1 quart [1 liter] water and 1 cup [¼ liter] stock	1¼ liters
1 tsp.	salt	5 ml.
2 tbsp.	butter	30 ml.
½ cup	salt pork, finely chopped	125 ml.
1	medium-sized onion, chopped	1
1	medium-sized carrot, chopped	1
2	leeks, green parts only	2
1 cup	chopped spinach or lettuce leaves	¼ liter
1	bay leaf	1
1	sprig thyme	1
	sugar (optional)	
	croutons (recipe, page 166)	

Put the peas in a saucepan with 1 quart [1 liter] of the water and the salt. Bring to a boil, skim, cover and cook slowly while preparing the following: melt half of the butter in a saucepan, add the salt pork and onion and cook until they soften and start to brown. Add the carrot, leeks, spinach or lettuce leaves, bay leaf and thyme and cook for a few minutes. Add this mixture to the peas. Continue cooking all together for about 1 hour or until the peas are soft. Rub through a sieve, add the remaining water or the stock if the soup is very thick. Bring to a boil, skim, and correct the seasoning, adding a little sugar if desired. Add the remaining butter. Serve with croutons.

LOUIS DIAT
FRENCH COOKING FOR AMERICANS

Black Bean Soup

This recipe is adapted from one used by the very fine Coach House restaurant in New York City.

To serve 10 to 12

2 cups	dried black beans, washed, soaked in water overnight and drained	½ liter
2½ quarts	cold water	2½ liters
2	ribs celery, chopped	2
1½	large onions, chopped	1½
4 tbsp.	butter or rendered bacon fat	60 ml.
1¼ tbsp.	flour	21 ml.
¼ cup	chopped fresh parsley	50 ml.
	rind and bone of a smoked ham	
1½	leeks, trimmed and thinly sliced	1½
1	bay leaf	1
2 tsp.	salt	10 ml.
½ tsp.	pepper	2 ml.
½ cup	Madeira	125 ml.
2	hard-boiled eggs, chopped	2
	lemon slices	

In a deep pot, combine the beans and water. Cook, covered, over low heat for 1½ hours.

In a soup pot over low heat, sauté the celery and onions in the butter or bacon fat until they are tender. Remove from the heat and blend in the flour and parsley. Return to low heat for a few minutes, stirring constantly. Gradually stir in the beans and their cooking liquid. Add the ham rind and bone, the leeks, bay leaf, salt and pepper. Simmer the soup, covered, for 4 hours.

Discard the ham rind and bone, and the bay leaf. Force the beans through a sieve, or purée them, a few cupfuls at a time, in a blender. In a pot, combine the puréed beans, their broth and the Madeira. Reheat the soup and remove from the stove. Stir in the chopped eggs and add a thin slice of lemon to each serving.

PAULA PECK
PAULA PECK'S ART OF GOOD COOKING

Black Turtle Soup

Turtle beans are another name for *frijoles negros* or, in other words, plain black beans. To prepare them, first soak the beans overnight in enough water to cover them by 2 inches [5 cm.]. The next day add 1 tablespoon [15 ml.] of salt to the soaking water, which will now be a deep, purplish black. Bring the beans to a boil and simmer for 2 hours, leaving the lid slightly askew. Check occasionally to see that the beans don't cook dry, and add boiling water if at any time the beans aren't completely covered with liquid.

To serve 4 to 6

2 cups	cooked black beans	½ liter
1 cup	beef broth	¼ liter
¼ cup	dry vermouth	50 ml.
1	garlic clove, finely chopped	1
½ tsp.	cumin	2 ml.
2 or 3	coriander pods, crushed	2 or 3
½	small, dried red chili	½
1	*chorizo* or pepperoni sausage, peeled and sliced	1
	water (optional)	
	lemon slices (optional)	
	finely cut fresh chives (optional)	
	sour cream (optional)	

Put the beans, broth, vermouth, garlic, cumin, coriander and chili into a blender and purée until smooth. Scrape the purée into a heavy pot and thin to the desired consistency with water—it should be about like split-pea soup. Stir in the sausage and heat carefully over low heat for about 25 minutes, stirring often to prevent sticking. Garnish each serving with lemon slices, chives or sour cream.

MIRIAM UNGERER
GOOD CHEAP FOOD

Red Pottage

To serve 6

1 cup	dried Great Northern or pea beans, soaked in water overnight	¼ liter
2 tbsp.	butter	30 ml.
1	medium-sized onion, sliced	1
1	rib celery or small parsnip, sliced	1
1	beet, boiled, peeled and sliced	1
4	medium-sized tomatoes, sliced	4
2 quarts	stock or water	2 liters
	salt and pepper	
1 tbsp.	finely chopped fresh mint	15 ml.

Drain the beans well. Melt the butter in a large, heavy saucepan, add the beans and fresh vegetables and fry gently for 5 minutes, stirring occasionally. Add the stock or water; season. Bring to a boil, skimming if necessary, and simmer for 3 hours or longer. Discard the beet, and pass all the rest through a sieve. Reheat and garnish with the mint.

F. MARIAN MC NEILL
THE SCOTS KITCHEN

Melon and Potato Soup

Sopa de Apatzingán

To make the thin sour cream called for in this recipe, mix 1 cup [¼ liter] of light cream with 2 tablespoons [30 ml.] of buttermilk. Cover the mixture and allow it to rest at room temperature for about 6 hours. Chill before using.

This soup is also good iced.

To serve 6

1 lb.	cantaloupe flesh (about 2 cups [½ liter]), diced	½ kg.
3	medium-sized potatoes (about 1 lb. [½ kg.]), boiled, peeled and diced	3
2 cups	milk	½ liter
4 tbsp.	butter	60 ml.
	salt and freshly ground pepper	
4	egg yolks	4
	thin sour cream	

Put half of the melon and potatoes into a blender with ½ cup [125 ml.] of milk. Blend to a purée, then repeat with the remaining melon and potatoes and ½ cup more milk.

Melt the butter, add the purée and cook gently for a few moments. Add the remaining milk, the salt and pepper and continue cooking for about 5 minutes over low heat.

Beat the egg yolks well until they are creamy and stir them gradually into the soup. Remove the saucepan from the heat as soon as the egg yolks have been added.

After serving the soup, add a little thin sour cream to each diner's bowl.

DIANA KENNEDY
THE CUISINES OF MEXICO

Raspberry Soup

Potage de Framboises

To serve 4

1 quart	fresh raspberries	1 liter
1 quart	milk	1 liter
	salt	

Select a few unblemished raspberries for a garnish, and purée the remainder, adding a little milk to make them pass easily through the sieve or food mill.

Bring the remaining milk to a boil, season it with a little salt and add the raspberry purée. Stir well, garnish with the reserved raspberries and serve.

LA VARENNE
LE VRAY CUISINIER FRANÇOIS

Apple Soup

To serve 12

4 or 5	medium-sized cooking apples (about 1½ lb. [¾ kg.]), peeled and cored	4 or 5
3 quarts	mutton or beef broth	3 liters
1 tsp.	ground ginger	5 ml.
½ tsp.	pepper	2 ml.

Clear the fat from the broth and strain the broth through a fine sieve into a large saucepan. Bring the broth to a boil, add the apples and stew them down very gently to a smooth pulp; press the whole through a strainer and add the ginger and pepper. Simmer the soup for a couple of minutes, skim, and serve it very hot, accompanied by a dish of boiled rice.

ELIZA ACTON
MODERN COOKERY

Game Soup

Potage Saint-Hubert

This recipe can be used for any game bird such as young partridge, quail or woodcock.

To serve 6 to 8

1	pheasant, cleaned, singed and trussed	1
	salt and pepper	
4 tbsp.	butter, melted	60 ml.
2½ cups	lentils	625 ml.
2 quarts	water	2 liters
1	onion	1
1	leek, white part only	1
1	sprig thyme	1
1	bay leaf	1
½ cup	heavy cream	125 ml.

Rinse the lentils and put them into a saucepan with the water, onion, leek, thyme and bay leaf. Season with salt and cook for 1 hour, or until the lentils are very soft.

Season the pheasant with salt and pepper, sprinkle with the melted butter, and roast in a preheated 350° F. [180° C.] oven for 30 minutes or until slightly underdone.

Cut the pheasant meat off the bones, saving the breast fillets to dice later. Pound the remaining meat in a mortar, strain the lentils, reserving their cooking liquid, and add them to the meat; pound again thoroughly until the mixture is perfectly smooth; rub it through a fine-meshed sieve into a saucepan; moisten the purée with the lentil stock. When quite hot, add the cream, taste to season, and pour the mixture into the tureen over the diced pheasant.

J. BERJANE
FRENCH DISHES FOR ENGLISH TABLES

Game-Bird Carcass Soup

To serve 6

1	leftover roasted game-bird carcass	1
1 cup	chopped onions	¼ liter
1 cup	chopped carrots	¼ liter
½ cup	sliced celery with the leaves	125 ml.
2	leeks, sliced	2
1	bouquet garni, composed of thyme, parsley and chervil	1
½ cup	cooked rice	125 ml.
6 cups	chicken or beef broth	1½ liters
	salt and pepper	
¼ cup	heavy cream	50 ml.
⅓ cup	port	75 ml.

Pound the carcass and put it in the bottom of a soup kettle. Add all of the ingredients except the cream and the wine. Cover and simmer the soup gently for 1 hour. Remove all of the bones, take off any meat clinging to them and purée the meat in a blender or food mill with the rest of the soup. Season with salt and pepper if needed. Bring the soup to a boil and add the cream and wine. Serve in soup cups.

STELLA STANDARD
STELLA STANDARD'S SOUP BOOK

Puréed Chicken Soup

Potage à la Reine

The technique of pounding chicken and almonds to a purée is demonstrated on pages 34-35. Hard-boiled egg yolks and strips of lemon peel may be pounded with the chicken and almonds to add flavor and thicken the purée. For a richer soup, up to 1 cup [¼ liter] of heavy cream may be stirred into the purée after it has been sieved.

To serve 4

3 to 3½ lb.	chicken	1½ to 1¾ kg.
1 quart	chicken broth	1 liter
1	slice white bread, crusts removed	1
6	blanched almonds	6
	croutons *(recipe, page 166)*	

Roast the chicken until it is slightly underdone, about 45 minutes, at 350° F. [180° C.]. Strip the meat from the bones, removing all tendons, gristle, and bits of meat that are too hard or too browned. If desired, simmer the skin and carcass of the chicken in the broth to add flavor to it.

In a large marble or ceramic mortar, pound the chicken meat with the almonds until smooth. Soak the bread in the broth, then incorporate the bread into the pounded chicken. Moisten the pounded mixture with a little of the broth, and purée this mixture through a fine sieve.

At serving time, reheat the purée over hot water in a double boiler. Heat the remaining broth in another pan and stir it into the purée. The purée should never boil. Stir in the croutons just before serving.

JULES BRETEUIL
LE CUISINIER EUROPÉEN

Purée of Chicken Soup à la Reine

Potage Purée de Volaille à la Reine

The original version of this recipe called for 12 sweet and 3 bitter almonds. Bitter almonds contain traces of poisonous prussic acid, and are unavailable in the United States. You may substitute ¼ teaspoon [1 ml.] of almond extract along with the consommé to give the soup a slightly bitter taste.

This recipe has been extracted from a 16th Century recipe book. Soup *à la reine* used to be served every Thursday at the court of the Valois. Queen Marguerite de Valois, it is said, was very fond of it.

To serve 4 to 6

1	whole chicken breast, cut from a slightly under-roasted, still warm chicken, skin removed and meat sliced	1
1	slice bread, crust removed	1
2¼ cups	consommé	550 ml.
15	blanched almonds	15
6	hard-boiled egg yolks	6
1¼ cups	light cream	300 ml.
	salt	

Add the bread to the consommé and bring to a boil. Pound finely in a large mortar the breast of chicken, almonds and egg yolks. When the mixture has been well pounded, add the consommé with the bread, and the cream. Rub the mixture through a sieve, season and keep the soup hot in a double boiler set over simmering water.

PROSPER MONTAGNÉ
THE NEW LAROUSSE GASTRONOMIQUE

Fennel and Almond Fish Soup

To serve 4 to 6

½	bulb fennel, julienned and blanched	½
2 tsp.	fennel seeds	10 ml.
24	blanched almonds	24
3	whole whiting (about ¾ lb. [⅓ kg.] each), cleaned	3
2 cups	water	½ liter
2 cups	dry white wine	½ liter
1	large Spanish onion	1
2 tsp.	peppercorns	10 ml.
1 cup	heavy cream	¼ liter
3 to 4 tbsp.	Pernod or other anise liqueur	45 to 60 ml.
	fresh parsley, chives or dill	

Poach the whiting in the water and wine, with the onion, peppercorns and fennel seeds. When done, skin and bone the fish. Strain the poaching liquid into a pan and reduce it by fast boiling to about 3 cups [¾ liter]. Put 2 cups [½ liter] of the skinned and flaked cooked fish into a blender with some of the stock and the blanched almonds. Blend to a cream, then force through a sieve. Add this purée to the stock remaining in the pan and reheat. Just before serving, stir in the cream, Pernod and blanched fennel. The soup is as white as snow, so sprinkle each bowl thickly with chopped parsley or chives before serving, or decorate with dill leaves.

MARGARET COSTA
MARGARET COSTA'S FOUR SEASONS COOKERY BOOK

Scallop Soup

To serve 6

½ lb.	scallops	¼ kg.
1 quart	water	1 liter
¾ cup	dry white wine	175 ml.
1	shallot, thinly sliced or 1 tbsp. [15 ml.] thinly sliced scallion	1
⅛ tsp.	ground saffron	½ ml.
⅛ tsp.	curry powder	½ ml.
¼ tsp.	dry mustard	1 ml.
1½ tsp.	salt	7 ml.
½ tsp.	pepper	2 ml.
¼ cup	heavy cream	50 ml.
2 tsp.	chopped fresh chives	10 ml.

In a nonaluminum 2-quart [2-liter] pot put the water, wine, shallot or scallion, saffron, curry powder, mustard, salt and

pepper. Bring to a boil, cover and simmer for 15 minutes. Add the scallops, cover and simmer for just 5 minutes more.

Purée the contents in a blender, half at a time. The scallops do not purée completely, but remain in tiny pieces. Return the soup to the pot and add the cream; stir thoroughly. Reheat, but do not boil.

When ladling soup from the pot make sure you stir up the bottom to include pieces of scallop which will have collected there. Pour into individual soup bowls and sprinkle with chives. Serve quite warm, but not hot.

CAROL CUTLER
THE SIX-MINUTE SOUFFLÉ AND OTHER CULINARY DELIGHTS

Cream of Shrimp Purée

Puré de Gambas

To serve 4

24	large raw shrimp, washed but not peeled	24
1½ quarts	water	1½ liters
1 cup	dry white wine	¼ liter
1	onion, very finely chopped	1
3	tomatoes, very finely chopped	3
2	carrots, very finely chopped	2
3 tbsp.	butter	45 ml.
3 tbsp.	flour	45 ml.
	fish broth or water	
	salt and pepper	
	ground saffron	
2	egg yolks, lightly beaten	2

Bring the water and wine to a boil, add the shrimp and cook for 5 minutes. Remove the shrimp, and then strain and reserve the liquid. Remove the tail meat of the shrimp and save it. Crush the rest of the shrimp—shells and all—into a smooth paste in a large mortar; or pass them through a food grinder or blender. In a bowl, combine the vegetables with this shrimp paste.

Melt the butter in a saucepan, sprinkle in the flour, and add the shrimp and vegetable mixture. Fry until golden, then slowly add the liquid in which the shrimp were boiled, stirring gently all the time. Cover and cook over low heat for 1 hour, adding fish broth or water from time to time if necessary. Pass the soup into a clean pan through a fine-meshed sieve, rubbing the vegetable pulp through. Season to taste with salt, pepper and saffron and add the shrimp tails. Beat some of the liquid with the egg yolks, then stir the egg-yolk mixture into the soup and reheat the soup without boiling it.

MARINA PEREYRA DE AZNAR AND NINA FROUD
THE HOME BOOK OF SPANISH COOKERY

Crayfish Bisque

The technique of shelling crayfish is shown on page 32.

	To serve 6	
30 to 40	live crayfish (about 2 lb. [1 kg.])	30 to 40
1	large onion, finely chopped	1
1 cup	chopped carrots	¼ liter
1	rib celery, chopped	1
1	bay leaf, crumbled	1
1 tsp.	thyme	5 ml.
4 tbsp.	butter	60 ml.
	Cognac	
1 cup	dry white wine	¼ liter
	salt	
	cayenne pepper	
5 cups	fish broth	1¼ liters
½ cup	stale bread crumbs	125 ml.
	heavy cream	

In a large skillet, sauté the chopped onion, carrots and celery with the bay leaf and thyme in the butter, until this mirepoix mixture is softened but not colored. Add first a dash of Cognac and then the white wine. The Cognac may flare up; if it does, stir the mirepoix until the flames die—or simply extinguish the flames with the wine.

Throw in the crayfish and stir them around until they redden. Season with salt and cayenne pepper, and cover the pan. Simmer for 7 to 8 minutes. Pour the crayfish and mirepoix into a colander set over a bowl.

When the crayfish cool, shell them and cut each tail section crosswise into three pieces. Set the pieces aside. In a mortar, pound the heads, shells and claws to a paste. Add the paste, the mirepoix and the strained cooking juices from the frying pan to a saucepan containing the fish broth. Bring to a boil, simmer for a few minutes and pass the mixture through a food mill. Taste for salt—the soup also may need to be heightened by a little more cayenne—and return the soup to the saucepan. Throw in the bread, simmer for 10 minutes or so and purée again; this time through a very fine sieve. Stir in some heavy cream; return to the boiling point and serve the bisque garnished with the crayfish tails.

PETITS PROPOS CULINAIRES

Compound Broths

Asparagus Tips Soup

Potage aux Pointes de Grosses Asperges

	To serve 4	
2 to 2½ lb.	thick fresh asparagus, tips only, cut into 1-inch [2½-cm.] lengths	1 kg.
	small croutons, fried in butter *(recipe, page 166)*	
1 tbsp.	cut chervil leaves	15 ml.
¼ tsp.	sugar	1 ml.
	coarsely ground pepper	
1 quart	consommé, heated to boiling	1 liter

Blanch the asparagus in boiling water for 5 to 10 minutes, or until just tender, to preserve their lovely springlike freshness. Drain the asparagus on a cloth and put them into a warmed soup tureen with the croutons and the chervil. Add the sugar, grind in a pinch of pepper, then pour in the hot consommé and serve.

ANTONIN CARÊME
L'ART DE LA CUISINE FRANÇAISE AU DIX-NEUVIÈME SIÈCLE

Sweet-and-sour Cabbage Soup

	To serve 6	
1	small cabbage (about 1½ lb.[¾ kg.]), trimmed, halved, cored and finely shredded	1
2 quarts	stock	2 liters
⅔ cup	tomato juice or sieved tomatoes	150 ml.
3	apples, peeled, cored and grated	3
1	onion, grated	1
	salt and pepper	
2 to 3 tbsp.	fresh lemon juice	30 to 45 ml.
	sugar	

Put the stock and the tomato juice in a large saucepan and bring to a boil; add the prepared cabbage, apples and onion, cover and cook gently for 30 minutes. Season with salt and pepper. Before serving, add lemon juice and sugar to taste.

FLORENCE GREENBERG
JEWISH COOKERY

Cabbage Soup with Cream

Soupe aux Choux à la Crème

To serve 6

1	small cabbage (about 1½ lb. [¾ kg.]), trimmed, quartered, cored and shredded	1
4 tbsp.	butter	60 ml.
½ lb.	saucisson or other mild-flavored fresh pork sausage	¼ kg.
1½ quarts	bouillon or water	1½ liters
	salt	
3	medium-sized potatoes, cut into pieces	3
1 cup	sour cream	¼ liter

Plunge the cabbage into boiling water. Boil for 1 minute, then strain off the water. Put the cabbage in a saucepan, add the butter, sausage and bouillon or water. Season lightly with salt. Bring to a boil, reduce the heat to low, cover and cook for 1 hour. Add the potatoes and cook, still covered, for a further 30 minutes. Remove the sausage, cut it into pieces and return it to the pan. The soup will be very thick. Serve the sour cream separately.

ÉDOUARD DE POMIANE
LE CARNET D'ANNA

Cauliflower and Broccoli Soup with Parsley

Potage de Choux-Fleurs et de Brocolis au Persil

To serve 4

1	cauliflower, stalks removed, divided into florets	1
2	heads broccoli, stalks removed, divided into florets	2
1	bouquet of parsley, tied together	1
1 quart	consommé	1 liter
	croutons (recipe, page 166)	

Blanch the cauliflower in boiling water for about 5 minutes, then plunge it into cold water and drain. Put it into a pan with a little of the consommé and the parsley, and simmer gently for 10 to 15 minutes, or until tender.

Meanwhile, blanch the broccoli in boiling water for 10 to 15 minutes, or until tender; drain it and place it in a warmed soup tureen. When the cauliflower is done, remove the parsley and pour the cauliflower with its cooking liquid into the tureen. Bring the remaining consommé to a boil and add it to the tureen with the croutons.

ANTONIN CARÊME
L'ART DE LA CUISINE FRANÇAISE AU DIX-NEUVIÈME SIÈCLE

Eggplant or Squash Soup

Sajur Terung atau Labu

Laos powder tastes like ginger, which may be substituted for it. Coconut oil comes in both solid and liquid form; either may be used in this recipe. Dried curry leaves have a slightly curry-like flavor. All three ingredients are available at shops specializing in Indonesian foods. Coconut milk may be obtained from stores that sell Caribbean or Oriental foods, or you can make it at home by mixing 2 cups [½ liter] of grated fresh coconut meat with 1 cup [¼ liter] of hot, but not boiling, water. Press the mixture through a fine sieve lined with dampened cheesecloth.

To serve 4

2	small eggplants or large zucchini or yellow squash, sliced or diced	2
½ tsp.	coriander seeds	2 ml.
½ ml.	cumin seeds	⅛ tsp.
3	macadamia nuts or almonds	3
¼ tsp.	ground turmeric	1 ml.
7	dried or fresh red chilies, stemmed and seeded, and sliced if fresh, or 2 tsp. [10 ml.] cayenne pepper	7
2 tbsp.	coconut or peanut oil	30 ml.
1½	Spanish onions, chopped	1½
1	large garlic clove, chopped	1
1	thin slice fresh ginger root	1
2 tbsp.	chopped, uncooked beef or chicken	30 ml.
	salt	
	water	
¼ tsp.	laos powder (optional)	1 ml.
2	curry leaves	2
2 cups	coconut milk	½ liter
½	lime or lemon	½

In a blender or mortar, grind or pound the coriander, cumin, nuts, turmeric and—if you are using it—the dried chili or cayenne. Heat the oil in a saucepan and fry the onions and garlic until they are just yellow. Add the ground spices, ginger and the sliced fresh chili, if using, and stir. Add the meat, salt to taste, cover with water and bring to a boil. Add *laos* powder, if using, and curry leaves and allow to simmer for about 15 minutes or until the meat is half-cooked.

Add the coconut milk to the pan and simmer, uncovered, for about 10 minutes. Finally, add the eggplants, zucchini or yellow squash and continue cooking without a lid until the vegetables are tender but not overcooked. Remove from the stove, add a squeeze of lime or lemon juice, stir and serve.

ROSEMARY BRISSENDEN
SOUTH EAST ASIAN FOOD

Spinach and Pork Soup

To serve 8

6 oz.	spinach, stems removed and cut into pieces about 1 inch [2½ cm.] square (about 1 cup [¼ liter])	175 g.
1 lb.	lean boneless pork, preferably loin, in 1 piece	½ kg.
6 tbsp.	light soy sauce	90 ml.
2 quarts	water	2 liters
1 tsp.	salt	5 ml.
½ tsp.	white pepper	2 ml.
1-inch	cube fresh ginger root, grated, squeezed and the juice reserved	2½-cm.

Marinate the pork in the soy sauce for 1 hour. In a large saucepan, bring the water to a boil and add the pork and its marinade. Cover and simmer until the pork is done, after about 40 minutes. Remove the piece of pork, putting it aside to cool. Add the salt and pepper, and the juice from the ginger root to the stock in the saucepan. Taste for seasoning and correct if necessary.

Shred the pork by hand, pulling it apart into thin strips about 1 inch [2½ cm.] long. Add the pork to the stock and heat. Add the spinach and cook for a minute. Serve immediately. This soup may be garnished with a one-egg omelette, fried thin, rolled and sliced crosswise into strips.

PETER AND JOAN MARTIN
JAPANESE COOKING

Green Soup with Fish Broth

Potage de Poisson aux Herbes

To serve 6

2	Boston lettuce hearts, roughly chopped	2
¼ cup	chopped chervil	50 ml.
1	celery heart, finely sliced	1
¾ cup	sorrel leaves, coarsely chopped	175 ml.
1½ quarts	fish broth	1½ liters
3	egg yolks	3
	slices of dry bread	
	olive oil or butter	

Put the broth in a saucepan over high heat. When it comes to a boil, put in the lettuce, chervil, celery and sorrel, reduce the heat and cook for about 15 minutes, or until the vegetables are tender.

Put the egg yolks into a small pan and stir in 4 or 5 tablespoons [60 or 75 ml.] of the hot broth. Stirring with a wooden spoon, cook over very low heat for a few moments until the mixture starts to thicken. Take the pan off the heat, stir in a little more of the broth, and then pour the yolk mixture into the soup.

Serve the soup ladled over slices of dry bread. Sprinkle the bread with good oil or put a lump of butter on each serving, if you like, before ladling on the soup.

CHARLES DURAND
LE CUISINIER DURAND

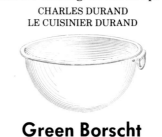

Green Borscht

Borchtch Vert

The salt pork called for may be replaced by spareribs or oxtail; the latter needs a longer cooking time, and both substitutions require adding more salt. At the end of the cooking, the ribs or oxtail should be boned, diced and returned to the soup.

To serve 6 to 8

½ lb.	salt pork with some meat attached, soaked in water overnight and drained	¼ kg.
2 quarts	water	2 liters
2 cups	stemmed sorrel leaves	½ liter
¾ cup	stemmed spinach leaves (optional)	175 ml.
4 tbsp.	butter	60 ml.
3	onions, finely chopped and lightly sautéed in butter	3
1 tbsp.	flour	15 ml.
5 or 6	potatoes, cut up	5 or 6
	salt	
¾ cup	heavy cream, whipped, or 1 cup [¼ liter] sour cream	175 ml.
3	hard-boiled eggs, chopped	3

Put the salt pork into the water, bring to a boil and simmer over low heat. Meanwhile, in another saucepan, gently cook the sorrel — and the spinach, if you are using it — in the butter until the leaves become a purée, about 10 minutes. Stir in the onions and flour, then add this mixture to the simmering soup and cook for 45 minutes to 1 hour.

Thirty minutes before the end of the cooking time, add the potatoes. These will help to neutralize the acidity of the sorrel. When the potatoes are tender, remove the pork from the soup, cut the rind and meat into serving pieces and return them to the soup. Taste for salt. Serve the cream and the chopped eggs in separate dishes.

H. WITWICKA AND S. SOSKINE
LA CUISINE RUSSE CLASSIQUE

Creamy Onion Soup

Tourin Bordelais

To serve 6

1	large onion, finely sliced	1
7 tbsp.	butter	105 ml.
3 tbsp.	flour	45 ml.
1½ quarts	milk, heated to simmering	1½ liters
	salt and pepper	
3	egg yolks	3
⅔ cup	heavy cream	150 ml.
	small rounds French bread, dried in a 375° F. [190° C.] oven for 5 minutes	

In a saucepan, sauté the onion in half of the butter, stirring constantly, until the slices are golden but not browned. Sprinkle in the flour and cook, stirring, for several more minutes. Pour in the hot milk. Bring to a boil, still stirring, season with salt and pepper, and let the soup simmer very gently for 15 minutes.

In a bowl, beat the egg yolks with the cream and then beat in a ladleful of the hot soup. Take the saucepan off the heat and allow the soup to cool for 5 minutes before stirring in the egg-and-cream liaison. Add the remaining butter. Put the dried bread rounds into a tureen and pour in the soup.

JEAN E. PROGNEAUX
LES SPÉCIALITÉS ET RECETTES GASTRONOMIQUES
BORDELAISES ET GIRONDINES

Onion and Garlic Soup

Le Tourin de Gastes

To serve 8

4	large onions, thinly sliced	4
6	garlic cloves, thinly sliced	6
1 tbsp.	rendered goose fat	15 ml.
2 quarts	water or 1¾ quarts [1¾ liters] water and 1 cup [¼ liter] consommé	2 liters
	salt and pepper	
1	egg	1
2 tsp.	wine, cider or sherry vinegar	10 ml.
8	slices homemade bread, toasted in the oven	8

In a large, heavy saucepan, gently sauté the onions and garlic in the goose fat without letting them color. When the

onions are soft and transparent, cover them with the water or water and consommé. Simmer, covered, for 30 to 40 minutes. Season with salt and pepper.

Beat the egg with the vinegar. Remove the soup from the heat and gradually stir in the egg mixture. Serve the soup at once in a warmed tureen, accompanied by toasted bread.

MADELEINE PETER
GRANDES DAMES DE LA CUISINE

Mushroom-Barley Soup

To serve 8

2 cups	thinly sliced fresh mushrooms	½ liter
1 cup	pearl barley	¼ liter
1 lb.	beef bones, in small pieces if possible	½ kg.
1	carrot, sliced	1
2	ribs celery, sliced	2
1 lb.	chicken backs and necks or wing tips	½ kg.
3 quarts	water	3 liters
1 tbsp.	salt	15 ml.
½ tsp.	freshly ground pepper	2 ml.
4 tbsp.	lard	60 ml.
1 cup	finely chopped onion	¼ liter
2 tbsp.	chopped fresh parsley	30 ml.
2 or 3	dried mushrooms, broken up (optional)	2 or 3

Place the beef bones, carrot, celery and chicken pieces in a soup pot. Add the water, salt and pepper. Bring to a boil, reduce the heat and simmer for 2 to 3 hours.

In 2 tablespoons [30 ml.] of the lard, sauté half of the barley until it starts to turn yellow and gives a crackling sound. Add the onion and continue cooking, stirring constantly, until the onion turns limp and glossy. Melt the remaining lard in another pan and quickly sauté the fresh mushrooms with the parsley. Set aside.

Strain the broth through a sieve. Discard the bones and vegetables. Add to the broth the remaining uncooked barley. Add the dried mushrooms, if using, and cook for 30 minutes. Add the sautéed barley-onion mixture and cook for 30 minutes more. Add the mushroom-parsley mixture and simmer for 10 additional minutes. Let the soup stand, covered, for at least 30 minutes before reheating and serving. The sautéed barley will keep its shape; the rest will cook to a pulp and give thickness to the soup.

LOUIS SZATHMARY
THE CHEF'S SECRET COOK BOOK

Fresh Mushroom and Cabbage Soup

Ch'ing Ts'ai Ma Ku T'ang

Dried Chinese mushrooms should be soaked in warm water for at least 30 minutes before being drained and sliced. Cellophane noodles need half an hour's soaking in hot water. Fried wheat gluten is wheat-flour dough often sold in small ball shapes in packages. All three ingredients are obtainable where Oriental foods are sold.

Mustard greens, watercress or lettuce may be used instead of bok choy. Soaked dried mushrooms may be used instead of fresh ones. For a substantial one-dish meal, add 10 to 20 pieces of fried wheat gluten to the soup and adjust the seasoning; or add 2 ounces [60 g.] of soaked cellophane noodles in addition to the fried wheat gluten.

To serve 4

1 cup	sliced fresh mushrooms	¼ liter
2 cups	bok choy leaves, cut into 1-inch [2½-cm.] pieces	½ liter
1 tbsp.	peanut or corn oil	15 ml.
3 cups	water	¾ liter
	salt	

Heat a cook-and-serve pot until hot. Add the oil and mushrooms and stir fry until the mushrooms begin to soften. Add the cabbage and stir fry for 2 more minutes. Add the water and bring to a boil. Cook uncovered for 2 to 3 minutes, or until the cabbage is soft. Add salt to taste and serve hot.

FLORENCE LIN
FLORENCE LIN'S CHINESE VEGETARIAN COOKBOOK

Mushroom Cream Soup

To serve 6

1 lb.	fresh mushrooms	½ kg.
1 quart	chicken broth	1 liter
¾ cup	finely chopped onion	175 ml.
7 tbsp.	butter	105 ml.
6 tbsp.	flour	90 ml.
3 cups	light cream	¾ liter
1 cup	heavy cream	¼ liter
1 tsp.	salt	5 ml.
½ tsp.	freshly ground white pepper	2 ml.
2 tbsp.	dry sherry or dry Madeira	30 ml.
1 tbsp.	fresh lemon juice	15 ml.
1 tbsp.	finely chopped fresh parsley	15 ml.

Reserve six mushroom caps, and chop the rest of the mushrooms, including the stems. Put the chopped mushrooms into a saucepan with the chicken stock and chopped onion, bring to a boil, reduce the heat to simmer, cover and cook for 30 minutes.

In another pan, melt 6 tablespoons [90 ml.] of the butter and stir in the flour. Cook, stirring with a wooden spatula, over high heat for 2 minutes—do not let this roux brown. Remove from the heat, change to a whisk, and add the light cream, whisking vigorously. Return the pan to high heat and cook, stirring, until the mixture is thick. Stir in the heavy cream and the mushroom mixture. Season with the salt and pepper.

When ready to serve, reheat the soup, adding the dry sherry or Madeira. Slice the reserved mushroom caps and sauté them quickly in the remaining 1 tablespoon [15 ml.] of butter, adding the lemon juice. Ladle the soup into bowls and garnish with the sliced mushrooms and the chopped parsley.

JULIE DANNENBAUM
MENUS FOR ALL OCCASIONS

Mushroom Vegetable Soup

Julienne aux Champignons

To serve 3 or 4

¼ lb.	fresh mushrooms, cut into julienne (about 1½ cups [375 ml.])	125 g.
1 or 2	carrots, cut into julienne	1 or 2
2	turnips, cut into julienne	2
2	potatoes, cut into julienne	2
2	leeks, trimmed and cut into julienne	2
3 or 4	cabbage leaves, cut into julienne	3 or 4
4 tbsp.	butter	60 ml.
1 quart	beef broth or pot-au-feu bouillon	1 liter
	croutons (recipe, page 166)	

Melt the butter in a saucepan over medium heat; add all of the prepared vegetables except the mushrooms and cook them until limp but not colored. Add the broth or bouillon, cover the pan and simmer until the vegetables are thoroughly cooked, about 30 minutes. Ten minutes before serving, add the mushrooms. While the mushrooms are cooking, lightly fry some diced bread in butter; place these croutons in a warmed soup tureen. Pour in the soup and serve.

MME. JEANNE SAVARIN (EDITOR)
LA CUISINE DES FAMILLES

Parsnip Chowder

To serve 6 to 8

1½ lb.	parsnips, peeled, cored and cut into ½-inch [1-cm.] cubes (about 3 cups [¾ liter])	¾ kg.
5	slices bacon	5
1	large onion, finely sliced (1 cup [¼ liter])	1
1½ lb.	new potatoes, cut into ½-inch [1-cm.] cubes (about 3½ cups [875 ml.])	¾ kg.
2 cups	boiling water	½ liter
3 cups	milk	¾ liter
3 tbsp.	butter	45 ml.
about 1 tbsp.	salt	about 15 ml.
about ¼ tsp.	freshly ground black pepper	about 1 ml.
1 cup	heavy cream	¼ liter
1 tbsp.	chopped fresh parsley	15 ml.

Fry the bacon gently until almost crisp. Remove the bacon and set the slices aside to drain on a paper towel. Add the onion to the remaining fat in the skillet, and cook gently until the onion is soft but only lightly browned (about 5 minutes). Lift the onion from the pan with a slotted spoon and place it in a large heavy casserole; reserve the fat. Add the parsnips and potatoes to the casserole and pour in the boiling water. Cover the casserole and cook over medium heat for about ½ hour until the vegetables are tender. When the vegetables are done, add the milk and bring the soup to the boiling point. Stir in the butter and leftover bacon fat; season to taste.

When the soup is scalding hot, gradually stir in the heavy cream and place the soup in a heated tureen. Sprinkle with the bacon, which you have cut into tiny pieces with scissors and reheated carefully in a separate small skillet. Sprinkle the soup with chopped parsley.

JUNE PLATT
JUNE PLATT'S NEW ENGLAND COOK BOOK

Leek and Potato Soup

Crème Bonne Femme

The vermicelles called for in this recipe are very thin French noodles, finer than Italian vermicelli. They may be found at French food markets.

To serve 8

4 or 5	leeks, white parts only, sliced	4 or 5
6 to 8	potatoes, sliced	6 to 8
½ cup	shredded sorrel leaves	125 ml.
2 tbsp.	butter	30 ml.
2 quarts	water, lightly salted	2 liters
3½ oz.	vermicelles	100 g.
1 cup	heavy cream	¼ liter

Melt the butter in a large saucepan, add the sorrel and cook gently until the sorrel wilts into a purée. Add the leeks and potatoes and pour in the salted water. Bring to a boil and simmer, covered, for 15 minutes or until half cooked. Add the *vermicelles* and continue cooking, uncovered, for about 2 to 3 minutes, until everything is done. Shortly before serving, stir in the cream.

CLARISSE OU LA VIEILLE CUISINIÈRE

Potato and Leek Soup

Potage aux Poireaux et Pommes de Terre

To serve 6

3 or 4	medium-sized potatoes (1 lb. [½ kg.]), peeled, quartered lengthwise and finely sliced	3 or 4
4 or 5	leeks (about 1 lb. [½ kg.]), tough green parts removed, cleaned and thinly sliced	4 or 5
2 quarts	boiling water	2 liters
	salt	
3 tbsp.	unsalted butter	45 ml.

Add the vegetables to the salted, boiling water and cook, covered, at a light boil until the potatoes begin to come apart—or until, when one slice is pressed against the side of the saucepan with a wooden spoon, it offers no resistance to crushing—after about 15 to 20 minutes, depending on the potatoes. Add the butter at the moment of serving, after removing the soup from the heat.

RICHARD OLNEY
SIMPLE FRENCH FOOD

Grated Potato Soup

Sopa de Patata Rallada

To serve 4

3	large potatoes (about 1 lb. [½ kg.]), finely grated	3
1½ quarts	stock	1½ liters
	salt and pepper	
1	hard-boiled egg, chopped	1

Bring the stock to a boil, then add the potatoes. Cook for 5 or 6 minutes, season to taste and serve with the chopped hard-boiled egg sprinkled on top.

MARINA PEREYRA DE AZNAR AND NINA FROUD
THE HOME BOOK OF SPANISH COOKERY

Algerian Tomato Soup

Cherbah

To serve 4

4	tomatoes, peeled, seeded and cut into large pieces	4
4	onions, cut into large pieces	4
2 tbsp.	butter	30 ml.
1	large sprig mint, coarsely chopped	1
2 or 3	fresh chilies, stemmed, seeded and finely chopped	2 or 3
	salt and pepper	
1 quart	hot water	1 liter
¾ lb.	lamb shoulder or neck	⅓ kg.
½ cup	dried apricots	125 ml.
2 oz.	vermicelli	60 g.

In a large saucepan, fry the tomatoes and onions lightly in the butter with the mint and chilies. Season with a little salt and pepper. Add the water, the meat and the apricots; cook slowly, covered, for about 1½ hours. Take out the lamb, bone it, cut the meat into tiny pieces and return them to the soup. Add the vermicelli and simmer for 10 more minutes, or until the pasta is cooked, then serve.

MRS. C. F. LEYEL & MISS OLGA HARTLEY
THE GENTLE ART OF COOKERY

Italian Tomato Soup

Minestra di Pomidoro

To make *crostini*, saturate slices of bread with melted butter, spread them thickly with grated Parmesan and cook them in a moderate oven for 10 minutes. An anchovy fillet may be placed on each slice.

To serve 4

1½ lb.	tomatoes, peeled and chopped	¾ kg.
⅓ cup	olive oil	75 ml.
1	garlic clove, crushed	1
1 tbsp.	chopped fresh parsley, basil or marjoram	15 ml.
2½ cups	meat or chicken stock	625 ml.
	salt and pepper	
	sugar	
	crostini (optional)	

Melt the tomatoes in the olive oil; add the garlic and the parsley or basil or marjoram. Cook for 5 minutes, then add the stock, salt and pepper, and a pinch of sugar. Cook for 5 minutes more only. By this method the flavor of the tomatoes is retained and the soup tastes very fresh. In the summer this soup can be eaten iced, accompanied by hot *crostini* of cheese and anchovy.

ELIZABETH DAVID
ITALIAN FOOD

Turnip Soup with Green Peas

Potage de Navets aux Petits Pois

To serve 4

6	turnips, peeled and diced	6
2 cups	freshly shelled young peas (about 2 lb. [1 kg.] unshelled), blanched in boiling water until bright green (about 1 minute)	½ liter
2 tbsp.	butter	30 ml.
1 quart	consommé	1 liter
	sugar	
	fried croutons (recipe, page 166)	

Sweat the turnips in the butter for about 10 minutes or until they are yellowed, stirring constantly with a wooden spoon. Drain the turnips in a strainer. Bring the consommé to a simmer and add the turnips and a pinch of sugar. Continue to simmer, skimming often, until the turnips are cooked, about 10 minutes. Put the peas and croutons into a warmed soup tureen. Pour in the turnips and consommé, and serve.

ANTONIN CARÊME
L'ART DE LA CUISINE FRANÇAISE AU DIX-NEUVIÈME SIÈCLE

Thrifty Housewife's Soups

Soupe de la Bonne Ménagère

This recipe produces two soups for serving on successive days. Any leftover roast-meat bones —lamb, beef, veal, fresh pork or smoked ham, or a combination of these —may be used in the bouillon for the soups. For a rich bouillon, you will need 3 to 4 pounds [1½ to 2 kg.] of bones and chicken carcasses.

To serve 6

2½ quarts	water	2½ liters
	leftover bones from roasted meat	
	raw or cooked chicken carcasses	
3	carrots	3
1	turnip	1
1	onion, stuck with 2 or 3 whole cloves	1
	salt	
1	bouquet garni	1
1	cabbage, halved, cored and coarsely shredded	1
2	hearts celery, cut into julienne	2
2	cabbage leaves, cut into julienne	2
3 or 4	leeks, cut into julienne	3 or 4
2 tbsp.	butter	30 ml.
3 or 4	large waxy potatoes	3 or 4
	sliced bread	

Pour the water into a soup pot and add the bones, carcasses, carrots, turnip, onion, salt and bouquet garni. Cover and simmer very gently for 3 hours. One hour before serving, pour off half of the bouillon and set it aside, in the refrigerator, for the next day. Strain the remainder, add the shredded cabbage and continue simmering gently until the cabbage is cooked. Serve this as cabbage soup.

The next day, lightly fry the julienned celery, cabbage and leeks in the butter over medium heat. When the vegetables are half-cooked and golden, add the reserved bouillon and the whole potatoes. Simmer until the potatoes are cooked, about 40 minutes, then mash the potatoes into the soup with a wooden pestle or potato masher. Place the slices of bread in a soup tureen and pour in the soup. Serve.

L. E. AUDOT
LA CUISINIÈRE DE LA CAMPAGNE ET DE LA VILLE

Mixed Vegetable Soup

Il Minestrone alla Milanese

In the summer, this soup may be served cold, topped with the slices of very lean salt pork that are cooked in the soup. Fresh pork rinds may be substituted for the salt pork, and the soup may be enriched by the addition of Parmesan cheese rinds. The cheese rinds should be added a few minutes before the end of the cooking time.

To serve 8 to 10

7 tbsp.	butter	105 ml.
2	small onions, chopped	2
1	leek, chopped	1
3½ oz.	salt pork, blanched in boiling water for 5 minutes, drained and cubed	100 g.
1	bouquet garni, composed of parsley, bay leaf and rosemary	1
2	medium-sized tomatoes, peeled, seeded and coarsely chopped	2
	salt and freshly ground pepper	
1	potato, diced	1
2	carrots, diced	2
1	zucchini, diced	1
1 cup	shelled broad beans (or substitute lima beans)	¼ liter
⅔ cup	shelled peas	150 ml.
1	celery heart, finely chopped	1
1 cup	fresh white beans, or ⅔ cup [150 ml.] dried beans, soaked in water overnight and precooked	¼ liter
2 quarts	veal or chicken stock	2 liters
1 cup	raw unprocessed rice	¼ liter
½	medium-sized green cabbage, cored, parboiled for 5 minutes and shredded	½
6	basil leaves	6
6	sprigs parsley	6
6	garlic cloves	6
1	fresh bay leaf (optional)	1
	freshly grated Parmesan cheese	

In a large saucepan melt 3 tablespoons [45 ml.] of the butter over low heat. Add the onions, leek, salt pork and bouquet garni; cover the pan and sweat the vegetables and pork for 15 to 20 minutes, without letting them brown. Discard the bouquet garni, add the tomatoes and season the mixture with a little salt and pepper.

Put the remaining butter into another pan and sweat the diced potato, carrots and zucchini, the broad beans, peas, celery and white beans in the butter for 8 minutes. Add these vegetables to the first saucepan, cook for a few minutes, and pour in the stock. Cover and simmer over medium heat for 30 to 40 minutes, or until the white beans are tender and the vegetables are cooked but not mushy.

Increase the heat and add first the rice, then the cabbage. Cook, uncovered, over medium heat for 15 to 20 minutes. A few minutes before removing the soup from the heat, finely chop together the basil, parsley, garlic and the fresh bay leaf—if available—and add them to the soup. Serve the soup with the cheese.

GIANNI BRERA AND LUIGI VERONELLI
LA PACCIADA

Farmer's Soup

Pächterin-Suppe

To serve 6

1 cup	freshly shelled peas (about 1 lb. [½ kg.] unshelled)	¼ liter
3 cups	water	¾ liter
	salt	
2 oz.	salt pork with the rind removed, coarsely chopped	50 g.
1	large carrot, finely chopped	1
3	leeks, white parts only, chopped	3
2	ribs celery, finely chopped	2
1 cup	sorrel with the stems removed, cut into thin strips	¼ liter
½ cup	spinach with the stems removed, cut into thin strips	125 ml.
2 tbsp.	butter	30 ml.
12	thin slices bread, buttered on both sides	12
1 quart	beef broth	1 liter
2 tbsp.	finely cut chervil leaves	30 ml.

Place the peas in a saucepan with the water and salt, bring to a boil and skim. Add the salt pork, carrot, leeks and celery, reduce the heat and simmer, covered, for about 40 minutes. Purée in a blender or food mill.

Meanwhile, cook the sorrel and spinach in the butter for 10 to 15 minutes over very low heat. Place the slices of bread in a baking pan and brown them in a 350° F. [180° C.] oven.

In a clean saucepan, blend the purée with the broth and bring the soup to the boiling point.

Layer the bread and the sorrel and spinach in a warmed soup tureen and pour in the soup. Sprinkle the soup with the chervil and serve.

M. RICHTER AND W. BICKEL
SUPPEN

Vegetable Soup

Be choosy about the size of the fresh vegetables. Select small-sized, firm ones. Then you can cut quite thick slices that will hold together during the cooking. Large vegetables are unattractive if cut thick, and thin slices fall apart.

To serve 6 to 8

18	whole baby carrots or 1 lb. [½ kg.] carrots cut into 2-inch [5-cm.] lengths	18
3	medium-sized onions, sliced	3
2	leeks, sliced	2
1 cup	sliced celery	¼ liter
1 cup	cut-up green beans	¼ liter
1 cup	green and red pepper strips	¼ liter
1 cup	corn kernels, cut from 2 large ears	¼ liter
1 cup	freshly shelled lima beans	¼ liter
1 cup	freshly shelled peas	¼ liter
1 cup	sliced but not peeled zucchini	¼ liter
1 cup	cubed turnip	¼ liter
4	tomatoes, peeled and sliced	4
1	garlic clove, crushed	1
	salt and pepper	
4 quarts	beef broth	4 liters
½ cup	chopped fresh parsley	125 ml.
1 tsp.	basil	5 ml.
1 tsp.	oregano	5 ml.

Measure the broth into a pot large enough to hold at least 10 quarts [10 liters]. Season to taste with salt and pepper—how much you want depends on the basic broth flavoring. Add all the vegetables and herbs to the kettle. Stir very gently to mix. Bring to the boiling point, cover and reduce the heat. Simmer without stirring—which may break up the more fragile vegetables—for about 1 hour or until the largest pieces, especially the carrots, are tender and cooked through. Taste, adding more salt and pepper if necessary.

ELEANOR GRAVES
GREAT DINNERS FROM LIFE

Mother Onésime's Soup

Soupe de la Mère Onésime

As hearty as you care to make it, and excellent reheated, this is the traditional hunter's breakfast. It is improved by the addition of bones from roasted meat, poultry carcasses and the cooking juices from meat or vegetables. Lamb bones, pork, duck and game are welcome. Everything you add must be perfectly fresh, and uncooked bones should be colored in a hot oven before going into the soup pot.

To serve 6 to 8

1 tbsp.	pork fat (or lard)	15 ml.
2 or 3	carrots, thinly sliced	2 or 3
1	turnip, thinly sliced	1
1	leek, white part only, thinly sliced	1
1 cup	thinly sliced, cored, halved cabbage	125 ml.
1½ quarts	water or broth	1½ liters
	meat bones or poultry carcasses (optional)	
1	bouquet garni	1
	salt	
1	sugar lump	1
½ cup	fresh white beans	125 ml.
½ cup	freshly shelled large peas	125 ml.
½ cup	cut-up green beans	125 ml.
2 to 2½ lb.	fresh or dried pork sausage	1 kg.
	pepper	

In a large heavy pot, melt the pork fat or lard and gently stew the carrots, turnip, leek and cabbage for about 10 minutes, keeping the pan tightly covered. The vegetables should not color. Add half of the water or broth, and leftover bones or carcasses if you have them. Bring to a boil over high heat. Skim if necessary and add the bouquet garni and the sugar. Cover and simmer gently for 45 minutes.

If you have used small or splintery bones, sieve the soup at this point, puréeing the vegetables. Wipe out the pot and return the liquid and the purée to it. Whether or not you have sieved the soup, now add the remaining water or broth and the white beans, peas, green beans and sausage. Return to a boil, reduce the heat and simmer, covered, for an additional 45 minutes.

To serve, remove the bouquet garni and the bones. Skim off the fat if you wish. Correct the seasoning. Slice the sausage and put the slices in the tureen with the soup, or serve them separately. Add a grind of fresh pepper to the tureen or to each of the individual bowls of soup.

MADAME SAINT-ANGE
LA CUISINE DE MADAME SAINT-ANGE

Vegetable Soup with Basil and Garlic

Soupe au Pistou

To serve 4 to 6

2	medium-sized leeks, white and tender green parts only, thinly sliced	2
1	large onion (about 6 oz. [175 g.]), sliced	1
3 or 4	carrots, quartered lengthwise, woody cores removed, and thinly sliced	3 or 4
2	medium-sized potatoes (about ¾ lb. [⅓ kg.]), quartered lengthwise and sliced	2
10 oz.	winter squash, seeded, peeled and coarsely diced	300 g.
1 lb.	fresh white beans, shelled, or ¾ cup [175 ml.] dried navy or pea beans, soaked overnight in water and cooked for 1 to 1¼ hours	½ kg.
1	bouquet garni, including 1 celery rib	1
	salt	
2½ quarts	boiling water	2½ liters
1½ cups	green beans (about 6 oz. [175 g.]), cut into ½-inch [1-cm.] lengths	375 ml.
2 or 3	small, firm zucchini (about ½ lb. [¼ kg.]), cut into ¼-inch [6-mm.] slices	2 or 3
1 cup	short or elbow macaroni	¼ liter

Pistou

4	large garlic cloves	4
1 cup	basil leaves and flowers	¼ liter
	salt and freshly ground pepper	
1 cup	freshly grated Parmesan cheese	¼ liter
1	medium-sized firm, ripe tomato, peeled, seeded and cut into pieces	1
about 1¼ cups	olive oil	about 300 ml.

Add the leeks, onion, carrots, potatoes, squash, white beans and bouquet garni to the salted boiling water and cook, covered, over medium heat for 30 minutes; test the beans for doneness and, if necessary, cook them a bit longer, or until they may be crushed with little resistance while still remaining completely intact. Add the green beans, zucchini and macaroni and cook the soup for about another 15 minutes, depending on the quality of the macaroni (it should be well cooked, but not falling apart) and on the tenderness of the green beans.

While the soup is cooking, prepare the *pistou*. Pound the garlic, basil, salt and pepper to a paste in a good-sized mortar (a 1-quart [1-liter] marble aioli mortar is perfect, but use a wooden bowl if nothing else is available), using a wooden pestle and alternating between pounding and turning with a grinding motion. Work in some of the cheese until you have a very stiff paste, then add about one third of the tomato, pounding and grinding to a paste; more cheese and a bit of the olive oil; more tomato, and so forth. The final addition of cheese will bring the consistency to that of a barely fluid paste. Add the remainder of the olive oil slowly and continuously, turning the pestle all the while. The mixture will not become a genuine emulsion (and should not); *pistou* should be thoroughly mixed each time it is served out.

Serve the soup boiling hot, the mortar of *pistou* at the table. Each guest stirs a small ladleful (about 1 or 2 tablespoons [15 or 30 ml.], depending on taste) into his soup.

RICHARD OLNEY
SIMPLE FRENCH FOOD

Rich Country Broth

La Sobronade

To serve 6

3 cups	dried white beans, soaked in water overnight and drained	¾ liter
½ lb.	lean, boneless smoked ham, diced	¼ kg.
1 lb.	fresh pork shoulder	½ kg.
1	turnip, sliced	1
¼ lb.	pork fat, chopped	125 g.
2 or 3	potatoes, sliced	2 or 3
3 or 4	carrots, sliced	3 or 4
1	rib celery, diced	1
1	large bouquet garni	1
1	onion, stuck with 2 whole cloves	1
2	garlic cloves, finely chopped	2
2 tbsp.	chopped fresh parsley	30 ml.
	salt and pepper	
	thinly sliced bread	

Put the beans into a soup pot and cover with cold water. Add the ham and pork and bring to a boil. Sauté half of the turnip in the pork fat until golden. Add this to the beans together with the remaining turnip, the potatoes, carrots, celery, bouquet garni, onion, garlic and parsley. Season the soup with a little salt and pepper. Pour in 1½ quarts [1½ liters] of hot water and bring the soup to a boil. Cover and simmer gently over low heat for 2½ hours, then pour this thick, very much reduced soup into a tureen lined with bread slices.

LA FRANCE À TABLE

Spanish Soup

Chorizos are spicy, garlicky Spanish sausages, obtainable at markets specializing in Spanish or Latin American foods. Any spicy fresh sausage may be substituted.

To serve 10 to 12

¼ lb.	dried chick-peas, soaked in water overnight and drained	125 g.
¼ lb.	dried white marrow beans, soaked in water overnight and drained	125 g.
¼ lb.	salt pork with the rind removed, diced	125 g.
¼ lb.	smoked ham, diced	125 g.
¼ lb.	*chorizos*	125 g.
2 quarts	water or stock	2 liters
2	garlic cloves, finely chopped	2
1	ham bone	1
2	medium-sized tomatoes, peeled, seeded and chopped	2
1½ tsp.	ground cumin	7 ml.
4	small potatoes, diced	4
	salt and pepper	
½ lb.	chopped dandelion greens (or substitute spinach or other leafy greens)	¼ kg.
3 tbsp.	butter	45 ml.
	croutons (recipe, page 166)	

In a large, heavy pot, sauté the salt pork until lightly browned. Add the ham and sausage. Sauté these meats until they are almost completely cooked. Remove them from the pot. Cut the sausage into thin slices. Reserve the meats. Drain off the fat from the pot.

Place in the pot the chick-peas, beans, the water or stock, garlic, ham bone, tomatoes, cumin, potatoes and salt and pepper. Simmer for 2½ to 3 hours, or until the chick-peas and beans are completely tender.

Melt the butter in a heavy skillet. Add the greens, and toss them over high heat until they are wilted and any liquid from the greens evaporates. Add the greens to the soup. If there is any meat on the ham bone, cut it into pieces; discard the bone and add the ham and the other meats to the soup. Correct the seasoning, and serve the soup with croutons.

PAULA PECK
PAULA PECK'S ART OF GOOD COOKING

Country Bean and Cabbage Soup

Make this soup at least one or two days before it's needed, which makes the flavor stronger and better. Reheating any leftover soup only improves it.

To serve 14

1 lb.	dried pea or navy beans (about 2 cups [½ liter])	½ kg.
3 lb.	cabbage, halved, cored and shredded	1½ kg.
3 lb.	smoked ham, bone in	1½ kg.
2 quarts	water	2 liters
1	rib celery, sliced	1
2	carrots, quartered lengthwise and sliced	2
1	bouquet garni, composed of 5 parsley sprigs and 2 bay leaves	1
1	onion, stuck with 2 whole cloves	1
2	onions, sliced	2
4	garlic cloves, crushed	4
½ tsp.	thyme	2 ml.
½ tsp.	pepper	2 ml.
1 tsp.	salt	5 ml.
8	medium-sized tomatoes (about 2 lb. [1 kg.]), peeled	8
2 tbsp.	puréed tomato	30 ml.
4 tbsp.	lard	60 ml.
3 tbsp.	flour	45 ml.

Rinse the beans and place them in a large soup pot. Add the water and let the beans soak overnight. If you are pressed for time, bring the water to a boil, turn off the heat and soak the beans for 1 hour.

Add the ham to the pot. The water should cover at least half of the ham; if not, add more. Bring the water to a boil, reduce the heat and simmer for 15 minutes, skimming off all the scum that rises to the top. When the scum stops rising, add the celery, carrots, bouquet garni, onions, garlic, thyme, pepper and salt. Cover the pot and simmer for 1½ hours.

Add the tomatoes and puréed tomato and simmer for another ½ hour. Stir the soup occasionally, mashing the tomatoes against the side of the pot to break them into smaller pieces. Add the shredded cabbage to the soup and simmer for another ½ hour, still stirring from time to time and mashing the tomatoes.

Make a very dark roux by melting the lard in a skillet, adding the flour and stirring constantly with a wooden spoon until the flour is well browned. The heat should be moderately high so that the browning can be accomplished in 7 to 10 minutes without burning the roux. The color should be al-most that of light chocolate. Add a ladleful of the soup to the roux and mix quickly and thoroughly. Be careful: a lot of steam will rise when the hot liquid meets the hot skillet. Add a few more ladlefuls of soup to the skillet, mixing well after each addition. Then pour the contents of the skillet into the soup pot. Simmer the soup briskly for 15 minutes more.

Retrieve the whole onion and the bouquet garni with a long-handled slotted spoon and discard them. Lift out the ham with two long forks. Strip away the fat and bone from the ham. Cut the meat into bite-sized pieces and return these to the pot. Correct the seasoning and serve the soup hot.

CAROL CUTLER
THE SIX-MINUTE SOUFFLÉ AND OTHER CULINARY DELIGHTS

Red Kidney Bean Soup

Bruine Bonensoep

To serve 4 to 6

2 cups	dried red kidney beans (about 1 lb. [½ kg.]), soaked in water overnight and drained	½ liter
3½ quarts	water	3½ liters
1	bouquet garni composed of 2 whole cloves, 1 small red chili and 1 bay leaf, wrapped in cheesecloth	1
2	medium-sized potatoes, diced	2
1	large onion, chopped	1
4 tbsp.	butter	60 ml.
2 tsp.	curry powder	10 ml.
	salt and pepper	
	Worcestershire sauce	
1	slice bacon, diced and fried (optional)	1
8	small sour gherkins, sliced (optional)	8
¼ cup	dry red wine or Madeira (optional)	50 ml.
	croutons (recipe, page 166)	

Put the beans in a soup kettle, cover them with the water and add the bouquet of cloves, chili and bay leaf. Bring slowly to a boil, reduce the heat and simmer for 1 hour. Add the potatoes and simmer for 30 minutes more.

Meanwhile, in a skillet, fry the chopped onion in the butter until golden brown. Stir in the curry powder. Discard the bouquet from the soup kettle and use a potato masher to coarsely mash the beans and potatoes in their cooking liquid. Add the fried, curried onion and simmer for some 20 minutes more until the soup thickens.

Season the soup to taste with salt, pepper and Worcestershire sauce. If you like, add the diced fried bacon and sliced gherkins, and stir in some red wine or Madeira. Serve the soup with croutons.

CULINAIRE ENCYCLOPEDIE

Tuscan Minestrone, Country-Style

Minestrone alla Contadina

The author suggests that a 1-ounce [30-g.] slice of salt pork plus a 2-ounce [60-g.] slice of boiled ham may be substituted for the prosciutto.

Tuscan minestrone is usually made in a large quantity so there will be enough left over to make *ribollita* the next day. *Ribollita* means, literally, "reboiled." To make it, leave the minestrone overnight to allow it to thicken even further. Bring it to a boil and cook for about 1 minute. With a wooden spoon, mix well, breaking up the bread slices until the texture of the soup is almost homogeneous. Ladle the soup into individual bowls, and pour 2 teaspoons [10 ml.] of good olive oil over each serving.

To serve 6 to 8

½ lb.	dried *cannellini* beans or any other dried white beans, soaked in cold water overnight	¼ kg.
	salt	
2 to 3 quarts	water, lightly salted	2 to 3 liters
3 oz.	prosciutto in 1 slice	100 g.
6 tbsp.	olive oil	90 ml.
1	large red onion, coarsely chopped	1
1	rib celery, coarsely chopped	1
2	large garlic cloves, chopped	2
1	carrot, coarsely chopped	1
7 or 8	sprigs flat-leafed parsley, chopped	7 or 8
½	small Savoy cabbage (about ½ lb. [¼ kg.]), cored and shredded	½
2 to 2½ lb.	kale, stripped from stems and shredded	1 kg.
1	potato, diced	1
2	small tomatoes, peeled	2
1 lb.	Swiss chard, leaves stripped from stems and shredded	½ kg.
	freshly ground pepper	
12	large, thick slices French or Italian bread, several days old or 9 to 12 tbsp. [135 to 180 ml.] croutons (recipe, page 166)	12
6 to 8 tbsp.	freshly grated Parmesan cheese	90 to 120 ml.

Drain the beans and cook them in a large heavy casserole with 2 quarts [2 liters] of salted water and the prosciutto for about 1 hour. As the beans cook they will absorb water, so more salted water must be added at frequent intervals; there should be 2 quarts of liquid in the casserole at the end of the cooking time. When the beans are tender, remove them from the heat and let them stand in their liquid until needed.

Heat the olive oil in a stockpot and sauté the onion, celery, garlic, carrot and parsley for 12 to 15 minutes. When the vegetables are light brown, add the cabbage, kale, potato and tomatoes to the stockpot. Cover and simmer for 15 minutes, then add the Swiss chard.

Remove the prosciutto from the bean casserole and discard. Purée two thirds of the beans in a food mill and add them to the stockpot. Simmer together for 30 minutes more, until the Savoy cabbage and kale are almost cooked.

Drain the remaining beans, reserving both them and the broth. Gradually add the bean broth to the stockpot in which the vegetables are cooking.

When the cabbage and kale are ready, add the remaining beans to the stockpot. Taste for salt and pepper, then cook the soup for 5 minutes more.

If you are using bread slices, put a layer of slices in the bottom of a tureen and pour two full ladles of soup over them. Add more layers of bread, each time pouring soup over them, until all the bread is used. Pour the remaining soup into the tureen, cover and let the soup stand for 20 minutes. Serve with a tablespoon [15 ml.] of grated Parmesan cheese sprinkled over each portion.

If you are using croutons instead of bread slices, allow the soup to stand for 20 minutes before serving, then place 1½ tablespoons [22 ml.] of croutons in each individual soup bowl and pour the soup over them. Sprinkle with Parmesan cheese and serve.

GIULIANO BUGIALLI
THE FINE ART OF ITALIAN COOKING

Rice Soup

Soupa Rizi Avgholemono

To serve 4

⅔ cup	raw unprocessed rice	150 ml.
1½ quarts	beef or chicken broth	1½ liters
	salt (optional)	
2	eggs	2
2 or 3 tbsp.	fresh lemon juice	30 or 45 ml.

Bring the beef or chicken broth to a boil. Add the rice, cover the saucepan and cook gently until the rice is tender, about 20 minutes. Add salt, if necessary. Beat the eggs and lemon juice in a bowl. Gradually add about ½ cup [125 ml.] of the broth, stirring constantly. Pour the egg-and-lemon mixture into the remaining stock in the saucepan.

Heat the soup over very low heat, stirring constantly. Take care that it does not boil. Serve at once.

CHRISSA PARADISSIS
THE BEST BOOK OF GREEK COOKERY

Indonesian Rice Soup

Nasi tim voor 2 zieken

This thick soup was traditionally cooked in a closed pot placed in a pan of boiling water, which was also closed—a sort of covered bain-marie.

To serve 2

1 cup	raw unprocessed long-grain rice	¼ liter
2	chicken drumsticks	2
1 quart	chicken broth	1 liter
	Spiced meatballs	
½ lb.	lean ground beef	¼ kg.
¼ tsp.	ground coriander	1 ml.
⅛ tsp.	ground cumin	½ ml.
⅛ tsp.	grated nutmeg	½ ml.
	salt	
1	egg yolk	1

Put half of the rice into a soup pot. Mix together all of the meatball ingredients, shape the mixture into small balls and arrange these on top of the rice. Cover with half of the remaining rice. Put the chicken legs on top and cover them with the rest of the rice. Pour on the broth, cover the pot tightly, bring to a boil and simmer very gently for 2 hours. Serve the soup very hot.

HUGH JANS
VRIJ NEDERLANDS KOOKBOEK

Rice and Chicken Liver Soup

Minestra di Riso e Fegatine

Chicken hearts and gizzards may be used in this recipe in addition to chicken livers; they should be thinly sliced and thoroughly cooked in broth before being added to the soup.

To serve 6 to 8

1 cup	raw unprocessed rice	¼ liter
5 oz.	chicken livers, cut into small pieces	150 g.
2 quarts	chicken broth	2 liters
3 tbsp.	butter (optional)	45 ml.
1 tbsp.	chopped fresh parsley	15 ml.
	freshly grated Parmesan cheese	

Bring the broth to a boil, add the rice and cook, covered, over medium heat for 18 to 20 minutes, or until the rice is tender.

Meanwhile, in another pan, cook the chicken livers in a few spoonfuls of the broth or, if preferred, sauté them in the butter for 5 minutes. When the rice is cooked, transfer the livers with their cooking juices to the rice pan. Add the parsley and serve very hot with the grated cheese.

GIANNI BRERA AND LUIGI VERONELLI
LA PACCIADA

Meat-Rice Barrel Soup, Epirus-Style

Yuvarelakia Soupa Avgolemono

To serve 6

1 lb.	ground beef, veal or lamb	½ kg.
1	onion, grated	1
2	garlic cloves, crushed (optional)	2
6 tbsp.	raw, unprocessed long-grain rice	90 ml.
3 tbsp.	chopped fresh parsley	45 ml.
2 tbsp.	chopped fresh mint, basil or dill	30 ml.
1 tsp.	dried oregano or thyme	5 ml.
	salt and freshly ground pepper	
3	eggs	3
5 cups	water or stock	1¼ liters
1	onion, chopped	1
1	rib celery, chopped	1
½	carrot, chopped	½
3 to 5 tbsp.	fresh lemon juice	45 to 75 ml.
2 tbsp.	chopped fresh parsley (optional)	30 ml.

In a large bowl, combine the meat, grated onion, garlic, rice, herbs, salt and pepper, and 1 egg, slightly beaten. Knead for a few minutes, then shape the mixture into walnut-sized barrels and set aside.

In a soup pot, bring the water or stock to a boil with the chopped vegetables, and salt and pepper to taste. Reduce the heat and add the meat-and-rice barrels. Simmer, covered, for 30 minutes, then remove from the heat. Beat the 2 remaining eggs for 2 minutes, then, continuing to beat, gradually add the lemon juice. Gradually beat in, by droplets, several ladlefuls of the hot soup. With a wooden spoon, stir the egg-and-lemon mixture back into the soup. Return to low heat and stir until the soup has thickened lightly, being careful not to let it boil. Serve hot, garnished with additional chopped parsley if desired.

VILMA LIACOURAS CHANTILES
THE FOOD OF GREECE

Pasta and Bean Soup

Pasta e Fagioli

One cup [¼ liter] of dried cranberry, white or kidney beans may be substituted for the fresh beans called for in this recipe. Dried beans should be soaked in water overnight and drained before they are used.

Nearly every region in Italy has its own version of this soup. It can be made with any small pasta (*tubetti*, elbow macaroni, broken-up spaghetti or linguini, as you wish).

To serve 8		
2 cups	small pasta	½ liter
2 cups	freshly shelled cranberry beans (about 1 ½ lb. [¾ kg.] unshelled)	½ liter
2	slices lean salt pork with the rind removed	2
1	small onion	1
1	garlic clove	1
1	rib celery	1
3 tbsp.	olive oil	45 ml.
3 or 4	plum tomatoes, peeled and coarsely chopped	3 or 4
2 quarts	hot water	2 liters
2 tsp.	salt	10 ml.
3 to 4 tbsp.	freshly grated Romano or Parmesan cheese	45 to 60 ml.

Put the slices of salt pork on a chopping board. Top them with the onion, garlic and celery and chop, then mince, until the pile has turned into a paste, or battuto. Put the battuto into a big soup pot with the olive oil. Over medium heat sauté the battuto until golden, then add the tomatoes and cook for about 3 minutes, or until the tomatoes have blended a bit and softened. Add the hot water, salt and beans, and bring to a boil. Reduce the heat and cook until the beans are tender—about 20 minutes. Then crush a few beans against the side of the pot, add the pasta and continue cooking until it is well done. By this time the soup will be really so thick you may want to add a little more water. Taste for salt and add some if necessary. Serve with a sprinkling of the Romano or Parmesan cheese.

MARGARET AND G. FRANCO ROMAGNOLI
THE ROMAGNOLIS' TABLE

"Little Chickens" Soup Antonio

Pulcini Zuppa all'Antonio

To serve 4 to 6		
½ cup	*pulcini* or other small pasta	125 ml.
3 tbsp.	butter	45 ml.
1	calf's sweetbread, parboiled for 10 minutes, drained and cooled, fat and membrane removed, and diced	1
1	carrot, chopped	1
½ tsp.	salt	2 ml.
	freshly ground pepper	
2	fresh artichoke bottoms, diced	2
2 quarts	chicken broth	2 liters
1 tbsp.	chopped fresh parsley	15 ml.

Melt the butter, sprinkle the sweetbread and carrot with the salt and pepper and sauté the pieces until they are brown. Stir in the artichoke bottoms and simmer for 5 minutes. Meanwhile, in a pot of boiling water, cook the *pulcini* until *al dente* and drain them.

In a separate pan, bring the chicken broth to a simmer, stir in the sweetbread-and-artichoke mixture and the pasta; simmer for 5 minutes. Serve in warmed soup bowls with parsley sprinkled on each serving.

JACK DENTON SCOTT
THE COMPLETE BOOK OF PASTA

Swedish Beer Soup

Schwedische Biersuppe

To serve 4		
3 cups	beer	¾ liter
1	cinnamon stick	1
2 tbsp.	flour	30 ml.
4 tbsp.	cold water	60 ml.
3	egg yolks	3
3 tbsp.	sugar	45 ml.
1 cup	milk, heated to boiling	¼ liter

First bring the beer to a boil with the cinnamon. Mix the flour with the cold water and stir this into the beer. Bring the soup back to a boil. Meanwhile, beat the egg yolks and sugar until light and frothy and pour in the boiling milk, beating with a whisk. Remove the soup from the heat, remove the cinnamon, and add the egg mixture, beating vigorously. Serve immediately.

GRETE WILLINSKY
KOCHBUCH DER BÜCHERGILDE

Vermont Cheddar-Cheese Soup

To serve 6 to 8

2 cups	shredded Cheddar cheese	½ liter
3 tbsp.	butter	45 ml.
3	scallions (including some of the green parts), chopped	3
1	small onion, chopped	1
1	rib celery, chopped	1
3 tbsp.	flour	45 ml.
⅛ tsp.	grated nutmeg	½ ml.
⅛ tsp.	pepper	½ ml.
2 cups	chicken broth	½ liter
1 quart	milk	1 liter
	salt	
	Worcestershire sauce	

In a large pot, melt the butter. Add the scallions, onion and celery. Cook until the onion softens. Sift in the flour, nutmeg and pepper and cook for 2 or 3 minutes longer. Gradually stir in the broth. Bring the mixture to a boil, cover, reduce the heat and simmer for 15 minutes. Cool the mixture slightly, then strain it into a bowl and return it to the pan.

Add the milk and bring the soup just to a boil. Gradually add the cheese, stirring to melt each batch before adding more. Return the soup to a boil, stirring often. Taste for seasoning, and add salt and Worcestershire.

THE GREAT COOKS' GUIDE TO SOUPS

Nigerian Peanut Soup

For this recipe, you can use either freshly roasted unsalted peanuts or dry-roasted peanuts.

To serve 6

1 cup	roasted peanuts	¼ liter
3 cups	fish broth	¾ liter
2 or 3	small dried chilies	2 or 3
½ cup	chopped green pepper	125 ml.
½ cup	chopped onion	125 ml.
	salt to taste	
	croutons *(recipe, page 166)*	

Crush the peanuts with a rolling pin, or grind them in a blender. (Do not blend them too fine or too long, or they will become peanut butter.) Heat the fish broth. Crush the chilies and add them to the broth along with the green pepper and

onion. Simmer covered for about 10 to 15 minutes, or until the vegetables are tender.

Stir in the peanuts. Simmer the soup for about 10 minutes, stirring frequently. Add salt to taste, depending on the saltiness of the roasted nuts. Pour the soup into cups and top with crisp croutons.

LOUISE DRIGGS
SOUPS AND STEWS THE WORLD OVER

Chicken and Fresh Corn Chowder

Accompaniments in keeping with the clear freshness and simplicity of this stew are fresh, ripe tomato wedges and freshly baked biscuits with sweet butter.

To serve 6

3½ lb.	chicken, cut up	1¾ kg.
1 quart	fresh corn kernels, cut from 8 large ears	1 liter
1 quart	water	1 liter
	salt	
1	rib celery, with leaves	1
1	sprig parsley	1
1	onion, quartered	1
1	bay leaf	1
10	peppercorns	10
6	hard-boiled eggs, chopped	6
	freshly ground black pepper	
1 cup	chopped fresh parsley	¼ liter
1 cup	heavy cream	¼ liter

Put the chicken pieces into a kettle with the water, 1 teaspoon [5 ml.] of salt, the celery, parsley sprig, onion, bay leaf and peppercorns. Bring to a boil, cover and simmer over low heat for 1 hour or until the meat is very tender.

Lift the chicken from the broth, discard the skin and bones, and break the meat into large pieces. Strain the broth and return it to the kettle. Add the chicken meat. Heat the broth to a gentle boil, add the corn and cook just until tender, about 5 minutes. Add the chopped eggs and correct the seasoning with salt and pepper. Stir in the parsley.

Salt the cream lightly and whip it until soft peaks are formed. Ladle the soup into warmed bowls and top each serving with a spoonful of whipped cream.

SHIRLEY SARVIS
SIMPLY STEWS

Cockie-Leekie

To serve 8 to 10

2½ quarts	chicken broth	2½ liters
4 to 6	leeks, thinly sliced	4 to 6
⅓ cup	oatmeal, pulverized in a blender or food processor	75 ml.
½ cup	water	125 ml.
	salt and pepper	
1 cup	cream	¼ liter
2 tbsp.	chopped fresh parsley	30 ml.

Bring the broth to a boil and add the leeks. Blend the oatmeal with the water and gradually stir the mixture into the broth. Season with salt and pepper, cover and cook until the leeks are tender. Skim if necessary. Put the cream and parsley in a warmed tureen and pour the boiling soup over them.

JANET MURRAY
WITH A FINE FEELING FOR FOOD

———◆———

Cock-a-Leekie

Like most traditional soup recipes, this one admits to variations. The leeks added at the beginning, which have given up all their flavor to the broth, may be removed before the second batch is added. At the end of cooking, the chicken may be skinned and boned, and the pieces of meat returned to the pot.

To serve 8

1	stewing chicken, trussed	1
10 to 12	medium-sized leeks (about 2 lb. [1 kg.]), trimmed, washed and sliced	10 to 12
2 quarts	veal or beef stock or water	2 liters
	bouquet garni of 1 whole clove, 1 blade mace, 1 sprig parsley and 6 peppercorns (optional)	
	salt	
	freshly ground allspice	
12	dried prunes	12

Place the fowl in a large pot with three or four of the leeks and the stock or water. If using water, add the bouquet garni, tied in a piece of cheesecloth. Bring to a boil, skim, and then cook gently for 2 hours or longer, until the fowl is tender, when it should be removed. Clear off all of the grease with paper towels. Add the remainder of the leeks (blanched if old and strong), cut into 1-inch [2½-cm.] lengths, which may be split. Add salt if required, and allspice to taste. Simmer very gently until the leeks are tender. Half an hour before serving, add the prunes. A little minced fowl may be added to the soup before serving it.

F. MARIAN MC NEILL
THE SCOTS KITCHEN

Chicken Gumbo

To serve 12

5 lb.	stewing chicken	2½ kg.
	flour	
¼ cup	rendered bacon fat	50 ml.
9 cups	boiling water	2¼ liters
2 cups	chopped, seeded, peeled tomatoes	½ liter
½ cup	green corn kernels, cut from 1 small ear	125 ml.
1 cup	sliced okra	¼ liter
1	large green pepper or 2 small red peppers	1
½ tsp.	salt	2 ml.
¼ cup	diced onion	50 ml.
¼ cup	raw unprocessed rice	50 ml.

Cut the chicken into pieces, and dredge each piece in flour. Brown the pieces in the bacon fat, then pour in 4 cups [1 liter] of boiling water. Simmer the chicken, uncovered, until the meat falls from the bones. Drain the broth. Bone, skin and chop the meat. Reserve the meat and broth.

In a soup kettle place the tomatoes, corn, okra, pepper, salt, onion and rice, and the remaining 5 cups [1¼ liters] of water. Simmer uncovered until the vegetables and rice are tender, about 25 minutes. Combine this with the chicken and broth, and correct the seasoning. Reheat the soup.

IRMA S. ROMBAUER AND MARION ROMBAUER BECKER
JOY OF COOKING

———◆———

Chicken and Cress Soup

Don Far Tong

To serve 6

1 quart	chicken stock, rich and well seasoned	1 liter
1 cup	watercress leaves	¼ liter
3	scallions, white and tender green parts, sliced	3
2	eggs	2
1 tsp.	soy sauce	5 ml.

Cook the scallions in the chicken stock for 3 minutes. Beat the eggs slightly, just enough to mix, and add to them the soy sauce. Now bring the soup to a merry boil, pour in the egg mixture, and stir, not too vigorously, until the egg sets in long threads. Add the watercress leaves and serve at once from a soup tureen.

HELEN EVANS BROWN
HELEN BROWN'S WEST COAST COOKBOOK

Mulligatawny Soup

The word mulligatawny came into English in the 18th Century, from the Tamil word, *milakutanni* (pepper-water).

To serve 4 to 6

4 lb.	stewing chicken cut into 6 or 8 pieces, or 4 lb. chicken drumsticks, thighs, giblets and backs	2 kg.
2	onions, sliced	2
6 tbsp.	butter	90 ml.
¾ to 1 cup	pot or farmer cheese or yogurt	175 to 250 ml.
	salt	
2 quarts	water	2 liters
4	whole cloves	4
3 tbsp.	fresh lemon juice	45 ml.
	Curry seasoning	
4 tsp.	finely chopped onion	20 ml.
1 tsp.	ground turmeric	5 ml.
1 tsp.	cayenne pepper	5 ml.
½ tsp.	ground ginger	2 ml.
¼ tsp.	finely chopped garlic	1 ml.
½ tsp.	ground coriander	2 ml.
¼ tsp.	ground cumin	1 ml.

To make the curry seasoning, pound together all the ingredients to a paste.

In a large saucepan, brown the onion slices in 4 tablespoons [60 ml.] of the butter with the chicken pieces. Stir in the curry seasoning, the cheese or yogurt and some salt, and stew for a little while until the juices turn into a brownish crust on the bottom of the pan. They should not burn, so this needs watching. Pour in the water, cover, and leave to cook over low heat.

Melt the remaining butter in a little pan with the cloves; after a few minutes you will be able to crush the cloves with a wooden spoon. Pour in the lemon juice, mix it all up well and pour this mixture into the large pan of soup. Stew the chicken, covered, for an hour or more depending on the age and toughness: the soup is ready when the meat parts easily from the bones, which should then be removed and thrown away.

Correct the seasoning, pour the soup into a tureen and serve with a separate bowl of boiled rice. This mulligatawny soup, unlike some of the other recipes, contains no apple, but if you like you can always serve a dish of chopped apple sprinkled with lemon juice, to be added to the soup with the rice by each diner.

JANE GRIGSON
ENGLISH FOOD

Turkey Chowder

To serve 6 to 8

1	leftover roast-turkey carcass	1
2 quarts	cold water	2 liters
1	bouquet garni	1
2	whole cloves	2
1 cup	finely diced potato	¼ liter
½ cup	finely diced carrot	125 ml.
¼ cup	finely chopped green pepper	50 ml.
⅓ cup	coarsely chopped onion	75 ml.
1	garlic clove	1
2	sprigs marjoram	2
2 cups	milk, scalded and slightly cooled	½ liter
2	egg yolks, beaten	2
1½ tbsp.	unsalted butter	22 ml.
2 or 3 tbsp.	dry sherry (optional)	30 or 45 ml.
½ to ¾ cup	chopped turkey meat (optional)	125 to 175 ml.
2	eggs, hard-boiled and chopped (optional)	2

In a large kettle, combine all of the bones and any leftover skin of the roast turkey with the bouquet garni and the cloves. Add the water, bring to a boil, reduce the heat to low, cover and simmer for 1½ hours. Strain the broth through a fine sieve into a clean kettle. Let it cool, then refrigerate and, when the broth is cold, skim off the cake of fat from the top.

Return the turkey broth to the heat. Add the potato, carrot, green pepper, onion, garlic and marjoram. Cook until the vegetables are tender—about 10 minutes—and season to taste with salt and black pepper. Stir in the milk mixed with the egg yolks and add, if used, the dry sherry, chopped turkey and hard-boiled eggs. Just before serving, stir in the butter. Serve with hot toasted, buttered crackers.

LOUIS P. DE GOUY
THE SOUP BOOK

Turkey Soup

When this recipe was first published, the soup may have been left to stand overnight in a cool pantry or—more likely—in the cool roofed shelter, or "house," above a well. Today you can keep the soup from spoiling by cooling it to room temperature, then refrigerating it.

	To serve 6	
1	leftover roast turkey carcass, with any remaining stuffing and gravy	1
1½ to 2 quarts	cold water	1½ to 2 liters
2 tsp.	flour, mixed to a paste with water	10 ml.
	salt and pepper	

Place the turkey carcass, stuffing and gravy in a pot and cover with cold water. Simmer gently for 3 or 4 hours, then remove the pot from the heat and let it stand till the next day. Take off all the fat and strain the liquid to remove the bones. Put the soup on to heat till it boils, then thicken slightly with flour wet up in water, and season to taste. Pick off all the bits of turkey from the bones, put them in the soup, boil up and serve.

THE OHIO HOUSEWIVES COMPANION

Pigeon Soup with Barley

Soupe de Pigeon à l'Orge

The water in this soup may be replaced by bouillon; at the end of the cooking time, the pigeon quarters may be skinned, boned, and diced, and the meat returned to the pot. The addition of green peas, when in season, gives an exquisite flavor to the soup.

	To serve 6	
2	large pigeons, cleaned, singed and quartered	2
⅓ to ½ cup	pearl barley	75 to 125 ml.
4 tbsp.	butter	60 ml.
1	large onion, finely chopped	1
2	carrots, diced	2
1½ quarts	water	1½ liters
2 tsp.	salt	10 ml.
	pepper	
1	bay leaf	1
¼ to ⅓ cup	freshly shelled peas (optional)	50 to 75 ml.

Melt the butter in a large pan, add the onion and cook for a few minutes over low heat. Add the pigeons and cook for 8 to 10 minutes, then put in the carrots, barley, water, salt, pepper and bay leaf. Cover and simmer over low heat for about 1¼ hours, or until the pigeons are very tender. Ten minutes before the end of the cooking time, add the peas if you are using them. Correct the seasoning and serve.

AUGUSTE ESCOFFIER
LE CARNET D'ÉPICURE

Marbled Partridge Soup

Potage de Perdrix Marbrées

To blanch the pistachios called for in this recipe, place them in a bowl and pour boiling water over them. Then drain the nuts and rub off their skins. If any skins resist removal, soak those nuts briefly in boiling water.

	To serve 4	
2	partridges, trussed and barded	2
1½ quarts	veal or chicken broth	1½ liters
	salt	
4 or 5	slices stale bread, crusts removed	4 or 5
1 cup	sliced fresh mushrooms	¼ liter
1 cup	water	¼ liter
1 cup	almonds (about ¼ lb. [125 g.]), pulverized in a mortar or food processor	¼ liter
½ cup	lamb roasting juices, degreased, or well-reduced lamb broth	125 ml.
⅓ cup	shelled green pistachios, blanched and pulverized in a mortar or food processor	75 ml.
2 tbsp.	fresh lemon juice	30 ml.

Half-roast the partridges for 15 minutes at 450° F. [230° C.]. Bring the veal or chicken broth to a boil, salt to taste and put in the partridges. Simmer until the partridges are tender—1 hour or more, depending on their age. Add the bread and simmer gently until it becomes a pulp; add the mushrooms and cook a few minutes longer.

Meanwhile, pour the water over the almonds, allow to steep for a few minutes and drain the liquid through a cloth, squeezing the cloth to extract all the almond milk.

Remove the partridges from the soup, split them and arrange the halves in a deep serving dish. Combine the almond milk, lamb juices or broth, pistachios and lemon juice and add the mixture to the soup. Pour the soup over the partridges and serve.

LA VARENNE
LE VRAY CUISINIER FRANÇOIS

Milanese Tripe Soup

Minestra di Trippe alla Milanese

If the tripe you purchase is precooked, it will require only about 1 hour of cooking.

To serve 10 to 12

4 lb.	honeycomb tripe, cleaned, washed and cut into 4-inch [10-cm.] squares	2 kg.
5 quarts	stock or lightly salted water	5 liters
1	onion, stuck with 2 whole cloves	1
2	ribs celery	2
1 cup	dried white beans, soaked in water overnight and drained	¼ liter
	salt	
1	medium-sized cabbage	1
4 tbsp.	butter	60 ml.
½ lb.	sliced bacon, cut into 1-inch [2½-cm.] pieces and parboiled for 5 minutes	¼ kg.
1	medium-sized onion, thinly sliced	1
3	leeks, white parts only, thinly sliced	3
1	heart celery, thinly sliced	1
4	small carrots, thinly sliced	4
2	tomatoes, peeled, seeded, drained and chopped	2
	freshly ground pepper	
3	medium-sized potatoes, cubed	3
¼ cup	chopped ham fat	50 ml.
1	garlic clove, chopped	1
	freshly grated Parmesan cheese	
	croutons (recipe, page 166)	

Put the tripe into a large flameproof, enameled-iron or earthenware pot. Add the stock (or lightly salted water, if you wish, although the soup will not be so flavorsome), the onion stuck with cloves and the celery ribs. Bring to a boil, reduce the heat to medium and cook, covered, for about 4½ hours. Drain the tripe, slice it into thin strips, and put it aside. Strain the broth through a very fine sieve and reserve it; discard the vegetables.

Meanwhile, in another pot, cook the beans in lightly salted water over low heat for 1½ hours or until tender. Cook the cabbage in boiling water for 10 minutes, drain, halve, core and cut into fine shreds.

Melt the butter in a large, heavy pot over medium heat, add the bacon, the onion and the leeks. As soon as they are lightly golden, add the celery heart, carrots and tomatoes and blend well. Cook gently, stirring occasionally, for 10 minutes. Add the sliced tripe, pour in 4 quarts [4 liters] of the reserved tripe broth, add salt and pepper if necessary, return to a boil and reduce the heat. Add the potatoes and simmer, covered, over medium heat for 20 minutes. Then add the beans and cabbage and simmer for about 5 minutes.

When ready to serve, sauté the chopped ham fat and garlic in a skillet for 5 minutes and add the fat pieces and garlic to the soup. Pour into soup bowls and serve the Parmesan cheese and the croutons separately.

LUIGI CARNACINA
GREAT ITALIAN COOKING

Mexican Tripe Soup

Menudo

To serve 10 to 12

4 lb.	tripe, precooked, cut into 1-inch [2½-cm.] cubes	2 kg.
2	calf's feet or 1 veal shank	2
6 quarts	water	6 liters
1¼ lb.	dried hominy, soaked in water overnight and drained, or two 1¾-lb. [875-g.] cans hominy, drained and rinsed under cold water	⅔ kg.
2	onions, chopped	2
4	garlic cloves, finely chopped	4
1 tbsp.	crushed dried oregano	15 ml.
2 tbsp.	chopped fresh coriander	30 ml.
	salt and freshly ground pepper	

Bring the water to a boil in a stockpot. If using calf's feet, add them to the pot; cover and simmer for 1 hour before adding the tripe and the rest of the ingredients. If veal shank is being used instead, add it to the pot with the tripe, the hominy, onions, garlic, oregano, coriander and a little salt and pepper. (If you are using canned hominy, this is added during the last hour of cooking.) Bring to a boil, cover, reduce the heat and simmer for 3 to 4 hours, or until the tripe is tender. Serve, providing dishes of additional chopped onions, chopped coriander and chopped fresh chilies for each person to add to his liking.

JANA ALLEN AND MARGARET GIN
INNARDS AND OTHER VARIETY MEATS

Tripe Soup

Soppi Mondongo

Cooks in Curaçao say this soup should be left to cool for 3 hours or so after it is cooked, then reheated, as this improves the flavor. They often add a tablespoon of dry sherry or brandy to each soup plate.

To serve 10 to 12

2 lb.	precooked tripe, washed and drained	1 kg.
¼ cup	fresh lime juice	50 ml.
2	pig's feet, split and cleaned	2
3 quarts	water, lightly salted	3 liters
½ lb.	uncooked corned beef	¼ kg.
1	onion, coarsely chopped	1
3	chopped shallots	3
1	rib celery, coarsely chopped	1
1 lb.	Hubbard squash or pumpkin, peeled, seeded, and cut into 1-inch [2½-cm.] cubes	½ kg.
1	sweet potato, cubed	1
3	potatoes, cubed	3
6	green olives, pitted	6
1 tbsp.	capers	15 ml.
1 tbsp.	seedless raisins	15 ml.
1	green pepper, seeded and coarsely chopped	1
1	green chili, stemmed, seeded and chopped	1
	freshly ground pepper	
¼ tsp.	grated nutmeg	1 ml.
¼ tsp.	ground cloves	1 ml.

In a bowl, pour the lime juice over the tripe and let it stand for 10 minutes. Transfer the tripe to a large saucepan. Add the pig's feet and the salted water. Simmer, covered, until tender—about 2½ to 3 hours.

Meanwhile, pour boiling water over the corned beef, and allow it to stand for 45 minutes. Drain, rinse, and add the corned beef to the pan in which the tripe is cooking.

When the meats are tender, remove them from the broth and allow them to cool. Cut the tripe into strips about ¾ inch [2 cm.] wide, and the corned beef into ½-inch [1-cm.] cubes. Remove the meat from the pig's feet and discard the bones. Put all the vegetables into the stock, with the meats and seasonings. Simmer gently for about 30 minutes, until the vegetables are tender. Serve with crusty French bread.

ELISABETH LAMBERT ORTIZ
THE COMPLETE BOOK OF CARIBBEAN COOKING

Philadelphia Pepper Pot

Legend has it that Philadelphia pepper pot was invented for George Washington and his troops during their winter at Valley Forge. The tripe called for is usually sold precooked; if uncooked tripe is to be used, simmer it in lightly salted water before starting to make the soup.

To serve 8 to 10

2 lb.	precooked honeycomb tripe cut into ½-inch [1-cm.] squares	1 kg.
1	veal shank	1
3 quarts	cold water	3 liters
1	bouquet garni, composed of 2 bay leaves, 10 parsley sprigs and 2 celery-leaf sprigs	1
1½ tsp.	salt	7 ml.
12	peppercorns, slightly bruised	12
2	onions, each stuck with 1 whole clove	2
4	medium-sized potatoes, cubed	4
Suet dumplings		
1 cup	chopped beef suet (about ½ lb. [¼ kg.])	¼ liter
2 cups	flour	½ liter
½ tsp.	salt	2 ml.
	chopped fresh parsley	

Put the tripe and veal shank into a kettle with the water, bring to a boil and skim carefully. Add the bouquet garni and simmer gently for 3 hours, adding—after 2 hours—the salt and peppercorns. Remove the meat from the bones, and cut it into small pieces. Strain the broth, return it to the kettle, then add the onions. Simmer the broth for 1 hour, then add the potatoes, meat and tripe. Taste for seasoning and let the soup simmer gently while you make the dumplings.

For the dumplings, combine the suet, the flour and salt. Add enough ice-cold water to make a workable dough and form it into dumplings about the size of marbles. Roll the dumplings in flour, coating them well to prevent sticking, and drop them into the simmering soup. Cook the dumplings for about 8 to 10 minutes.

Stir some chopped parsley into the soup and serve, in heated soup plates, accompanied by finger-shaped sandwiches of brown bread and butter.

LOUIS P. DE GOUY
THE SOUP BOOK

Mock Turtle Soup

Soupe Fausse Tortue

If water is substituted for broth, the quantity of beef should be doubled. The classic turtle-soup herbs are basil, thyme, bay leaf and marjoram, all fresh if possible; this recipe adds sage, savory and rosemary. By association, these herbs are intended to make calf's feet (or the calf's head, sometimes used instead) taste like turtle: in fact, the only similarity is in the smooth, firm, gelatinous texture of the meat.

To serve 12 to 14

2	calf's feet, split, blanched in boiling water for 10 minutes, drained and rinsed	2
1 lb.	veal shank	½ kg.
2 to 2½ lb.	beef shank, cut into 2-inch [5-cm.] pieces	1 kg.
2 tbsp.	butter	30 ml.
1	onion	1
2	carrots, sliced	2
¼ cup	water	50 ml.
4 quarts	broth or water	4 liters
2	whole cloves	2
½ tsp.	peppercorns	2 ml.
1	bay leaf	1
1 tbsp.	flour	15 ml.
¼ cup	puréed tomato	50 ml.
1	shallot, finely chopped	1
1	sprig thyme	1
1	sprig sage	1
1	sprig savory	1
1	sprig rosemary	1
1	sprig basil	1
1	sprig marjoram	1
½ cup	Madeira	125 ml.
⅔ cup	sliced mushrooms, sautéed in butter	150 ml.
	cayenne pepper	
5 or 6	hard-boiled egg yolks, chopped	5 or 6

Melt half of the butter in a large, heavy-bottomed saucepan. Add the onion, carrot, veal shank, beef and calf's feet. Add the ¼ cup [50 ml.] of water, cover, and cook over low heat until the water has completely evaporated and the meats are lightly colored—in 30 to 40 minutes. Pour in the broth or water and add the cloves, peppercorns and bay leaf. Bring to a boil, put the lid on slightly ajar, and cook the meats very slowly until they are tender—about 3 hours. Take out the calf's feet, bone them and put their meat on a plate with a

weight on top to press it as it cools. Strain and degrease the broth, discarding the beef and veal shanks.

In a large saucepan, melt the remaining butter, stir in the flour and add the broth and the puréed tomato. Simmer over very low heat for about 30 minutes, removing the skin as it forms on the surface of the soup.

Meanwhile, put the shallot and the herbs into a small pan with the Madeira. Simmer, covered, for 5 minutes. Cut the meat from the calf's feet into small dice and put it into a saucepan. Strain in the Madeira and herb infusion, add the mushrooms and cover to keep the meat warm.

Remove any remaining traces of fat from the soup and season the soup with the cayenne pepper. Pour the soup through a strainer into a warmed tureen, add the herb infusion with the diced meat and the mushrooms, and serve the soup garnished with the chopped egg yolks.

JEAN DE GOUY
LA CUISINE ET LA PATISSERIE BOURGEOISES

Mary's Portuguese Soup

To serve 10 to 12

3 lb.	boneless beef chuck roast	1½ kg.
	salt and freshly ground black pepper	
2 tbsp.	oil	30 ml.
3	onions, sliced	3
6 cups	water	1½ liters
1 cup	dried red kidney beans, soaked in water overnight	¼ liter
1 cup	dried pea beans, soaked in water overnight	¼ liter
3 or 4	*chouriço* or *chorizo* sausages, each pricked with a fork in 2 or 3 places	3 or 4
4 cups	shredded cabbage (about 1 lb. [½ kg.])	1 liter
3 to 4 cups	small broccoli florets	¾ to 1 liter
1 lb.	spinach, roughly shredded	½ kg.

Sprinkle the beef generously with salt and pepper and, with your fingers, rub in the seasoning. Cover the meat and let it stand in the refrigerator overnight or for up to three days.

Heat the oil in a large, heavy casserole or kettle, add the beef and brown it quickly on all sides. Add the onions and water, bring to a boil, cover and simmer slowly for about 1 hour. Drain the beans and add them to the casserole. Bring to a boil, cover and simmer for 45 minutes or until the meat and beans are tender. Remove the meat, dice it finely and return it to the casserole.

Add the sausages and cook for 5 minutes. Stir in the cabbage and cook, covered, for 5 minutes; stir in the broccoli and cook, covered, for 5 minutes; add the spinach and cook, covered, for 3 minutes. Check the seasoning and serve.

JEAN HEWITT
THE NEW YORK TIMES WEEKEND COOKBOOK

Wrexham Soup

For the "bladder" used in this recipe to cover the top of the jar, the modern cook may substitute a piece of aluminum foil. The vegetables should be prepared according to their type: root vegetables cut into small pieces, onions and leeks sliced, lettuce shredded, and so on. The jar or deep bowl of soup should be simmered gently in a water bath over low heat or baked at a temperature of 250° F. [120° C.].

To serve 4

1 lb.	lean, boneless stew beef	½ kg.
2 to 2½ lb.	mixed vegetables (carrot, turnip, celery, potato, leek, onion, peas, lettuce, etc.), cut into small pieces	1 kg.
	salt and pepper	

Cut the beef into very small pieces; put the pieces into a half-gallon [2-liter] stoneware jar; fill it up with every description of vegetable, even lettuce. Tie the jar over with a bladder, and put it over the fire in a deep saucepan of boiling water, or cook it in the oven, which is far better, for at least 6 hours. This generally makes sufficient soup for four persons. A little salt and pepper must be added.

MARY JEWRY (EDITOR)
WARNE'S MODEL COOKERY AND HOUSEKEEPING BOOK

Irish Farm Broth

To serve this soup country fashion, a pot of boiled potatoes was in readiness. The meat was removed from the pot, cut in small pieces and distributed round the plates (or bowls most likely), to which the broth was added. Peeled potatoes were broken up in each plate, and all was eaten with a spoon.

To serve 8

2 lb.	boneless chuck beef	1 kg.
2 to 3 quarts	water	2 to 3 liters
¾ cup	split peas	175 ml.
¾ cup	pearl barley	175 ml.
1	small cabbage, cored and shredded	1
1 cup	celery leaves, shredded	¼ liter
1	carrot, diced	1
1	small turnip, diced	1
	salt and pepper	

Put the beef into the pot with the amount of water required for the broth; add the peas and the barley. Put on the lid and cook slowly, while you prepare the vegetables. Add the vegetables to the pot and simmer all for 2 or 3 hours over low heat. Season to taste and serve.

FLORENCE IRWIN
IRISH COUNTRY RECIPES

Jamaica Pepper-Pot Soup

The coco used in this soup is a Jamaican variety of sweet potato. Ordinary sweet potato may be substituted for coco. Shrimp may replace the crayfish; like the crayfish, they should be parboiled for about 5 minutes in salted water, drained and shelled. To make coconut milk, pour ½ cup [125 ml.] of boiling water over ½ cup of grated fresh coconut, allow to steep for a few minutes, and then strain the resulting milk through a cloth, squeezing hard.

To serve 12

1½ lb.	beef soup meat, such as boneless shank, cubed	¾ kg.
2	pig's tails	2
4 quarts	water	4 liters
2	coco, coarsely chopped	2
1 or 2	sprigs thyme	1 or 2
2½ lb.	spinach, finely chopped	1¼ kg.
12	okra, sliced into thin rounds	12
1	medium-sized onion, chopped	1
1	garlic clove, crushed	1
1	small eggplant, peeled and coarsely chopped	1
1½ lb.	kale, finely chopped	¾ kg.
	salt	
1	green chili	1
1 lb.	crayfish, parboiled and shelled	½ kg.
½ cup	coconut milk	125 ml.

Place the soup meat and pig's tails in a large soup kettle with the water. Bring to a boil, reduce the heat and simmer, covered, until the meat is nearly cooked, which should be in about 2 hours. Add the *coco*.

Place the thyme and all of the vegetables except the chili in a separate saucepan without any water, and steam, covered, for about 10 minutes or until cooked. Rub the vegetables through a coarse strainer or colander into the kettle.

Add the chili and salt to taste. Add more boiling water, if needed. Simmer until the soup has thickened, then add the crayfish. Lastly add the coconut milk and cook for just 5 minutes more. Remove the chili before serving.

LEILA BRANDON
A MERRY-GO-ROUND OF RECIPES FROM JAMAICA

Catalan Soup

Sopa de Mandonghuilles a la Casolana

To blanch the almonds and hazelnuts called for in this recipe, place them in a bowl and pour boiling water over them. Then drain the nuts and rub off their skins. (Alternatively, you can buy the almonds already blanched.) Toast the nuts in a shallow pan in a 350° F. [180° C.] oven for 10 minutes, turning them frequently to brown them evenly.

	To serve 4	
1	small garlic clove, crushed	1
½ lb.	ground beef	¼ kg.
2 tbsp.	chopped fresh parsley	30 ml.
	salt and black pepper	
⅓ cup	flour	75 ml.
	oil or lard for frying	
1 quart	chicken broth	1 liter
4	slices toast	4

Picada

2	garlic cloves	2
2	sprigs parsley	2
¼ tsp.	ground saffron	1 ml.
⅛ tsp.	salt	½ ml.
2 tbsp.	hazelnuts, blanched and toasted	30 ml.
2 tbsp.	almonds, blanched and toasted	30 ml.
½ tsp.	ground cinnamon	2 ml.
1 tbsp.	dry sherry	15 ml.
	water	

To make the *picada*, pound the garlic and parsley together with all of the dry *picada* ingredients in a mortar, then add the sherry and enough water to make a fine paste.

Mix the crushed garlic with the ground beef, chopped parsley, salt and pepper. Make this into tiny balls and roll them in flour. Heat a little oil or lard in a skillet and brown the meatballs lightly all over.

In a separate pan, bring the chicken broth to a boil, add the toast and let it disintegrate, then add the meatballs and the *picada* and cook gently for 15 to 20 minutes.

ANNA MACMIADHACHÁIN
SPANISH REGIONAL COOKERY

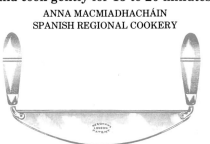

Ham and Winter Melon Soup

The winter melon called for in this recipe is a round, green melon with a white pulp; the flavor is similar to that of a zucchini. Winter melon is sold fresh in slices at Chinese specialty stores. If not available, use peeled, seeded zucchini or cucumber, but cook them for only 8 to 10 minutes.

Sliced pork may be substituted for ham, but then ½ teaspoon [2 ml.] of salt should be added.

	To serve 4 to 6	
¼ lb.	Smithfield or country ham, skin and any black surface removed, sliced	125 g.
1 lb.	winter melon (about 2½ cups [625 ml.]), peeled, seeded and cut into ½-by-2-inch [1-by-5-cm.] slices	½ kg.
2 cups	water	½ liter
2 cups	chicken broth	½ liter
1	slice fresh ginger root	1

Cook the sliced melon with the water in a saucepan. Bring to a boil. Boil slowly over low heat for 20 to 30 minutes until the melon is translucent and tender. Add the ham, chicken broth and ginger root. Cook for another 10 minutes. Remove the ginger root and serve the soup hot.

JOYCE CHEN
JOYCE CHEN COOK BOOK

Beef, Okra and Tomato Soup

	To serve 8	
3 lb.	meaty beef shank, sawed into several pieces	1½ kg.
2 cups	sliced okra (about ¾ lb. [⅓ kg.])	½ liter
2 cups	peeled and diced tomatoes (about 2 large tomatoes)	½ liter
2 quarts	cold water	2 liters
1	bouquet garni, composed of bay leaf, oregano and parsley	1
1 cup	diced onions	¼ liter
1 cup	diced green beans	¼ liter
½ cup	diced celery	125 ml.
½	green pepper, halved, deribbed, seeded and diced	½
½ cup	diced carrots	125 ml.
½ tsp.	salt	2 ml.
¼ tsp.	pepper	1 ml.
	boiled rice, made from about 2 cups [½ liter] raw rice	

Put the meat in a soup kettle with the water. Slowly bring to a boil and after 5 minutes of boiling, reduce the heat to a simmer and skim thoroughly. Add the bouquet garni and continue simmering, partially covered, for 2 hours or until the broth is flavorful and the meat nearly tender. Add the okra, tomatoes and all of the other vegetables; season with the salt and pepper. Cover and simmer gently for about 45 minutes. Remove the beef shank from the soup, dice the meat and return it to the kettle, discarding the bones. Cook gently for 10 minutes longer. Taste for seasoning and serve in heated soup plates with side dishes of plain boiled rice.

LOUIS P. DE GOUY
THE SOUP BOOK

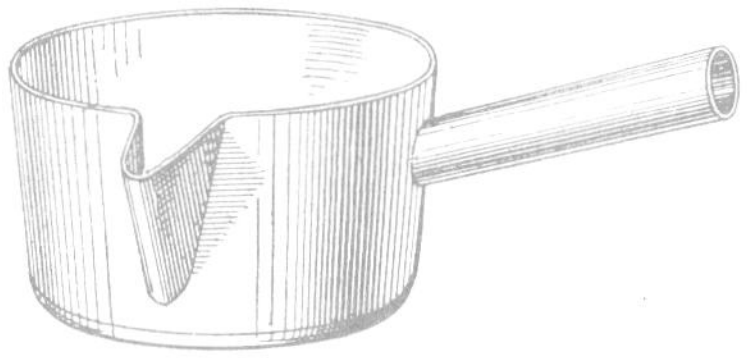

Scotch Broth

The vegetables for flavoring the soup may be included for the first hour of cooking, then discarded and replaced by fresh vegetables to be served with the soup.

To serve 8

1½ to 2 lb.	lamb neck or shoulder, trimmed of excess fat	¾ to 1 kg.
2½ quarts	water	2½ liters
¼ cup	pearl barley, soaked in water for 2 hours	50 ml.
1 cup	freshly shelled peas or ¾ cup [75 ml.] dried peas soaked in water overnight	¼ liter
	salt	
1	turnip, diced	1
2	carrots, diced	2
1	small onion, chopped	1
1	leek, white part only, chopped	1
½ lb.	cabbage, cored and finely shredded (about 2½ cups [625 ml.] when shredded)	¼ kg.
	pepper	
1 tbsp.	chopped fresh parsley	15 ml.

Put the lamb into a large saucepan with the water and barley. If you are using dried peas, add them now. Add salt. Bring to a boil and skim. Cover and simmer gently for about an hour, then add the remaining vegetables, except the cabbage. Allow to simmer, covered, for at least 2 hours longer.

As soon as the lamb is cooked, lift it out of the broth, cut the meat off the bones and return the meat to the broth. Ten minutes before serving, add the cabbage. Skim off the fat, season the broth to taste and, just before serving, add the parsley. Serve very hot.

F. MARIAN MC NEILL
THE SCOTS KITCHEN

Oxtail Soup

For a richer soup, you can brown the oxtails and vegetables in a 475° F. [250° C.] oven, as demonstrated on page 46, before combining the oxtails with the ham and adding the water.

An inexpensive and very nutritious soup may be made of oxtails, but it will be insipid in flavor without the addition of a little ham, smoked pig's knuckle or other meat. To increase the savor of this soup when meat is not served in it, the onions, turnips and carrots may be gently fried until of a fine light brown, before they are added to it.

To serve 12

2 or 3	small oxtails (2 to 4 lb. [1 to 2 kg.] in all), washed and soaked in water for 15 minutes	2 or 3
1	pig's knuckle, about 1½ lb. [¾ kg.]	1
4½ quarts	water or beef broth	4½ liters
	salt	
4	medium-sized carrots	4
2 to 4	onions	2 to 4
1	bouquet garni	1
1	stalk celery, trimmed and cored	1
2	turnips	2
6 to 8	whole cloves	6 to 8
½ tsp.	peppercorns	2 ml.
1 tbsp.	arrowroot or rice flour	15 ml.
	cayenne pepper	

Put the oxtails and the pig's knuckle into a large pan and pour in the water or broth. Bring gradually to a boil, throw in 2 tablespoons [30 ml.] of salt and clear off the scum carefully as soon as it forms upon the surface; when it ceases to rise, add the carrots, onions, bouquet garni, celery, turnips, cloves and peppercorns. Stew these gently from 3 to 3½ hours if the tails be very large; lift the tails out, strain the liquor and skim off all the fat; divide the tails into joints and put them into 2 quarts [2 liters], or rather more, of the stock; stir in, when these begin to boil, the arrowroot mixed with as much cayenne and salt as may be required to flavor the soup well, and serve it very hot.

If stewed down until the flesh falls away from the bones, the oxtails will make stock which will be quite a firm jelly when cold; and this, strained, thickened and well flavored with spices, catsup or a little wine, would, to many tastes, be a superior soup to the above.

ELIZA ACTON
MODERN COOKERY

Fife Broth

This soup is traditionally served with flat oatmeal cakes cooked on a griddle.

	To serve 6	
12 or more	leftover pork ribs, saved from chops or roasts	12 or more
1 cup	pearl barley, soaked in water overnight	¼ liter
	salt and pepper	
2 quarts	water	2 liters
1	large onion, finely chopped	1
12	potatoes, sliced	12

Put the pork bones, barley, salt and pepper into a pan with the water. Cover and cook gently for about 2 hours, then add the onion and potatoes. Cook for another 30 minutes and, when ready, serve with oatcakes.

JANET MURRAY
WITH A FINE FEELING FOR FOOD

Mackerel Soup

	To serve 6	
2 or 3	mackerel with heads removed, cleaned and cut into 1-inch [2½-cm.] pieces	2 or 3
1½ quarts	water	1½ liters
10	white peppercorns	10
2 tbsp.	salt	30 ml.
8	sprigs dill	8
¼ cup	light cream	50 ml.
2 to 3 tbsp.	fresh lemon juice	30 to 45 ml.
2	egg yolks	2

In a large saucepan, simmer the mackerel pieces in the water with the peppercorns, salt and six of the dill sprigs for 10 minutes, then remove the pieces of fish and let them cool.

Strain the fish stock into another saucepan and add half of the cream and 2 tablespoons [30 ml.] of the lemon juice. Simmer for a few minutes. Bone and skin the mackerel pieces carefully and add them to the soup. Remove the saucepan from the heat; mix together the egg yolks and the remaining cream and gradually stir the mixture into the soup to thicken it.

Finely chop the remaining dill and add it to the soup. Check the seasoning, adding more lemon juice if necessary, and then serve.

BENGT PETERSEN
DELICIOUS FISH DISHES

Rockfish Soup

Soupe de Poisson du Moulin de Mougins

This soup is traditionally made from whitebait or other small fish, which are used uncleaned. The important thing is to have a selection of several varieties of fish. Whiting, bass, sole, small bream, fish heads and carcasses, and trimmings from conger eel or angler may also be used.

For instructions on how to make rouille, the red-pepper sauce accompaniment, see the demonstration on page 51 (recipe, page 165).

	To serve 6 to 8	
3 to 4 lb.	mixed fish	1½ to 2 kg.
3 or 4	large yellow onions, chopped	3 or 4
1 cup	olive oil	¼ liter
4	large, very ripe tomatoes, sliced	4
½	bulb garlic, crushed but not peeled	½
2	sprigs thyme	2
1	bay leaf	1
2	sprigs dried fennel	2
2 quarts	water	2 liters
	salt	
½ tsp.	ground saffron	2 ml.
	freshly ground pepper	
	freshly grated Parmesan cheese (optional)	
12	slices dried French bread, rubbed with garlic	12
	rouille (optional)	

Sweat the onions in the olive oil, without letting them color, until they are soft and transparent. Turn up the heat and add the fish with the tomatoes, garlic and herbs. Mix vigorously with a wooden spatula while cooking for about 10 minutes, then pour in the water. Salt lightly and boil vigorously for 20 minutes.

Put the soup through a food mill, then through a fine sieve, pressing hard to extract all the juices. Return the soup to the heat and bring to a gentle boil. Add the saffron and pepper (pepper added too early gives a disagreeable flavor), and season to taste with salt. Add the grated cheese if you wish. Serve the soup garnished with the bread slices, and with *rouille* if desired.

LES PRINCES DE LA GASTRONOMIE

Smoked Fish Chowder

To serve 6

1½ lb.	finnan haddie, cut into 1-inch [2-cm.] pieces	¾ kg.
¼ lb.	salt pork with the rind removed, blanched in boiling water for 5 minutes, drained and diced	125 g.
1	large onion, sliced	1
4	medium-sized potatoes, sliced	4
	water	
	salt and freshly ground pepper	
1	bay leaf	1
5 cups	milk	1¼ liters

In a large saucepan, brown the salt pork. Add the onion and sauté until soft. Add the potatoes and enough water to cover them. Add salt, pepper and the bay leaf. Cover and simmer until the potatoes are barely tender.

Add the milk and fish and simmer for 15 to 20 minutes. Remove the bay leaf and serve.

MARJORIE PAGE BLANCHARD
TREASURED RECIPES FROM EARLY NEW ENGLAND KITCHENS

Octopus Soup

Sopa de Pulpo

To clean octopus, remove the thin, purplish skin, empty the body sac and cut off the hard beak. In Spain, olive oil would be used for frying the bread called for in this recipe.
This soup is equally delicious made with skate.

To serve 6

1	medium-sized octopus (2 lb. [1 kg.]), cleaned and cut into small pieces	1
1	medium-sized onion, sliced	1
2 or 3	tomatoes, peeled and sliced	2 or 3
2 tbsp.	oil	30 ml.
2 tbsp.	chopped fresh parsley	30 ml.
2 quarts	water	2 liters
	salt and pepper	
12	slices firm-textured white bread, fried in oil	12

In a large, heavy saucepan, fry the onion and tomatoes in the oil over medium heat for 5 to 10 minutes. Add the octopus pieces and fry for 10 to 15 minutes more. Add the parsley and water and simmer, covered, over very low heat for 2 to 3 hours. Season to taste. Drop the fried bread slices into the soup, cook for another 15 minutes and serve.

MARINA PEREYRA DE AZNAR AND NINA FROUD
THE HOME BOOK OF SPANISH COOKERY

Fish Stew, Leghorn-Style

Cacciucco alla Livornese

All or any of the following fish and shellfish can be used for this dish: whiting, hake, mullet, turbot, eel, shrimp, crayfish, squid, octopus or cuttlefish.

To serve 6

4 to 5 lb.	assorted fish and shellfish, cleaned, fish heads removed and reserved, large fish or octopus cut into pieces	2 to 2½ kg.
1 cup	olive oil	¼ liter
	salt and pepper	
1	onion, finely chopped	1
1	carrot, finely chopped	1
2	ribs celery, finely chopped	2
3 tbsp.	finely chopped fresh parsley	45 ml.
2	garlic cloves	2
2	small dried hot chilies	2
2	bay leaves	2
1	sprig thyme	1
1¼ cups	dry red wine	300 ml.
6	medium-sized tomatoes (about 2 lb. [1 kg.]), peeled and chopped	6
1½ quarts	water	1½ liters
	small bread slices, fried in oil or toasted in the oven	

Put the fish and shellfish into a shallow dish and sprinkle them with a little olive oil and with salt and pepper. Leave for 30 minutes.

Meanwhile, heat ½ cup [125 ml.] of the olive oil in a large pan. Add the aromatic vegetables, parsley, garlic, chilies, bay leaves, thyme and, finally, the fish heads. Brown the heads well, moisten with the wine and continue cooking until the wine has reduced to a thick sauce. Add the tomatoes and water. Season and continue cooking for 30 minutes. Rub the soup through a fine sieve.

In another large pan, preferably an earthenware one, heat the remaining olive oil. Add the squid, cuttlefish and octopus and cook these for 15 minutes. Add the shrimp and, 5 minutes later, the remaining fish and shellfish. Add salt, if needed, and plenty of pepper and cook for 10 minutes.

Put two or three slices of toasted bread for each person into the bottom of a large soup tureen or into large individual soup bowls. Add the fish and shellfish, and pour the soup over the top.

ADA BONI
ITALIAN REGIONAL COOKING

Mixed Seafood Stew

Cioppino

To serve 8

1½ lb.	boned sea bass, cut into 2-inch [5-cm.] slices	¾ kg.
3	live lobsters (1½ lb. [¾ kg.] each), cut up	3
1 lb.	shrimp, shelled and cleaned	½ kg.
12	live hard-shell clams	12
24	live mussels	24
2 cups	chopped onions	½ liter
½ cup	chopped green pepper	125 ml.
6	garlic cloves, minced	6
½ cup	olive oil	125 ml.
4 cups	Italian tomatoes canned with basil	1 liter
¾ cup	tomato paste	175 ml.
2 cups	dry red wine	½ liter
1	lemon, thinly sliced	1
1 cup	chopped fresh parsley	¼ liter
1 tsp.	dried basil	5 ml.
1 tsp.	dried oregano	5 ml.
1 tsp.	salt	5 ml.
	freshly ground black pepper	

Combine the onion, green pepper and garlic with the olive oil in a large pot or kettle. Cook over low heat for 10 minutes, stirring occasionally. Add the tomatoes, tomato paste, wine, lemon, ½ cup [125 ml.] of the parsley and all of the other seasonings. Bring to a boil, reduce the heat, cover and simmer for 20 minutes. Add the bass, lobsters and shrimp and simmer, covered, for 20 minutes. Scrub the clams and mussels with a stiff brush under cold running water. Remove the "beard" that may be attached to the mussels. Add the clams and mussels to the pot and simmer, covered, for 10 minutes more or until the clams and mussels open and the fish is done. Serve the *cioppino* sprinkled with the remaining chopped parsley.

ELEANOR GRAVES
GREAT DINNERS FROM LIFE

Barcares Fish Soup

Boullinada du Barcares

For this recipe from the Ariège, France, a wide variety of fish may be used. Among the possibilities are mullet, whiting, flounder, hake, angler, conger eel and small squid. The origi- *nal recipe specifies "slightly rancid" lard—typical of the cooking of this region, but an acquired taste that will not please most palates.*

To serve 8 to 10

4 lb.	mixed fish, cleaned, whole or cut up depending on size	2 kg.
6 tbsp.	lard, diced	90 ml.
¼ cup	finely chopped fresh parsley	50 ml.
3	garlic cloves, finely chopped	3
	salt	
	cayenne pepper	
12	medium-sized potatoes (4 lb. [2 kg.]), finely sliced	12
2 tbsp.	flour	30 ml.
3 tbsp.	olive oil	45 ml.

Spread the lard over the bottom of a large saucepan or fire-proof earthenware pot. Mix the parsley and garlic and scatter them over the lard, then season the mixture with salt and cayenne pepper. Cover this base with a layer of potatoes, followed by a layer of fish. Sprinkle over the flour. Continue alternating layers of potatoes and fish until the pot is filled. Add enough cold water to reach the top layer of fish.

Cover the pot and place it over high heat. Bring quickly to a boil; this will bind the sauce and give flavor to the dish. As soon as the water has come to a boil, add the oil. Cover the pot and continue to cook rapidly for 15 to 20 minutes, or until the potatoes are just tender. Serve hot.

CURNONSKY
RECETTES DES PROVINCES DE FRANCE

New England Soup

Soupe de la Nouvelle Angleterre

To serve 6

2 to 2½ lb.	cod or haddock fillets	1 kg.
1 quart	water	1 liter
3	medium-sized potatoes, diced	3
2 oz.	salt pork with rind removed, diced	60 g.
1	onion, thinly sliced	1
2 cups	heavy cream	½ liter
	salt and white pepper	

Put the fish and the water into a saucepan, bring to a boil and cook over medium heat for 15 minutes. Remove and flake the fish. Put the potatoes into the fish's cooking liquid and cook over low heat for 10 minutes. The potatoes should be tender but still firm.

Meanwhile, sauté the salt pork in a skillet. Add the onion and cook until golden. Pour in the cream and bring to a boil. Pour the mixture into the saucepan with the potatoes. Add the salt and pepper and the flaked fish. Reheat without boiling, check the seasoning, and serve.

LES PETITS PLATS ET LES GRANDS

Old-fashioned Fish Chowder

To serve 8 to 10

4 lb.	fresh cod or haddock, skinned, filleted and cut into 2-inch [5-cm.] pieces; the head, tail and bones reserved and broken into pieces	2 kg.
2 cups	cold water	½ liter
1½-inch	cube fat salt pork with the rind removed, diced	4-cm.
1	onion, thinly sliced	1
4 or 5	medium-sized potatoes, thinly sliced (about 4 cups [1 liter])	4 or 5
2 cups	boiling water	½ liter
1 quart	milk or cream, scalded by heating until bubbles form around the sides of the pan	1 liter
1 tbsp.	salt	15 ml.
⅛ tsp.	pepper	½ ml.
3 tbsp.	butter	45 ml.

Put the pieces of head, tail and bones in a deep kettle. Add the cold water. Bring to a boil and simmer slowly for 10 minutes, drain and save the liquid.

Put the diced salt pork in a small skillet. Cook slowly for 5 minutes. Add the onion and cook until it is soft—about 5 minutes. Strain the fat into a deep pan and set aside the onion and salt pork.

Add the potatoes and boiling water to the fat. Cook for 5 minutes. Add the fish and the reserved liquid; cover and simmer for 10 minutes. Add the onion and salt pork pieces, the scalded milk or cream, the salt, pepper and butter. Heat, but do not boil, before serving.

WILMA LORD PERKINS (EDITOR)
THE FANNIE FARMER COOKBOOK

Fish Chowder, Roman Tavern-Style

Zuppa di Pesce delle Osterie Romane

To serve 4

4 lb.	mixed fish (mullet, flounder, halibut, eel, sole, etc.), cleaned, boned, sliced, fish heads and bones reserved	2 kg.
24	live mussels (about 2 lb. [1 kg.]), scrubbed and the beards removed	24
½ lb.	squid, cleaned and sliced	¼ kg.
2 tbsp.	chopped onion	30 ml.
½ cup	chopped fresh parsley	125 ml.
1 tbsp.	salt	15 ml.
6	peppercorns	6
3 cups	water	¾ liter
2½ cups	dry white wine	625 ml.
10 tbsp.	olive oil	150 ml.
2	leeks, chopped	2
2	heads Boston lettuce, cored and shredded	2
	thyme	
1	bay leaf	1
	pepper	
4	anchovy fillets, pounded to a paste	4
2	garlic cloves, chopped	2
4	slices French or Italian bread, toasted	4

Put the fish heads and bones into a pot with the onion, half of the parsley, the salt and peppercorns, water and 2 cups [½ liter] of the wine. Simmer this court bouillon for 30 minutes, then strain through a fine sieve.

In a heavy pan, heat 4 tablespoons [60 ml.] of the oil, put in the mussels, cover and cook them over medium heat until they open. Remove the mussels from their shells and strain the pan juices over them.

Heat 4 tablespoons more of the oil in a soup kettle and sauté the sliced squid for 5 minutes. Add the leeks, lettuce, a pinch of thyme, the bay leaf, salt and pepper. Cook over medium heat for about 30 minutes. When the squid slices are almost cooked, pour in the remaining ½ cup [125 ml.] of wine. Simmer until the wine evaporates. Add the anchovies and sliced fish. Simmer for a few minutes, stirring constantly. Add the court bouillon and continue cooking the chowder for 10 minutes. Add the mussels and their pan juices.

In a small pan, sauté the garlic in the remaining 2 tablespoons [30 ml.] of oil until golden. Remove and discard the garlic, then pour the oil into the chowder. Put the bread into warmed soup dishes, pour the chowder over it and sprinkle with the remaining parsley.

WAVERLEY ROOT
THE BEST OF ITALIAN COOKING

Bahama Seafood Chowder

Conch is a mollusk with a spiral shell, and coquina is a small marine clam. Although both are native to the Caribbean and unavailable in many parts of the United States, this soup may be made with any selection of available fish and shellfish.

To serve 8

2 lb.	assorted red snapper, mullet, jack and bluefish fillets, cut into 1½-inch [4-cm.] pieces	1 kg.
2 lb.	assorted cleaned, shelled conch, crab, coquina, mussels, clams and cleaned squid, cut into bite-sized pieces	1 kg.
	juice of 1 large Seville orange or 2 large limes	
2	dried red chilies	2
¼ lb.	fat salt pork with the rind removed, coarsely ground	125 g.
6	yellow onions, diced	6
1	large sweet green pepper, halved, seeded, deribbed and diced	1
3	small garlic cloves, crushed	3
1 quart	diced potatoes	1 liter
3 quarts	water	3 liters
½ tbsp.	dried thyme	7 ml.
1	small bay leaf	1
	ground mace	
5 or 6 drops	Angostura bitters	5 or 6 drops
2 cups	light cream	½ liter
	salt	
⅓ cup	finely chopped fresh coriander	75 ml.

Put the fish and shellfish into a large nonmetallic bowl and add the orange or lime juice and chilies. Mix gently but thoroughly and let stand at room temperature for 1 hour. Toss the mixture occasionally.

Fry the salt pork in a large soup kettle until golden. Remove the solid bits and reserve. In the fat left in the kettle, sauté the onions, green pepper and garlic until soft but not brown. Add the potatoes, water, thyme, bay leaf, a pinch of mace and the bitters. Bring to a boil, then cover and simmer for 40 minutes. Add the drained fish and shellfish, and simmer for 20 minutes. (If conch or squid is used, simmer it for about 15 minutes before adding the rest of the seafood.) Stir in the cream and the reserved pork bits. Season with salt to taste, add the coriander and serve.

JACQUELINE E. KNIGHT
THE COOK'S FISH GUIDE

Manhattan Clam Chowder

To serve 10

36	live hard-shell clams	36
¾ lb.	salt pork, rind removed and the pork diced	⅓ kg.
4	small onions, chopped	4
4 cups	peeled, seeded and chopped tomatoes	1 liter
2½ cups	chopped celery	625 ml.
1½ cups	chopped carrots	375 ml.
3 tbsp.	finely chopped fresh parsley	45 ml.
½ tsp.	thyme	2 ml.
1	large bay leaf	1
3	potatoes, cut into ½-inch [1-cm.] cubes	3
	salt and freshly ground pepper	
4	oyster crackers, crushed	4

Place the clams in a soup kettle, cover with water and steam them open. Remove the clams from the shells and mince them very finely. Strain the clam liquid through a sieve lined with several thicknesses of cheesecloth and reserve.

Render the salt pork in a soup kettle. Remove the browned bits. Sauté the onions in the pork fat until golden and transparent. Add the tomatoes to the onions and simmer for several minutes, stirring constantly. Add the celery, carrots, parsley, thyme and bay leaf. Measure the clam liquid and add enough water to make 2½ quarts [2½ liters]. Add this to the vegetables and simmer, covered, for 1 hour.

Add the potatoes to the soup and simmer for 15 minutes. Add the minced clams and simmer for 8 minutes, or until the potatoes are tender. Adjust the seasonings. Put some crushed crackers in the bottom of each soup bowl and pour in the soup. Serve steaming hot.

YVONNE YOUNG TARR
THE NEW YORK TIMES BREAD AND SOUP COOKBOOK

New England Clam Chowder

The clams called for in this recipe are sometimes called steamers or long necks.

	To serve 6 to 8	
24	live soft-shelled clams	24
3 cups	water	¾ liter
2	slices salt pork with the rind removed, finely chopped	2
1	medium-sized onion, sliced	1
3	medium-sized potatoes (about 1 lb. [½ kg.]), diced	3
3 tbsp.	butter	45 ml.
1¾ cups	half milk and half cream	425 ml.
1 tbsp.	salt	15 ml.
	pepper	
	crackers (optional)	

Combine the clams, their liquor and the water and bring to a boil. Drain the clams, reserving the broth. Remove the shells, finely chop the necks and coarse membranes of the clams and coarsely chop the remainder of the clam meat. Set the clams aside. In a heavy saucepan, fry the salt pork until lightly browned. Stir in the onion and cook until limp but not brown. Add the clam broth and potatoes and cook until the potatoes are tender, about 20 minutes. Stir in the butter, milk-and-cream mixture, salt and pepper and the clams. Heat, but do not boil, and pour immediately into large, warmed soup bowls. Serve with crackers, if desired.

THE EDITORS OF AMERICAN HERITAGE
THE AMERICAN HERITAGE COOKBOOK

Lobster Stew

To obtain the lobster meat called for in this recipe, first twist off the cooked lobster's large pincers, or claws. Use a nutcracker or mallet to crack the shell of the claws in several places. Pick out the claw meat. Then break off the meaty tail section from the main part of the lobster's body; pull off the small tail piece on the end, and use your thumb or a small fork to push out the tail meat. Pull the legs off the main section and pick out the meat from inside them. Finally, lift out the two reddish sacs of roe (coral) and the greenish liver (tomalley) from the main body cavity and pick out the bits of meat there.

	To serve 3 or 4	
3	live lobsters, about 1¼ lb. [⅔ kg.] each	3
8 tbsp.	butter	120 ml.
1 quart	light cream or half-and-half cream	1 liter

Steam the live lobsters in a small amount of water for about 15 minutes. Leave them to cool and, as soon as you can handle them, remove the meat and cut it into bite-sized pieces. Save the lobster fat, tomalley (liver) and coral (roe).

In a heavy saucepan melt the butter. Simmer the fat, tomalley and coral for 7 to 8 minutes. Add the pieces of lobster meat and cook over low heat for a few minutes. Very slowly, pour in the cream, stirring constantly. Remove from the heat. Cool and refrigerate.

Leave for at least 12 hours (some recommend 24). Reheat without boiling.

MARJORIE PAGE BLANCHARD
TREASURED RECIPES FROM EARLY NEW ENGLAND KITCHENS

Jane's Lobster Stew

	To serve 2	
1½ lb.	live lobster	¾ kg.
4 quarts	water	4 liters
4 tbsp.	salt	60 ml.
6 tbsp.	unsalted butter	90 ml.
2 cups	milk	½ liter
2 cups	heavy cream	½ liter

In a large kettle, bring to a boil the water, into which you have put the salt. When the water is rapidly boiling, plunge the live lobster, head first, into the pot; cover, and bring the water back to just a simmer. Simmer the lobster for 7 minutes, then turn off the heat, and let the lobster remain in the salted water until cool enough to handle.

Split the lobster open and extract every little bit of the meat, discarding only the shell, the intestinal vein that runs down the back, the gills and the sac that lies in the head. Reserve the green liver (tomalley) and the pink roe (coral). Cut the meat into good-sized chunks.

In a heavy saucepan heat 6 tablespoons [90 ml.] of the butter, and in it simmer the tomalley and coral for 7 minutes. Then add the lobster meat and cook over very low heat for 5 minutes longer, stirring and tossing the lobster occasionally in the mixture. Remove the saucepan from the heat. Very gradually pour in first the milk and then the cream, just a trickle at a time, stirring constantly; continue to stir until the rich milk turns to a delicate pink color. Cover and refrigerate for at least 6 hours, or overnight.

To serve, reheat the stew until it is steaming hot, but do not let it boil.

ANN SERANNE
ANN SERANNE'S GOOD FOOD & HOW TO COOK IT

Seafood Gumbo

The techniques of shelling crabs and making brown roux are demonstrated on page 44.

	To serve 8	
24	live blue crabs, steamed for 5 minutes	24
3 lb.	raw shrimp, unpeeled, with heads left on, if possible	1½ kg.
5 quarts	water	5 liters
1	carrot	1
1	onion, quartered	1
½ cup	coarsely chopped celery	375 ml.
1 cup	finely chopped green pepper	¼ liter
3	garlic cloves, finely chopped	3
3 lb.	okra, cut into ¼-inch [6-mm.] pieces	1½ kg.
about 1 cup	oil	about ¼ liter
2 tbsp.	flour	30 ml.
3	medium-sized tomatoes, peeled, seeded and chopped	3
½ cup	diced, cooked ham	125 ml.
1 tsp.	thyme	5 ml.
1 tsp.	basil	5 ml.
3	bay leaves	3
¼ cup	finely chopped fresh parsley	50 ml.
	salt and pepper	
	Tabasco	
	Worcestershire sauce	
2 cups	cooked rice	½ liter

To make the stock, fill a 6- to 8-quart [6- to 8-liter] stockpot with 5 quarts [5 liters] of water. Pull off the back shells of the crabs, adding the shells to the stockpot. Discard the inedible spongy fingers of the crabs, break their bodies in half and set them aside. Peel the shrimp, adding the heads and shells to the pot. Set the shrimp meat aside.

Add the carrot, onion quarters and ½ cup [125 ml.] of the celery to the pot, cover and simmer for 2 hours. Strain the stock and return it to the pot.

Meanwhile, sauté the chopped onions, celery, green pepper and garlic in ¼ cup [50 ml.] of oil until they are soft. Set the vegetables aside off the heat. Fry the okra separately in ¾ cup [175 ml.] of oil over medium heat for about 45 minutes

or until it is soft and the ropy texture is gone. Stir often, adding more oil if the okra sticks. Set the okra aside.

In a separate skillet, make a brown roux with 1 tablespoon [15 ml.] of oil and the flour. Cook for 45 minutes, then add the tomato pulp and cook the mixture into a paste. Add the ham, thyme, basil and bay leaves. Cook for 5 minutes and set aside.

Add the sautéed vegetables and the okra to the strained stock and, while stirring, slowly add the roux mixture. Simmer for 1 hour. Add the peeled shrimp, crab halves and parsley and cook for an additional ½ hour. Season with salt, pepper, Tabasco and Worcestershire to taste. Serve in gumbo bowls over rice.

THE JUNIOR LEAGUE OF NEW ORLEANS
THE PLANTATION COOKBOOK

Mussel Soup with Milk

Kraeklingasúpa úr Mjólk

	To serve 4	
2 lb.	live mussels (about 24), scrubbed and bearded	1 kg.
2 cups	milk, or a mixture of milk and cream	½ liter
1¼ cups	water	300 ml.
¼ lb.	salt pork with the rind removed, blanched in boiling water for 5 minutes, drained and diced	150 g.
1	medium-sized onion, chopped	1
3 or 4	medium-sized potatoes, diced	3 or 4
1	small bay leaf	1
1	sprig thyme	1
	salt and white pepper	
2 tbsp.	butter (optional)	30 ml.

Bring the water to a boil and put in the mussels. Cover the pot and boil the mussels until the shells open, in 3 or 4 minutes. Remove the mussels, extract the meat from the shells, chop it up and set it aside in a covered dish so that it does not dry out. Strain the cooking broth and reserve it.

In a large, heavy saucepan, fry the salt pork until light brown. Remove the salt-pork pieces, and add the onion to the fat left in the pan. Cook the onion gently, without letting it color. Pour the strained broth into the pan and add the potatoes, bay leaf, thyme and a light seasoning of salt and pepper. Simmer for 15 to 20 minutes, then add the milk, or milk and cream, and simmer for another 5 minutes.

Return the mussels to the soup together with the salt-pork pieces, and the butter if used. Heat the soup through and serve it with crackers.

HELGA SIGURDARDÓTTIR
MATUR OG DRYKKUR

Velouté of Mussels

To give the soup a yellow color and delicately musky flavor, a pinch of ground saffron or saffron threads may be dissolved in a tablespoon [15 ml.] of hot water, and stirred into the velouté before the final thickening with egg yolks and cream.

	To serve 4 to 6	
3 lb.	live mussels (about 36), scrubbed and bearded	1½ kg.
½ cup	dry white wine	125 ml.
1	onion, thinly sliced	1
2	garlic cloves, crushed	2
1	bouquet garni	1
4 tbsp.	butter	60 ml.
⅓ cup	flour	75 ml.
1 quart	fish broth	1 liter
	salt and pepper	
2	egg yolks	2
⅔ cup	heavy cream	150 ml.

Pack the cleaned mussels into a large saucepan with the wine, onion, garlic and bouquet garni. Cover tightly and steam over high heat for 5 to 10 minutes or until all the mussels have opened. Remove the mussels from their shells and keep them warm in a covered dish; strain the cooking liquor into a bowl through a sieve lined with several layers of dampened cheesecloth; reserve the liquor.

Melt the butter in a saucepan over low heat, and stir in the flour to make a roux. Whisk in the fish broth, and stir until the soup comes to a boil. Simmer slowly for at least 40 minutes, skimming the skin that forms on the surface. Add the mussel cooking liquor and return the soup to a boil, skimming if necessary.

In a small bowl, whisk the egg yolks and cream together. Gradually whisk in a ladleful of the hot soup. Stir the egg mixture into the soup and heat slowly, without boiling, until the soup thickens lightly. Add the shelled mussels to the soup and pour into a warmed tureen to serve.

GEORGE LASALLE
THE ADVENTUROUS FISH COOK

Oyster Soup

This excellent recipe comes from the *Restaurant de la baie des Anges* at Aber-Wrach, in Finistère, the extreme northwest corner of France. Mussels may be substituted for oysters: open them in a covered pan over high heat, add their liquor to the soup and cut them into fourths if they are large, into halves if they are small, before reheating with cream.

	To serve 6 to 8	
48	live oysters, shucked and the liquor reserved, or 1 quart [1 liter] shucked oysters	48
½ lb.	leeks, white part only, chopped	¼ kg.
4 tbsp.	butter	60 ml.
1	medium-sized potato, diced	1
1 cup	light cream	¼ liter
2 tbsp.	chopped fresh parsley	30 ml.
	Fish stock	
2	sole carcasses	2
1	carrot, sliced	1
1	medium-sized onion, sliced	1
1	small leek, sliced	1
1	rib celery	1
1	bouquet garni	1
¾ cup	dry white wine	175 ml.
1 quart	water	1 liter
	salt and freshly ground black pepper	

Simmer the stock ingredients together for 25 minutes, then strain. Melt the chopped leeks gently in the butter for 10 minutes, add the potato and pour in the strained stock. When the leeks and potato are cooked, in about 15 minutes, purée the soup in an electric blender, or put it through a food mill: the result should be very smooth.

Put the oysters and their liquor into a shallow pan, and cook gently for a moment or two over moderate heat, until the edges curl. Strain the liquor into the puréed soup and pour the cream onto the oysters. Bring the oysters and cream to just below a boil, being careful not to overcook the oysters, then pour into a large warmed soup tureen. Add the purée mixture gradually, sprinkle with the parsley and serve.

Lightly salted butter and rye bread are good accompaniments for this soup.

JANE GRIGSON
FISH COOKERY

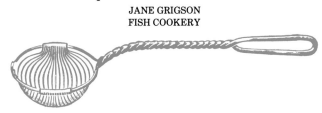

Panades

Asturian Garlic Soup

Sopa de Ajo Asturiana

To serve 4

4 or 5	large garlic cloves, chopped	4 or 5
6 tbsp.	olive oil	90 ml.
8 to 10	thick slices stale bread, torn into walnut-sized pieces	8 to 10
1 quart	water	1 liter
½ tsp.	salt	2 ml.
2 or 3	tomatoes, peeled and chopped (optional)	2 or 3

Heat the oil gently in a large saucepan and allow the garlic to stew in the oil. Gradually add the bread to the oil and garlic, stirring well. Do not allow the bread to brown. Add the water and the salt. Throw in the tomatoes (which may be omitted if not available). Allow the soup to simmer gently for about 15 minutes, until the bread is very soft but not completely disintegrated.

ANNA MACMIADHACHÁIN
SPANISH REGIONAL COOKERY

Panade with Sorrel or Leek

La Panade avec Oseille ou Blanc de Poireau

To serve 6 to 8

8	slices bread, cut into small pieces	8
1 cup	sorrel leaves, coarsely chopped, or 1 large leek, white part only, very finely chopped	¼ liter
6 tbsp.	butter	90 ml.
2 quarts	water, heated to simmering	2 liters
6	egg yolks, lightly beaten	6
	salt	

Melt 2 tablespoons [30 ml.] of the butter in a deep, heavy-bottomed saucepan and lightly sauté the sorrel or leek over low heat for 10 minutes. If using a leek, do not allow it to color. Add the bread and pour in the water. Cover the saucepan, remove it from the heat and let it stand for 10 minutes to allow the bread to absorb the water.

Bring the soup to a boil over high heat, stirring constantly with a wooden spoon. Cover the pan again and simmer the soup very gently for at least 30 minutes. Do not stir during this time: stirring will make the bread stick to the pan.

Stir vigorously to break up any remaining lumps. When the soup is cooked, it should be a very smooth purée or cream. Off the heat, slowly whisk in the egg yolks, then the remaining butter and salt to taste. Return the pan to gentle heat and whisk the soup until it thickens. Serve.

MADAME SAINT-ANGE
LA CUISINE DE MADAME SAINT-ANGE

Pumpkin Supper

A whole pumpkin makes a dramatic table presentation; unfortunately, shops sell pumpkins for a relatively short period. Acorn squash, on the other hand, enjoy a long market season. They work just as well, and are far easier to clean.

To serve 6 to 8

3 to 4 lb.	whole pumpkin, preferably with the stem intact, or six 1-lb. [½-kg.] acorn squash	1
4	slices firm-textured white bread	4
1 tbsp.	oil	15 ml.
3½ cups	half-and-half cream	875 ml.
1 tsp.	salt	5 ml.
½ tsp.	pepper	2 ml.
¼ tsp.	grated nutmeg	1 ml.
1 cup	freshly grated Swiss cheese	¼ liter

Preheat the oven to 350° F. [180° C.]. Cut the bread into pieces about ½ inch [1 cm.] square; precision doesn't matter at all. Put the pieces on a baking sheet and toast them in the oven until golden brown—about 7 minutes.

Meanwhile, wash and dry the pumpkin. Using a strong, serrated knife, slice about one fourth of the way down from the top to cut off a cap. Pull out as many of the fibers and seeds as possible, then scrape out the rest of the fibers with a spoon. Rub the outside of the pumpkin and the cap with the oil. In a bowl, beat together 2½ cups [625 ml.] of the cream and the salt, pepper and nutmeg.

Place the pumpkin on a large, strong piepan or baking sheet. Layer into the pumpkin the bread cubes and cheese, finishing with a layer of cheese. Fill three fourths of the space in the pumpkin. Pour in enough cream to just cover the filling, using the remaining cream if necessary. Replace the cap on the pumpkin.

Place the pumpkin in the preheated oven and bake for about 2 hours. Stir from time to time. Pumpkin Supper is done when the skin turns a rust-orange and the pulp is tender when pierced with a small, sharp knife. At the table remove the pumpkin cap and ladle out the thickened, custardy soup and the pumpkin pulp into the soup dishes.

CAROL CUTLER
THE SIX-MINUTE SOUFFLÉ AND OTHER CULINARY DELIGHTS

Saffron Soup

Le Mourtaïrol

To serve 4		
¼ tsp.	ground saffron	1 ml.
10 to 12	thin slices homemade bread (recipe, page 165)	10 to 12
1 quart	chicken broth	1 liter

Place the bread slices in an earthenware casserole. In a saucepan, bring the broth to a boil, remove the pan from the heat and mix a spoonful of the broth with the saffron. When the saffron is dissolved, after about 5 minutes, stir it into the broth. Pour the saffron-flavored broth over the bread until the bread refuses to absorb any more. Set the casserole to simmer in a preheated 350° F. [180° C.] oven for about 30 minutes, adding some of the remaining broth from time to time, if necessary, to keep the bread moist. Serve the soup from the casserole in which it has been cooked.

LA FRANCE À TABLE

Bread and Tomato Soup

Pappa al Pomodoro

It is most important that the bread used in this recipe not be soggy. It should be sufficiently old, several days at least, rather hard and, if possible, dark rather than light. Though considered a soup, the consistency of this dish is not liquid at all. It may be eaten hot, lukewarm or cold, or reheated and served hot on the following day.

To serve 4		
1 lb.	bread, cut into small pieces	½ kg.
3	medium-sized very ripe tomatoes (1 lb. [½ kg.]), peeled, seeded and quartered	3
½ cup	olive oil	125 ml.
3	large garlic cloves, coarsely chopped	3
	crushed, dried red chili	
3 cups	hot chicken or meat broth	¾ liter
	salt and freshly ground black pepper	
4 or 5	basil leaves	4 or 5

Place half of the oil in a stockpot, preferably of flameproof terra cotta, and add the garlic and a pinch of chili. Sauté very gently for 10 to 12 minutes. Add the tomatoes to the pot and simmer for a further 15 minutes.

Add the bread to the pot, along with the broth, salt, pepper and whole basil leaves. Stir the mixture very well and

simmer for 15 minutes longer, then remove the pot from the heat, cover and let rest for 1 to 2 hours.

When ready to serve, stir very well and spoon the soup into individual soup bowls. At the table, sprinkle 1 tablespoon [15 ml.] of the remaining olive oil on each serving and grind some fresh black pepper into each bowl.

GUILIANO BUGIALLI
THE FINE ART OF ITALIAN COOKING

Stuffed Bread Soup

Zuppa di Pane Farcito

The instructions for extracting beef marrow from a marrowbone appear on page 18.

To serve 6		
48	1½-inch [4-cm.] rounds cut from thinly sliced bread	48
½ lb.	cooked chicken, boned and skinned	¼ kg.
2 oz.	prosciutto, thinly sliced	60 g.
1 oz.	beef marrow, extracted from a 2-inch [5-cm.] bone	30 g.
1	egg, lightly beaten	1
½ tsp.	salt	2 ml.
⅛ tsp.	freshly ground pepper	½ ml.
6 tbsp.	freshly grated Parmesan cheese	90 ml.
about 6 tbsp.	butter	about 90 ml.
2 quarts	broth, heated to boiling	2 liters

Chop and mix thoroughly (or put through the medium blade of a food grinder) the chicken, prosciutto and marrow; add the egg, salt, pepper and 1 tablespoon [15 ml.] of grated cheese, and mix thoroughly until smooth. Spread half of the bread rounds with the chicken mixture and cover with the remaining rounds, pinching the edges of these sandwiches together firmly. Melt 2 tablespoons [30 ml.] of the butter in a skillet and fry the stuffed sandwiches to a golden brown on both sides, adding more butter as necessary.

Distribute the sandwiches in deep soup plates, pour over them the boiling broth and serve immediately, passing additional grated cheese separately.

LUIGI CARNACINA
GREAT ITALIAN COOKING

Portuguese Bread Soup

Açorda Alentejana

This soup is often served as an accompaniment to broiled fresh sardines.

	To serve 6 to 8	
8	slices dry bread, broken up	8
1	sprig coriander	1
3 or 4	garlic cloves	3 or 4
½ tsp.	salt	2 ml.
3 tbsp.	olive oil	45 ml.
2 quarts	boiling water	2 liters

In a mortar, pound to a paste the coriander, garlic and salt. Put the mixture in a serving bowl and add the oil, stirring well. Pour in the boiling water and add the bread. Mix all together well until smooth.

CAROL WRIGHT
PORTUGUESE FOOD

Auvergne Bread and Cheese Soup

Soupe d'Auvergne au Fromage, Mitonnée

At the turn of the century, a French culinary magazine published this reminiscence by A. Colombié, a famous chef, of the Christmas soup his mother used to make during his childhood in the rugged Auvergne. Preserved goose (confit d'oie) is a speciality of the region. Cantal cheese is a hard, strong-flavored yellow cheese. If it is unavailable, a sharp, mature Cheddar or a hard Gouda may be substituted.

	To serve 6	
2 to 2½ lb.	cabbage, trimmed, halved, cored and cut into 2-inch [5-cm.] pieces	1 kg.
1½ quarts	water	1½ liters
	salt	
1	garlic clove	1
¼	preserved goose, with some of its fat clinging to it	¼
	thinly sliced dark bread	
5 oz.	Cantal or white Cheshire cheese, thinly sliced	150 g.

Generally, the finest cabbage was left in the garden for the Christmas soup, and a marked, prime pot of preserved goose was carefully put aside. The sops, or slices of bread, were taken from the familiar round whole-meal loaf and put on the tilted wrought-iron grill to be toasted in front of the fire.

The cabbage, water, salt, garlic and the preserved goose were put together in the soup pot, which was hung over the fire. When it came to a boil, Mother let the soup boil for 30 to 40 minutes while she toasted the bread and cut the cheese; she layered toasted bread and the cheese in the brown earthenware soup tureen, interspersed with ladles of cabbage. She poured in the liquid, setting the piece of goose aside to eat cold, covered the tureen and put it on the glowing cinders at the side of the fire so that it would simmer very gently until we returned from midnight Mass.

The result was a sort of cream that formed strand after strand, and how happy I was to see these strands stretch from the plate to my mouth. A happy age and how little it took to delight children in those days!

MME. JEANNE SAVARIN (EDITOR)
LA CUISINE DES FAMILLES

Bread and Cheese Soup

La Soupe au Fromage et au Pain Bis

Pain bis is a large round loaf of peasant-style bread, usually made from a mixture of unbleached white, whole-meal and rye flours, leavened with a sourdough sponge as described in the preface to the bread recipe on page 165. For this soup, cut a large wedge from the round loaf and slice it thinly. The Cantal cheese called for is a hard, strong-flavored yellow cheese. If it is unavailable, a sharp, mature Cheddar or a hard Gouda may be substituted.

	To serve 4 to 6	
24	thin slices stale or dry *pain bis,* or other firm-textured, whole-wheat bread	24
2 cups	grated Cantal cheese	½ liter
6	onions, sliced	6
3	garlic cloves, sliced	3
2 tbsp.	butter	30 ml.
	salt	
1 quart	water	1 liter

In a large saucepan, sauté the onions and garlic in the butter. Season with a little salt, then pour in the water and bring to a boil. Reduce the heat and let this onion bouillon simmer, uncovered, while you prepare the soup tureen.

Warm an ovenproof tureen (preferably of the bulbous shape used in Auvergne), and cover the bottom of the tureen with a layer of bread slices. Cover the bread with grated cheese. Repeat, alternating layers of bread and cheese, until both are used up and the tureen is full.

Pour the onion bouillon into the tureen, and put the tureen—uncovered—into a preheated 350° F. [180° C.] oven for 45 minutes to 1 hour. The soup should be thick enough for a spoon to stand upright in the middle, and there should be a golden crust on top.

SUZANNE ROBAGLIA
MARGARIDOU

Italian Bread Soup

Zuppa Mitunà

To vary this recipe, 5 ounces [150 g.] of Fontina or other soft Italian cheese may be sliced thinly and placed on top of each layer of the bread.

	To serve 6	
10 to 12	thin slices stale homemade bread, (recipe, page 165)	10 to 12
2	garlic cloves, halved	2
2 quarts	chicken or beef broth, heated	2 liters
2 tbsp.	finely chopped fresh parsley	30 ml.

Place the bread on a baking sheet and bake it in a preheated 350° F. [180° C.] oven until thoroughly dried—about 10 minutes. Rub the slices with the cut sides of the garlic cloves. Place the bread in an ovenproof tureen, and pour in the hot broth a little at a time so that it is absorbed by the bread.

Put the tureen in a preheated 425° F. [220° C.] oven, and let the surface of the soup brown for 10 to 15 minutes. Sprinkle the parsley over the soup just before serving.

LAURA GRAS PORTINARI
CUCINA E VINI DEL PIEMONTE E DELLA VALLE D'AOSTA

Black-Bread Soup, Franconian-Style

Brotsuppe

This soup has several variations. Two chopped, pared apples may be sautéed with the onion, and a little grated lemon peel added to the broth. The leftover gravy may be replaced by sour cream. Five minutes before serving, sliced bratwurst may be added to the soup.

	To serve 6 to 8	
6	slices slightly stale, dark rye bread, cubed	6
2 quarts	beef broth or water, heated to boiling	2 liters
1	medium-sized onion, chopped	1
1 to 2 tbsp.	meat drippings	15 to 30 ml.
2 to 3 tbsp.	leftover meat gravy (preferably pork gravy)	30 to 45 ml.
	salt (optional)	

Cover the bread cubes with the boiling broth or water and let stand until the bread is soft, about 10 minutes. Meanwhile, in a saucepan, sauté the onion in the meat drippings until it is soft and yellow. Add the bread and broth, and simmer for 30 minutes. If water is used, add salt to taste. Stir in the gravy and serve.

BETTY WASON
THE ART OF GERMAN COOKING

Fisherman's Soup

Soupe du Pêcheur

This is not a fish soup, but a special onion soup obtained by the author from a fisherman friend.

	To serve 4	
4	medium-sized onions, thinly sliced	4
½ lb.	homemade bread (recipe, page 165), sliced ½ inch [1 cm.] thick	¼ kg.
7 tbsp.	butter	105 ml.
1¼ cups	grated Gruyère cheese	300 ml.
3 tbsp.	puréed tomato	45 ml.
about 1 quart	boiling water	about 1 liter
	salt	

Toast the slices of bread. Leave them to get quite cold, then spread them with 6 tablespoons [90 ml.] of the butter. Cover each slice with a generous coating of grated cheese. (The layers of butter and cheese together must be the same thickness as the slices of bread.) Sauté the onions in the remaining butter until they are golden brown.

Arrange a layer of the bread slices spread with butter and cheese at the bottom of a large fireproof earthenware casserole, and sprinkle with a third of the onions. Make another layer of bread and onions, and sprinkle with 2 tablespoons [30 ml.] of the puréed tomato. Layer the remaining bread and onions, and add the remaining tomato. Cover the top with a coating of grated cheese. Since the bread swells considerably during cooking, it is important that the casserole be no more than two thirds full.

Take a funnel and push the stem into the casserole so that it touches the base. Pour boiling water slowly through the funnel until the contents of the casserole just begin to float upwards. Salt should be added to the water unless the cheese is very salty. Place the casserole on top of the stove, uncovered, and let it simmer over low heat for 30 minutes. Add enough additional boiling water at the end of this time to keep the bread from drying out.

Put the casserole, uncovered, into a preheated 325° F. [160° C.] oven for 1 hour, adding more water and more salt during the cooking if necessary. The soup is cooked when the cheese topping forms a nicely golden, rather crisp crust. By this time the interior will have been reduced to a purée. Serve each guest a portion of the smooth, thick interior and a section of the crisp crust.

B. RENAUDET
LES SECRETS DE LA BONNE TABLE

Onion Soup

Soupe à l'Oignon

Instead of pouring the soup over the bread, you may float the bread slices topped with the cheese on the soup and melt the cheese under the broiler.

	To serve 4	
2 or 3	large onions, finely chopped	2 or 3
2 tbsp.	butter	30 ml.
2 tsp.	flour	10 ml.
1 quart	hot water	1 liter
4	slices bread, cut from a large, round loaf	4
⅓ cup	freshly grated Gruyère or Parmesan cheese (optional)	75 ml.

Melt the butter in a saucepan, and sauté the onions until they are lightly colored. Stir in the flour, and continue to cook until the onion mixture has turned as brown as it can become without burning. Add the water, cover the pan and simmer the soup for 30 minutes. Put the slices of bread into a warmed soup tureen. If you are using cheese as well, alternate layers of bread with layers of cheese. Season the soup with salt, pour it into the tureen and serve.

JULES BRETEUIL
LE CUISINIER EUROPÉEN

Onion and Bread Soup

The English cookery writer, Hannah Glasse, published this recipe in the 1747 volume she signed only "By a Lady."

	To serve 4 to 6	
10 to 12	medium-sized onions, chopped	10 to 12
16 tbsp.	butter	240 ml.
2 tbsp.	flour	30 ml.
1 to 1½ quarts	water, heated to boiling	1 to 1½ liters
4	slices stale bread, cut into small pieces	4
	salt	
2	egg yolks	2
2 tsp.	vinegar	10 ml.

Take the butter, put it into a stewpan on the heat, let it all melt and boil it till it has done making any noise; then have ready the onions, throw them into the butter and let them fry for 15 minutes. Shake in the flour and stir the onions round; shake your pan and let them do a few minutes longer. Pour in the boiling water, stir round, take the bread and throw it in. Season with salt to your taste. Let it boil for 10 minutes, stirring it often; then take it off the heat and have ready the

egg yolks beaten with the vinegar; mix some of the soup with them, then stir this into your soup and mix it well and pour it into your dish. This is a delicious dish.

THE ART OF COOKERY MADE PLAIN AND EASY

Soup with Eggs

La Zuppa Pavese

	To serve 2	
4	eggs	4
8	thin slices bread, buttered	8
⅓ cup	freshly grated Parmesan cheese	75 ml.
2 cups	boiling stock	½ liter
	freshly ground white pepper	

Sprinkle the bread with the cheese and place the slices in individual ovenproof ramekins or bowls. Pour in the stock and gently break the eggs into the ramekins, taking care to keep the yolks whole. Season with a dash of pepper and put into a hot oven, preheated to 450° F. [230° C.], for 10 minutes or long enough to set the eggs. Serve very hot, accompanied by additional grated cheese.

GIANNI BRERA AND LUIGI VERONELLI
LA PACCIADA

Cold Soups

Yogurt Soup

Tarator: Soupe de Yaourt à la Bulgare

	To serve 6	
1½ quarts	plain yogurt	1½ liters
2	medium-sized cucumbers (about 1 lb. [½ kg.]), peeled, halved, seeded and cut into small dice	2
1½ cups	shelled walnuts, pounded in a mortar	375 ml.
½ cup	olive oil	125 ml.
1 tbsp.	finely cut fresh dill	15 ml.
1	garlic clove, crushed	1
	salt	

Put the yogurt into a chilled soup tureen and stir in all the other ingredients. If the soup is not sufficiently chilled, add a few ice cubes just before serving.

LES PETITS PLATS ET LES GRANDS

Cold Yogurt and Cucumber Soup

Cacik

To serve 2 to 4

2 cups	plain yogurt	½ liter
1	medium-sized cucumber, peeled, halved, seeded and grated (about 1 cup [¼ liter])	1
2 tsp.	white vinegar	10 ml.
1 tsp.	olive oil	5 ml.
2 tsp.	finely cut fresh mint leaves or 1 tsp. [5 ml.] dried mint	10 ml.
½ tsp.	finely cut fresh dill or ¼ tsp. [1 ml.] dried dill weed	2 ml.
1 tsp.	salt	5 ml.

In a deep bowl, stir the yogurt with a wire whisk or large spoon until it is completely smooth. Gently but thoroughly beat in the grated cucumber, vinegar, olive oil, mint, dill and salt. Do not overbeat. Taste for seasoning, adding more salt if necessary, and refrigerate the soup for at least 2 hours, or until it is thoroughly chilled.

Serve the soup in chilled individual soup plates, and add an ice cube to each portion if you like.

FOODS OF THE WORLD/MIDDLE EASTERN COOKING

Cucumber and Cream Soup

Minestra di Cetriolo alla Crema

To serve 2 to 4

1	large cucumber, peeled, seeded and cut into pieces	1
1	large or 2 small dill pickles, cut into pieces	1
3 tbsp.	fresh lemon juice	45 ml.
3 tbsp.	grated onion	45 ml.
¾ cup	heavy cream	175 ml.
	salt and pepper	
1 tbsp.	finely cut dill	15 ml.
	diced cucumber	

Put the cucumber pieces in a blender and blend with the dill pickle, lemon juice and onion. When the mixture is smooth, pour into a chilled tureen and stir in the cream, salt and pepper and dill. Garnish with a little diced cucumber and serve chilled.

JANET ROSS AND MICHAEL WATERFIELD
LEAVES FROM OUR TUSCAN KITCHEN

Avocado Bisque

To serve 2 to 4

1	large, ripe avocado, peeled and pitted	1
½ cup	fresh lemon juice	125 ml.
	salt and freshly ground pepper	
1 ½ cups	rich chicken broth	375 ml.
¾ cup	heavy cream	175 ml.

Cut the avocado into large chunks and immediately dip them into the lemon juice. With a fork, mash the avocado into the lemon juice—not mashing too finely, as you want some of the pulp to remain in nuggets about the size of peas. Season with salt and pepper. Turn the mixture into a saucepan, preferably one with an enamel lining, and place over low heat. Slowly add the chicken broth, stirring to blend, then add the cream. Bring the soup just to a boil and simmer for 2 minutes. Serve hot, or chill in the refrigerator for several hours before serving.

DORIS TOBIAS AND MARY MERRIS
THE GOLDEN LEMON

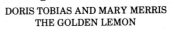

Avocado Summer Soup

To serve 4 to 6

1	large ripe avocado, peeled, pitted and sieved (about 1 cup [¼ liter])	1
1 cup	chicken stock, heated to the boiling point	¼ liter
1 cup	heavy cream	¼ liter
½ cup	dry white wine	125 ml.
2 tsp.	fresh lemon juice	10 ml.
	salt and white pepper	
	cayenne pepper	
	fresh chives or dill	

Add the hot chicken stock to the sieved avocado. Mix well and strain through a sieve, then combine with the cream and the white wine. Add the lemon juice, salt and white pepper, and a tiny speck of cayenne. Cover the container and chill well. Chop the chives or dill and sprinkle them over the soup just before serving.

HELEN EVANS BROWN
HELEN BROWN'S WEST COAST COOKBOOK

Greek Eggplant Soup

To serve 8

1 lb.	eggplant, peeled and cut into 1-inch [2½-cm.] cubes	1 kg.
6 tbsp.	olive oil	90 ml.
1	green pepper, halved, seeded, deribbed and cut into chunks	1
½ cup	water	125 ml.
	salt and pepper	
1	garlic clove, sliced	1
1 tsp.	finely cut fresh mint	5 ml.
3 cups	plain yogurt	¾ liter
½ cup	milk (optional)	125 ml.
2 tbsp.	finely cut fresh chives	30 ml.

Heat the olive oil in a pan, add the eggplant and green pepper, mixing to coat all the pieces thoroughly. Cover and simmer for a minute. Add the water, a little salt and pepper and the garlic, and simmer for 15 minutes.

Purée the cooked vegetables and their liquid, and the mint leaves and yogurt in a blender (or pass the vegetables and liquid through a food mill into a bowl and stir in the mint and yogurt). If you prefer a thinner soup, add the milk. Chill the soup for at least 4 hours. Sprinkle each serving of cold soup with chives.

CAROL CUTLER
THE SIX-MINUTE SOUFFLÉ AND OTHER CULINARY DELIGHTS

Vichyssoise

To serve 4 to 6

2	large leeks, white parts only, chopped (about 1 cup [¼ liter])	2
3 cups	thinly sliced potatoes	¾ liter
4 tbsp.	butter	60 ml.
1	small onion, chopped (about ⅓ cup [75 ml.])	1
1	small rib celery, finely chopped (about ¼ cup [50 ml.])	1
1 quart	chicken broth	1 liter
	salt	
	white pepper	
1 cup	heavy cream	¼ liter
2 tbsp.	finely cut fresh chives	30 ml.

Melt the butter very slowly in a large, heavy skillet. As soon as the butter melts, mix into it the chopped onion, celery and leeks. Cook slowly for about 20 minutes, stirring every now and then and adjusting the heat so that the vegetables barely color. When they are soft and transluscent, use a rubber spatula to scrape the contents of the skillet into a 3- or 4-quart [3- or 4-liter] saucepan. Pour in the broth, add the sliced potatoes and bring it all to a boil. Reduce the heat at once, partially cover the pan and simmer until the potatoes are soft and crumble easily when pierced with a fork.

Purée the soup in a food mill, or use a fairly coarse sieve and the back of a large spoon. Force the soup through the mill or sieve into a large mixing bowl. Do not use a blender; a blender, no matter how carefully controlled will reduce the soup to an irretrievable, bland cream. Stir in the seasonings—the salt liberally and the white pepper discreetly; use much more of the seasonings than you would ordinarily, for the cold will dull the soup's flavor later.

Cover the bowl and refrigerate the soup until it is thoroughly chilled. Before serving the soup in chilled cups, stir into it the cream, and taste again for salt. If the vichyssoise seems too thick for your taste, thin it with more cream, heavy or light, and adjust the seasonings accordingly. Garnish each cup with a teaspoon [5 ml.] of chives.

MICHAEL FIELD
MICHAEL FIELD'S COOKING SCHOOL

White Garlic Soup with Grapes

Sopa de Ajo Blanco con Uvas

The original version of this Malagan soup is made with fresh almonds, that is, not green almonds but simply ripe ones recently removed from their shells and not kept for months. They are skinned, dried slightly in the oven and ground down in a mortar. Powdered almonds can be used but something of the flavor is lost.

To serve 3 or 4

5	garlic cloves	5
1 lb.	white grapes, peeled, halved and seeded	½ kg.
2 tbsp.	ground almonds or 30 fresh almonds	30 ml.
⅓ cup	brown-bread crumbs	75 ml.
	salt	
2 tbsp.	olive oil	30 ml.
1 tbsp.	vinegar	15 ml.
2 cups	water	½ liter
6	ice cubes	6

Pound the garlic, almonds, bread crumbs and salt together in a mortar. Add the oil gradually, mixing well, then add the vinegar. Put this mixture into a soup tureen and pour in the water. Add the grapes and the ice and leave in a cool place for about 30 minutes before serving.

ELIZABETH CASS
SPANISH COOKING

Cream of California Herbs

Any harmonious herbs will do for this soup; just be careful not to overdo them.

	To serve 6	
2 cups	chopped lettuce leaves	½ liter
¼ cup	finely chopped fresh parsley or chervil	50 ml.
¼ cup	finely chopped shallots or scallions	50 ml.
1 tsp.	finely chopped tarragon	5 ml.
1 tsp.	finely chopped rosemary	5 ml.
1 quart	chicken stock	1 liter
	salt and pepper	
3 or 4	spinach leaves (optional)	3 or 4
1 cup	light cream	¼ liter
3	egg yolks, lightly beaten	3
	finely cut fresh chives	

Simmer the lettuce in the stock for 10 minutes, along with the parsley or chervil, shallots or scallions, and the tarragon and rosemary, then press through a strainer. If the color is not good, add a few leaves of spinach, ground to a paste in a mortar. Correct the seasoning, then bind with the cream and the egg yolks. Serve hot or cold, topped with the chives.

HELEN EVANS BROWN
HELEN BROWN'S WEST COAST COOKBOOK

Savory Summer Soup

	To serve 6 to 8	
4	medium-sized zucchini, sliced	4
1	green pepper, seeded, deribbed and sliced	1
3	medium-sized onions, sliced	3
2	large garlic cloves, sliced	2
4 tbsp.	butter	60 ml.
	salt and white pepper	
2 tbsp.	chopped fresh thyme	30 ml.
6 cups	chicken broth	1½ liters
1 cup	heavy cream	¼ liter
	finely cut fresh chives or chopped fresh parsley	

In a heavy pot, sauté three of the sliced zucchini with the green pepper, onions and garlic in 3 tablespoons [45 ml.] of the butter over very low heat. Cook, stirring often, for about 10 minutes, or until the vegetables are tender but have not browned. Add the thyme, and salt and pepper to taste. Stir in

the chicken broth and simmer, uncovered, for 15 minutes.

Meanwhile, sauté the remaining zucchini in 1 tablespoon [15 ml.] of butter until it is barely tender and still bright green. This should take about 3 minutes—stir, and watch closely that it doesn't overcook and become mushy. Immediately turn the sliced zucchini out onto a plate to cool quickly. Reserve.

Cool the vegetable-and-broth mixture slightly and purée it in a blender or food mill. In a bowl, stir the cream into the purée and add the sliced sautéed zucchini. Adjust the seasoning—the soup should be rather highly seasoned as chilling vitiates flavors. Chill for 24 hours and serve the soup with a scattering of fresh chives or parsley.

MIRIAM UNGERER
GOOD CHEAP FOOD

Potato Soup with Tomato and Basil

	To serve 4	
4	medium-sized potatoes, diced	4
3	large tomatoes	3
	basil leaves	
2	carrots, thinly sliced	2
	sugar	
	salt and pepper	
2 cups	chicken broth	½ liter
1	large onion, sliced	1
1	garlic clove, crushed	1
1 cup	heavy cream	¼ liter

To make a tomato purée, stem the tomatoes, cut them in half crosswise, squeeze out most of the seeds and reserve the juice. Finely chop the tomatoes and place them in a pan with the carrots, sugar and seasoning. Simmer until the carrots are soft, adding a bit of reserved tomato juice if necessary to prevent sticking. Pass through a strainer and chill.

Put the broth, potatoes, onion and garlic in a saucepan. Simmer for about 15 minutes, until the potatoes are tender and the onion soft. Purée the mixture in a blender or food processor. Add the cream, season to taste, and chill the soup.

When ready to serve, swirl the tomato purée into the chilled potato soup. Sprinkle with finely torn basil leaves.

JUDITH OLNEY
SUMMER FOOD

Andalusian Gazpacho

To serve 4

1	garlic clove	1
2 to 3 tbsp.	olive oil	30 to 45 ml.
5	tomatoes, sliced	5
1	onion, sliced	1
½ tsp.	salt	2 ml.
¼ tsp.	pepper	1 ml.
¼ tsp.	paprika	1 ml.
1½ tbsp.	vinegar	22 ml.
1 cup	cold water	¼ liter
1	medium-sized cucumber, peeled, seeded and chopped (about 1½ cups [375 ml.])	1
4	slices firm-textured white bread	4
	ice cubes	

Pound the garlic clove with a wooden spoon in a salad bowl. Stir in the oil to form a paste. Add the tomatoes, onion, salt, pepper, paprika, vinegar and water. Leave for half an hour. Ten minutes before serving, add the chopped cucumber, slices of bread, more water if necessary and the ice cubes.

MARINA PEREYRA DE AZNAR AND NINA FROUD
THE HOME BOOK OF SPANISH COOKERY

Yogurt Gazpacho

To serve 4

3 cups	plain yogurt	¾ liter
4	tomatoes, peeled, seeded and coarsely chopped	4
1 tbsp.	finely chopped green chilies	15 ml.
1	onion, finely chopped	1
¼ cup	chopped fresh parsley	50 ml.
	radish or cucumber slices	
	watercress sprigs	

Combine the tomatoes, chilies, onion, parsley and salt in a large bowl. Chill the mixture in the refrigerator for at least 2 hours. Stir in the yogurt just before serving. Garnish each of the servings with the radish or cucumber slices and a sprig of watercress.

JEAN HEWITT
THE NEW YORK TIMES NATURAL FOODS COOKBOOK

Gazpacho

To serve 6

4	medium-sized ripe tomatoes, peeled and chopped	4
1 or 2	garlic cloves	1 or 2
	salt	
1 cup	soft bread cubes with the crusts removed	¼ liter
¼ cup	wine vinegar	50 ml.
1	medium-sized cucumber, peeled, halved, seeded and chopped	1
1	large green pepper, halved, seeded, deribbed and diced	1
¼ cup	olive or vegetable oil	50 ml.
2 cups	cold water	½ liter
2 cups	tomato juice	½ liter
	pepper	
	chopped scallions (optional)	
	croutons (optional) *(recipe, page 166)*	

Pound the garlic and a little salt in a mortar with a pestle or in a bowl with a wooden spoon. Add the bread cubes and vinegar and work into a paste. Add three of the tomatoes and half of the cucumber and mash as fine as possible or whirl in a blender. Mix the purée with the remaining chopped tomato and cucumber and the diced pepper. Chill. Before serving, stir in the oil, water and tomato juice. Add more vinegar if desired. Season to taste with salt and pepper. Serve garnished with scallions or croutons, if desired.

KAY SHAW NELSON
SOUPS AND STEWS

Iced Soup for a Very Hot Day

Soupe Glacée pour Grosse Chaleur

This recipe is a creation of Gérard Vié, chef at Les Trois Marches in Versailles.

To serve 1

2	tomatoes	2
	salt and freshly ground pepper	
1 tbsp.	fresh lemon juice	15 ml.
1 tbsp.	olive oil	15 ml.
1 tsp.	coarsely chopped fines herbes	5 ml.

Put the tomatoes in a blender with the salt and pepper, lemon juice and oil. Blend at high speed for 2 minutes. Serve the soup chilled, with the herbs sprinkled on top.

LA CUISINE NATURELLE À L'HUILE D'OLIVE

Hot-and-cold Onion Soup

To serve 6

3	large onions, sliced	3
2 tbsp.	butter	30 ml.
1 tsp.	ground cumin	5 ml.
½ tsp.	ground turmeric or saffron	2 ml.
½ tsp.	white pepper	2 ml.
1	cardamom pod, crushed	1
1	large potato, diced	1
1 quart	boiling chicken broth	1 liter
1 cup	light cream or milk	¼ liter
	salt	
	finely cut fresh chives or parsley	

Melt the butter in an enamel-lined iron kettle. Add the cumin, the turmeric or saffron, white pepper and cardamom. Stir and cook gently for 5 minutes. Add the sliced onions, stir them around, cover, and cook until they are quite limp but not browned. Swirl the potato into the onions and spices and pour in the hot chicken broth. Simmer, covered, for 20 minutes. Cool the soup for about 10 minutes, then purée it in a blender. Pour the soup into a nonmetallic container, blend in the cream or milk, and taste for salt. Chill the soup overnight if possible, or for at least 4 hours. Serve cold and sprinkle with fresh chives or parsley.

MIRIAM UNGERER
GOOD CHEAP FOOD

Chilled Green Split-Pea Soup with Mint

To serve 6 to 8

2 cups	dried green split peas	½ liter
1 cup	finely cut fresh mint leaves, well packed	¼ liter
6 cups	chicken broth	1½ quarts
1 cup	finely chopped onions	¼ liter
½ cup	finely chopped celery	125 ml.
1	small bay leaf	1
	salt and white pepper	
½ to 1 cup	heavy cream	125 to 250 ml.
6 to 8	sprigs mint	6 to 8

In a heavy 4- to 5-quart [4- to 5-liter] casserole, combine the peas, finely cut mint leaves, broth, onions, celery, bay leaf and a little salt and pepper. Bring to a turbulent boil over

high heat, partially cover the pot and reduce the heat. Simmer, stirring occasionally, for anywhere from 1 to 1½ hours, or until the peas have disintegrated almost completely and can be mashed easily against the sides of the pot with a fork.

Remove the bay leaf and purée the soup through the finest disk of a food mill set over a bowl, or force the soup through a fine strainer with the back of a spoon. Stir in ½ cup [125 ml.] of the cream, taste for seasoning, and let the soup cool to room temperature. Then cover the bowl with plastic wrap and refrigerate until the soup is thoroughly chilled.

The soup will thicken considerably as it chills. Thin it with as much of the remaining cream (or even more) as you think it needs—it should not be too dense. Taste for seasoning again, since chilling will have dulled the soup's flavor, and serve in chilled soup plates. Garnish each serving with a sprig of mint.

MICHAEL FIELD
ALL MANNER OF FOOD

Chilled Pea Soup

To serve 6

5 cups	freshly shelled peas (about 5 lb. [2½ kg.] unshelled)	1¼ liters
½ cup	chopped onion	125 ml.
1 tbsp.	butter	15 ml.
1¼ cups	beef broth	300 ml.
1 quart	water	1 liter
1 tsp.	chervil	5 ml.
1½ tsp.	salt	7 ml.
	freshly ground pepper	
	fresh mint	
½ cup	chilled dry white wine	125 ml.
2 cups	light cream	½ liter

Sauté the onion in the butter in a large saucepan until the onion is soft. Add the peas, broth, water, chervil, salt and a little pepper and bring to a boil. Reduce the heat and simmer uncovered until the peas are very soft—after about 30 minutes. Purée the soup in a blender or food mill. Strain the soup, cut up six mint leaves and stir them in. Chill the soup for at least 3 hours. Before serving, stir in the wine and cream and correct the seasoning. Garnish with more mint.

ELEANOR GRAVES
GREAT DINNERS FROM LIFE

Iced Soup, Simplified

Soupe à la Glace Simplifiée

The author of this recipe suggests that cantaloupe can be substituted for the cucumber. To extract the cucumber (or cantaloupe) juice, grate or grind about 2 cups [½ liter] of peeled and seeded flesh, salt the flesh lightly and let it drain for 30 to 45 minutes in a cheesecloth-lined colander. Squeeze and twist the cheesecloth to extract all the liquid. Buttermilk may be substituted for the sour milk.

To serve 4

1 cup	chopped sorrel leaves	¼ liter
1 tbsp.	butter	15 ml.
1 quart	sour milk	1 liter
½ cup	cucumber juice	125 ml.
3 tbsp.	chopped fennel or dill leaves	45 ml.
2 tbsp.	finely cut fresh chives	30 ml.
1	small cucumber, peeled, seeded and thinly sliced	1
2	hard-boiled eggs, sliced	2
	salt	
6 to 8	ice cubes, crushed in a cloth	6 to 8

Sauté the sorrel in the butter over low heat for 3 to 4 minutes. Put it into a soup tureen and mix with the milk, cucumber juice, fennel, chives and sliced cucumber and eggs. Salt to taste. Just before serving, stir in the crushed ice.

L. E. AUDOT
LA CUISINIÈRE DE LA CAMPAGNE ET DE LA VILLE

Cold Cherry and Rice Soup

To be used safely, cherry pits must be immersed in water and cooked as soon as they are removed from the fruit.

To serve 6

½ lb.	sour cherries, pitted and the pits reserved	¼ kg.
¼ cup	raw, unprocessed rice	50 ml.
1½ quarts	water	1½ liters
2½ tbsp.	sugar	37 ml.
5 tbsp.	heavy cream	75 ml.

Put the cherry pits in the water, bring to a boil, and boil for 10 minutes. Strain. Put the rice and sugar into the cherry-pit stock and simmer for 30 minutes or until the rice is very soft. Five minutes before the end of cooking, add the cherries. Cool the soup and serve it very cold with a spoonful of cream on each serving.

SOFKA SKIPWITH
EAT RUSSIAN

Hungarian Cherry Soup

Meggy leves

Morellos are sour cherries; they may be either light red or dark, almost black, red. Any other sour cherries may be substituted. To be used safely, cherry pits and stems must be combined with the other ingredients and cooked as soon as they are removed from the cherries.

This recipe comes from the Gay Hussar restaurant in London's Soho district.

To serve 6

1 lb.	morello cherries, pitted, pits and stems reserved	½ kg.
3 cups	Riesling or other dry white wine	¾ liter
¼ cup	sugar	50 ml.
1 inch	stick cinnamon	2½ cm.
2	lemons, 1 peeled and the peel reserved, both squeezed	2
½ cup	brandy (optional)	125 ml.
2 cups	sour cream	½ liter

Crush a few of the cherry pits, then put all the pits and stems into a pan with the wine, sugar, cinnamon stick and the juice of both lemons and peel of one. Simmer for 5 minutes, then leave to steep for at least 15 minutes. Strain, bring back to a boil and add the cherries and their juice. Remove from the heat immediately and allow to cool to tepid. Stir in the brandy. Put the sour cream into a tureen, then gradually pour in the cherry soup, mixing thoroughly. Serve chilled.

JANE GRIGSON
OBSERVER MAGAZINE

Chilled Cantaloupe Soup

To serve 4

1	3-lb. [1½-kg.] ripe cantaloupe, halved, seeded and the flesh scooped out	1
¼ cup	sugar	50 ml.
½ cup	dry sherry	125 ml.
1 tbsp.	fresh lime juice	15 ml.

In a blender, combine the cantaloupe flesh with the rest of the ingredients. Blend until smooth. Refrigerate, covered, until very cold.

THE WOMEN'S COMMITTEE OF THE WALTERS ART GALLERY
PRIVATE COLLECTIONS: A CULINARY TREASURE

Cold Pear and Watercress Soup

To serve 4

8	ripe pears, peeled, quartered and cored, skins and cores reserved	8
2	bunches watercress, leaves and stems chopped, with a few leaves kept whole for garnishing	2
1 quart	chicken broth	1 liter
2 to 3 tbsp.	fresh lemon juice	30 to 45 ml.
	salt and pepper	
¾ cup	heavy cream	175 ml.

As you prepare the pear quarters, plunge them into half of the chicken broth to prevent them from discoloring. Boil the pear skins and cores in the remaining broth for a few minutes to extract their maximum flavor, then strain the broth into another saucepan. Add the chopped watercress to the strained broth, simmer for 10 minutes, then purée the mixture in a blender or food mill.

Purée the pear quarters with their broth through a sieve or in a blender, and combine the two purées. (More chicken broth may be stirred in at this point to bring the purée to the desired consistency.) Add a little lemon juice and mill in salt and pepper to taste. Chill the mixture thoroughly.

Plunge the remaining watercress leaves into boiling water to wilt them and brighten their green hue, then quickly refresh them in cold water. To serve, whisk heavy cream to taste into the soup, check the seasoning, pour into a tureen, and float the watercress leaves on top.

PETITS PROPOS CULINAIRES

Chilled Lemon Soup with Mint

To serve 6

2 tbsp.	fresh lemon juice	30 ml.
1 tbsp.	grated fresh lemon peel	15 ml.
2 tbsp.	fresh mint, finely cut with scissors	30 ml.
1 quart	chicken broth	1 liter
2 tbsp.	quick-cooking tapioca	30 ml.
3	egg yolks	3
½ tsp.	salt	2 ml.
⅛ tsp.	cayenne pepper	½ ml.
1 cup	heavy cream	¼ liter

In a heavy, 2-quart [2-liter] saucepan, bring the broth to a boil and slowly sprinkle in the tapioca. Cook rapidly for 2 or 3 minutes, then reduce the heat and simmer, partially covered, for about 5 minutes.

Meanwhile, with a wire whisk or fork, beat together in a small bowl the egg yolks and the lemon juice, grated peel, salt and cayenne pepper. When they are just about combined, mix in the heavy cream. Now, spoonful by spoonful, add the simmering stock to the cream mixture, stirring well after each addition. After about the tenth spoonful, pour the now-heated cream back into the saucepan all at once, stirring constantly.

Place the saucepan over medium heat and, stirring deeply and around the sides of the pan with a wooden spoon, cook the soup until it begins to thicken. Still stirring, lift the pan away from the heat to cool it a bit, then return it to the heat once more. Continue to cook, lifting the pan from time to time, until the soup has thickened enough to coat the back of the spoon lightly. Do not worry if the soup seems thin; it will thicken more as it cools. Pour it at once into a cold bowl, preferably stainless steel, and allow the soup to come to room temperature before covering it tightly with plastic wrap or waxed paper. Refrigerate the soup until icy cold. Garnish each serving with fresh mint.

MICHAEL FIELD
MICHAEL FIELD'S COOKING SCHOOL

Senegalese Soup

The best curry powders to use for a spicy effect are those made in, or in the style of, Madras, India.

To serve 6

2 tbsp.	chopped onion	30 ml.
2 tbsp.	butter	30 ml.
2 tsp.	curry powder	10 ml.
1 tbsp.	flour	15 ml.
3½ cups	chicken stock	875 ml.
4	egg yolks	4
2 cups	heavy cream	½ liter
¼ cup	finely diced, cooked white meat of chicken, or peeled, cooked shrimp	50 ml.

Sauté the onion in the butter until soft, but do not brown it. Add the curry powder and flour and cook slowly for 5 minutes. Add the stock and bring to a boil, stirring until smooth. Beat a few spoonfuls of soup into the egg yolks and return the yolk mixture to the soup, stirring constantly. Cook for 1 minute without allowing the soup to boil. Pour the soup through a sieve into a tureen and chill thoroughly. Add the cream and chicken (or shrimp). Serve very cold in bowls surrounded by crushed ice.

HELEN CORBITT
HELEN CORBITT'S COOKBOOK

Cold Fish Soup

Botvinya

Dark beer, ale or stout may be substituted for kvas, the Russian rye beer included in this recipe. In place of the sorrel and spinach you may use 1½ pounds [¾ kg.] of young beet greens or chard leaves, parboiled for 10 minutes and very finely chopped. If you wish to have shrimp or crayfish tails to garnish the soup, as described on pages 68-69, use about two dozen of the shellfish. But be sure to purchase them raw and unshelled so that after cooking them, you can use the shells to enhance the flavor of the kvas.

To serve 12

2 to 2½ lb.	salmon, sea trout or firm-fleshed fish steaks or fillets	1 kg.
4 cups	sorrel leaves, stemmed, chopped and cooked in 1 tbsp. [15 ml.] butter until soft	1 liter
1 lb.	spinach, parboiled for 3 minutes, squeezed dry and very finely chopped	½ kg.
1	cucumber, peeled, halved, seeded and diced	1
4	scallions, chopped	4
2 tbsp.	finely cut fresh dill	30 ml.
3 tbsp.	chopped fresh parsley	45 ml.
	salt	
½ cup	dark molasses	125 ml.
	grated horseradish	
Kvas		
8	slices stale rye bread, dried out in a 325° F. [160° C.] oven and broken into pieces	8
2 quarts	boiling water	2 liters
¼ cup	dark molasses	50 ml.
2 tbsp.	compressed fresh yeast, or ½ tsp. [2 ml.] dry yeast	30 ml.
	raisins	

To make the *kvas*, put the rye bread into a bowl and pour in the boiling water. Cover the bowl immediately with a thick cloth and let the liquid cool until lukewarm. Strain the liquid into another bowl through a sieve lined with a clean cloth; do not squeeze the cloth. Add the molasses to the strained liquid, stirring well to dissolve the molasses. Dissolve the yeast to a thin paste with a bit of the liquid, and stir the mixture into the bowl. Cover, and let stand in a warm room for 12 hours. Strain the liquid again and bottle it, putting two raisins in each bottle. Cork or seal the bottles well

and store them in a cool place. The *kvas* will be ready for use in two days, and should be used within about two months.

To make the soup, poach the fish in salted water for about 10 minutes or until it flakes easily. Drain the fish, cool it, then remove any skin or bone and cut the flesh of the fish into bite-sized pieces. Refrigerate the fish until you are ready to serve the soup.

Put the sorrel and the spinach into a cold soup tureen and add the cucumber, scallions, dill, parsley, salt and molasses. Stir in 2 quarts [2 liters] of the *kvas*, and then chill the soup thoroughly.

At serving time, add the pieces of fish to the soup. Serve a bowl of grated horseradish separately.

ELENA MOLOKHOVETS
PODAROK MOLODÝM KHOZYAÍKAM

Cold Fish and Vegetable Soup

Chlodnik z Ryby

The redfish called for in this recipe is an ocean perch. Hamburg parsley root is a hardy parsley with a parsnip-shaped root. If unavailable, a small parsnip may be substituted.

This is a refreshing summer dish, but also a filling one. I have suggested using redfish, but almost any white fish with firm flesh will do. A section of cod or hake would be quite suitable. You will need enough to provide at least 1½ pounds [¾ kg.] of cleaned flesh.

To serve 6

1	whole redfish (2½ lb. [1 kg.]), cleaned	1
3	medium-sized carrots, coarsely grated	3
1	medium-sized turnip, coarsely grated	1
1	medium-sized onion, coarsely grated	1
1	large beet, coarsely grated	1
1	Hamburg parsley root, coarsely grated (optional)	1
1 quart	water	1 liter
	salt and pepper	
	sugar	
1	large cucumber, peeled, seeded and cut into strips	1
1 tbsp.	finely cut fresh chives	15 ml.
1 tbsp.	finely cut fresh dill	15 ml.
1 tbsp.	finely chopped fresh parsley	15 ml.
3 tbsp.	fresh lemon juice	45 ml.
3	hard-boiled eggs, quartered	3
½ cup	sour cream	125 ml.

Put the grated vegetables into a large saucepan with the water and cook over medium heat for 30 minutes. If you wish to have a clear broth, strain out the vegetables at this point. Add salt, pepper and sugar to taste, and put in the fish. Cook for another 20 minutes or so, covered, until the fish is cooked through. Take the pan off the heat, lift out the fish, let it cool, remove all of the skin and bones and break the flesh into fairly small pieces. Refrigerate the fish until you are ready to serve the soup. Chill the liquid, and then add the cucumber and the chopped herbs to the soup and season to taste with the lemon juice. Stir well.

Arrange some pieces of fish and two egg quarters in each soup plate. Bring the soup to the table in a tureen and ladle it over the fish. Let each person add a dollop of sour cream to his own portion.

ALAN DAVIDSON
NORTH ATLANTIC SEAFOOD

Chilled Consommé Madrilène

Consommé Glacé à la Madrilène

For a firmer consommé, you may want to add chopped chicken parts, particularly feet, to supplement the gelatin in the basic broth.

	To serve 8 to 10	
3 quarts	beef or chicken broth	3 liters
1½ lb.	lean ground beef chuck, finely chopped	¾ kg.
1	egg white	1
⅓ cup	finely diced carrot	75 ml.
1	large leek, white part only, finely diced	1
12 to 15	tomatoes, halved, seeded and chopped	12 to 15
3 tbsp.	puréed tomato (optional)	45 ml.
	cayenne pepper (optional)	

In a stockpot or deep saucepan, mix the broth with the ground beef, egg white, carrot, leek and tomatoes. Bring to a boil, stirring. Reduce the heat, partially cover and allow to simmer very slowly, undisturbed, for 1½ hours. Add the puréed tomato, if you are using it, at this point. Strain the consommé through a colander lined with a napkin, or several layers of cheesecloth, wrung out in cold water. Degrease the consommé thoroughly and season it with a little cayenne pepper, if liked.

Chill the consommé until lightly set and serve it in chilled porcelain cups.

PROSPER MONTAGNÉ
MON MENU

Full-Meal Soups

Ukrainian Borscht

Borscht Malorossiskii

This soup is traditionally served with a variety of garnishes: small, fried fresh pork sausages; the small meat pies called piroshki; and boiled buckwheat groats, or kasha. A bowl of sour cream also is passed as a side dish. To make the fermented beet liquid called for in the recipe, see the demonstration on page 84. Vinegar may be substituted, but much less is needed, since it is more pungent.

	To serve 6	
3 lb.	beef brisket or shank, or a mixture of beef and smoked ham	1½ kg.
2½ quarts	water	2½ liters
2	onions	2
1	bay leaf	1
	salt and pepper	
1	cabbage, halved, cored and coarsely chopped	1
about 2 cups	fermented beet liquid	about ½ liter
6	beets, washed but not peeled	6
1½ tbsp.	flour	22 ml.
	finely chopped fresh parsley	

Put the meat into a large pot with the water, onions, bay leaf, salt and pepper. Bring to a boil, skim, partially cover, reduce the heat to low and simmer for 2 to 3 hours.

Strain the stock, reserving the meat, and return the stock to a clean pot. Add the cabbage, and fermented beet liquid to taste. Simmer for 1 hour.

Meanwhile, bake 5 beets in a 350° F. [180° C.] oven for 2 to 3 hours or until soft; or boil the beets in water for the same length of time, then drain them. Peel and chop the beets, and mix them with the flour. Add the mixture to the simmering soup and return the soup to a boil. Correct the seasoning.

Grate the remaining beet and press out the juice. Cut the reserved meat into small pieces and add it to the soup to reheat it for 2 or 3 minutes.

Put the parsley into a warmed tureen, add the juice from the grated beet and pour in the soup.

Serve the borscht accompanied by a choice of garnishes.

ELENA MOLOKHOVETS
PODAROK MOLODÝM KHOZYAĬKAM

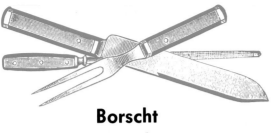

Borscht

Borisch

This is the authentic recipe for the borscht served at the court of Czar Nicholas II. As a modern variation, the vegetables with a short cooking time—onion, cabbage, leek—may be added to the soup 10 to 15 minutes before the beef is done. The parsley root may be added whole and removed before serving. The chipolata sausages called for are mildly seasoned pork sausages available at French food markets; any other mild pork sausages may be used in their place.

To serve 8

8 to 10	beets (about 2 lb. [1 kg.]), peeled	8 to 10
4 to 5	leeks (about 1 lb. [½ kg.])	4 to 5
1	celeriac	1
2	Hamburg parsley roots or 1 parsnip	2
1	onion	1
1	small Savoy cabbage	1
5 tbsp.	butter	75 ml.
2 quarts	pot-au-feu bouillon or veal stock	2 liters
½ cup	fermented beet liquid, or vinegar or fresh lemon juice	125 ml.
1	4- to 5-lb. [2- to 2½-kg.] duckling, roasted for 1 hour at 350° F. [180° C.]	1
2 to 2½ lb.	beef brisket	1 kg.
1	bouquet garni (including marjoram, bay leaf, whole clove)	1
	salt and pepper	
½ cup	sour cream	125 ml.
1 tbsp.	chopped fresh parsley	15 ml.
1 tbsp.	finely cut dill leaves	15 ml.
1 lb.	*chipolata* sausages, broiled and skinned	½ kg.

Reserve two of the beets, and cut the rest into julienne. Cut the leeks, celeriac, parsley roots or parsnip, onion and cabbage into julienne. Melt the butter in a large saucepan and sauté the vegetables until they are lightly colored. Stir in the bouillon and the fermented beet liquid; add the partly roasted duckling, the beef and the bouquet garni. Cover and simmer very gently.

Remove the duckling when done, after about 1 hour; continue to simmer the soup until the beef is done, after about

another 1½ hours. Remove the beef, remove and discard the bouquet garni, degrease the soup and season with salt and pepper. Grate the remaining beets and press out their juice; mix the juice with the sour cream and stir it into the soup with the parsley and dill.

Cut the duckling and the beef into serving pieces, and arrange on a warmed platter with the *chipolatas*. If necessary, reheat briefly in an oven at 350° F. [180° C.].

Pour a ladleful of the soup over the meats, and serve the rest of the soup separately from a tureen. Alternatively, the meats can be arranged in a deep dish and all the soup poured over them for serving.

MME. JEANNE SAVARIN (EDITOR)
LA CUISINE DES FAMILLES

Polish Borscht

Borshch Pol'skii

Instructions for making fermented beet juice are on page 84; a dash of vinegar may be substituted. The beets for this soup may be either baked or boiled; beets require 1 to 3 hours of baking or boiling time, depending on their age and size. Borscht is often served with buckwheat groats, meat dumplings or piroshki. For recipes, see pages 161 to 163.

To serve 6

5	beets, baked or boiled	5
3 tbsp.	fermented beet juice	45 ml.
1 to 2 cups	sour cream	¼ to ½ liter
	salt	
2 tbsp.	finely chopped fresh parsley	30 ml.
2 tbsp.	finely cut dill	30 ml.
Beef and ham broth		
2 to 3 lb.	beef brisket or chuck	1 to 1½ kg.
1 lb.	ham hock (optional)	½ kg.
1½ quarts	water	1½ liters
5 or 6	peppercorns	5 or 6
1 or 2	bay leaves	1 or 2
2	onions, chopped (optional)	2
2 oz.	dried mushrooms, preferably dried Polish mushrooms, soaked in warm water for 30 minutes and drained (optional)	50 g.

To make the broth, place all the broth ingredients in a large saucepan, bring to a boil and skim. Partly cover the pan and simmer the broth very slowly for 3 to 4 hours. Strain the broth, reserving the meats, and allow the broth to cool slightly. Skim off the fat.

Peel the baked or boiled beets and cut them into very fine strips. Put the strips into a saucepan and add the strained broth, the fermented beet liquid and the sour cream. Season with salt, parsley and dill. Bone and finely chop the reserved ham, if used, and add it to the soup. Heat the soup, but do not allow it to boil lest it lose its color.

The beef may be served as a main course after the soup, or made into salad for another meal.

ELENA MOLOKHOVETS
PODAROK MOLODÝM KHOZYAĬKAM

Garlic Soup

Soupe Languedocienne

To serve 4

20	garlic cloves, crushed	20
3 tbsp.	rendered goose fat	45 ml.
2	large boneless slices smoked ham hocks	2
1 tbsp.	flour	15 ml.
2½ quarts	water or bouillon	2½ liters
2	large tomatoes, sieved	2
	salt and pepper	
1	sprig thyme	1
3	egg yolks	3
⅓ cup	olive oil	75 ml.
	thick slices homemade bread (recipe, page 165)	
	grated Gruyère or Parmesan cheese	

Melt the goose fat in a large saucepan and sauté the ham slices until they are golden on both sides. Remove the ham and keep it warm between two plates.

Put the garlic in the pan and cook it gently, without letting it brown. Sprinkle the garlic with the flour and cook until the flour is absorbed. Pour in the water or bouillon and add the sieved tomatoes. Season lightly with salt and generously with pepper. Add the thyme and boil the soup rapidly, uncovered, for 12 to 15 minutes.

In a tureen, beat the egg yolks with the oil and pour in the soup gradually, mixing well.

Serve the soup with slices of bread sprinkled with grated cheese and lightly browned in a preheated 375° F. [190° C.] oven. Slice the ham, arrange it on a warmed plate with the bread and serve as an accompaniment to the soup.

70 MÉDECINS DE FRANCE
LE TRÉSOR DE LA CUISINE DU BASSIN MÉDITERRANÉEN

Beef and Lamb Soup, Roman-Style

Brodetto alla Romana

In Italy, this dish is traditionally served at Easter.

To serve 6

2 to 2½ lb.	beef brisket, shank or chuck	1 kg.
2 to 2½ lb.	lamb breast	1 kg.
6 quarts	water	6 liters
1	small onion, stuck with 2 whole cloves	1
1	small carrot	1
1	rib celery	1
1	sprig parsley	1
2 tbsp.	coarse salt	30 ml.
6	egg yolks	6
⅔ cup	freshly grated Parmesan cheese	150 ml.
2 tbsp.	fresh lemon juice	30 ml.
	white pepper	
1 tbsp.	chopped marjoram	15 ml.
	bread slices, dried for 5 minutes in a 375° F. [190° C.] oven	

Put the meats into a fireproof, earthenware pot with the water and bring to a boil over medium heat. Skim, then add the vegetables, parsley and salt. Simmer, uncovered, over very low heat. After about 1½ hours remove the lamb, and after another 1½ hours remove the beef. Trim and bone the meats and cover them with some of the stock. Cover the meats with foil and keep them warm in an oven preheated to its lowest setting. Take the stock off the heat.

Beat the egg yolks with 2 tablespoons [30 ml.] of the cheese, and the lemon juice. Strain the stock through a sieve into a bowl and return it to the pot. Pour in the egg mixture gradually, stirring briskly. Return the pot to low heat; stir the soup until the eggs thicken it slightly. Add the pepper and marjoram. Arrange the bread slices in soup bowls and pour in the soup. Serve the soup, accompanied by the remaining grated cheese. Serve the meats as a second course, accompanied by fresh vegetables.

LUIGI CARNACINA
GREAT ITALIAN COOKING

Thick Lamb Soup

Soupe Courte

To serve 4 to 6

1½ lb.	leg of lamb, in 1 thick slice	¾ kg.
2 tbsp.	lard	30 ml.
3½ oz.	lean salt pork with the rind removed, cut into coarse julienne	100 g.
1	onion, chopped	1
2 to 3 tbsp.	broth or water	30 to 45 ml.
	salt and pepper	
1½ quarts	hot water	1½ liters
1 cup	raw unprocessed rice	¼ liter
¼ tsp.	ground saffron	1 ml.
1	onion, studded with 3 whole cloves	1
1	bouquet garni, composed of 1 rib celery, 1 sprig chervil, 1 bay leaf	1

Put the lamb in a tin-lined copper pan with the lard and the salt pork; brown the meat on both sides, add the chopped onion, stir, and moisten with 1 tablespoon [15 ml.] of the broth. Season with salt and pepper, cover and cook over very low heat, occasionally turning the meat and moistening it lightly, if necessary, with additional broth. When you judge the meat to be cooked (normally this takes not less than 2 hours, but it will depend on the thickness of the meat), add the water. Increase the heat and, when the water is boiling, throw in the rice, saffron, as much salt as is necessary, the clove-studded onion and the bouquet garni. Cook, covered, over low heat for at least 25 minutes; a few more minutes if you like the rice well cooked. This soup should be almost as thick as a pilaf. Remove the bouquet garni and the clove-studded onion. Serve the lamb separately.

J. B. REBOUL
LA CUISINIÈRE PROVENÇALE

Bean Soup

Zuppa di Fagioli

This soup may be enriched by adding other meats—for example, a piece of ham, pig's ears or a fresh pork sausage. Adjust the cooking time accordingly; some meats may need to sim-

mer for 2 to 3 hours to be tender. To ensure that the flavoring vegetables do not lose their fresh taste, the onion, garlic and tomato may be omitted from the preliminary stages of cooking but sautéed in oil and added a few minutes before serving. The meats may be sliced and served separately.

To serve 4

½ lb.	dried white beans (about 1 cup [¼ liter]), soaked in 1 quart [1 liter] water overnight	¼ kg.
½ lb.	salt pork with the rind removed, diced	¼ kg.
1	onion, finely chopped	1
1	garlic clove, finely chopped	1
1	rib celery, chopped	1
3 tbsp.	oil	45 ml.
3	tomatoes, peeled, seeded and chopped	3
	salt and pepper	
1 tbsp.	chopped fresh parsley	15 ml.

Cook the salt pork, onion, garlic and celery in the hot oil until they begin to brown, then add the tomatoes, the beans and their water, salt and pepper. Simmer gently until the beans are very well cooked. The time will depend on the type of beans and whether they are the new season's or the last. The cooking could take anywhere from 1½ to 3 hours. Serve the soup sprinkled with the chopped parsley.

BERYL GOULD-MARKS
THE HOME BOOK OF ITALIAN COOKERY

Broad Bean and Lamb Soup

Soupe de Fèves au Collet de Mouton

To serve 6

2 lb.	broad beans, shelled and peeled	1 kg.
4 lb.	lamb neck	2 kg.
4 quarts	water	4 liters
2½ tbsp.	salt	37 ml.
1	bouquet garni	1
4 tbsp.	butter	60 ml.
	pepper	
1 tbsp.	chopped fresh winter savory	15 ml.
12	slices day-old French bread	12

Put the lamb in a large saucepan with the water, salt and bouquet garni. Bring to a boil and skim. Simmer for 2 hours with the lid half on. Add the beans and increase the heat. As soon as the soup has come to a boil, turn the heat down so that the soup will do no more than simmer gently.

When the beans are cooked, in 10 to 20 minutes, lift out the lamb with a slotted spoon and transfer it to a warmed serving dish. Discard the bouquet garni. Lift the beans out of the soup, drain them in a strainer, then toss them briefly in a saucepan over moderate heat with the butter, pepper, a little salt if necessary, and the savory.

Put the bread in a warmed soup tureen and pour in the soup. Put the beans into the serving dish around the lamb, and serve after the soup.

JULES GOUFFÉ
LE LIVRE DES SOUPES ET DES POTAGES

Swedish Pea Soup

Ärter Med Fläsk

If split peas are substituted for whole dried yellow ones, the soaking time should be reduced to 2 to 3 hours and the cooking time to that of the pork.

To serve 6

1 cup	yellow dried peas (about ½ lb. [¼ kg.]), rinsed and soaked in water overnight	¼ liter
2 quarts	water	2 liters
1 lb.	lean, boneless pork, fresh or lightly cured	½ kg.
2 tsp.	salt	10 ml.
¼ tsp.	ground ginger	1 ml.

Put the peas in a saucepan with the water, let them come to a boil slowly, then cook vigorously for 1 hour, to make the skins come off more easily. As the skins float to the surface, skim them off. Put in the pork and simmer the peas for about another 2 hours. Season with the salt and ginger. Remove the pork, slice it and serve separately from the soup.

Leftover pea soup is very good made into a purée.

INGA NORBERG
GOOD FOOD FROM SWEDEN

Poached Chicken Soup

Poule au Pot

This is the broth for holidays and it is a point of honor with the good housewife to prepare it herself. The cooking is usually begun the evening before, because the quality of the broth is dependent on the slowness of the simmer. The chicken can be served together with its stuffing and vegetables or as a separate course. Or it may be served on a bed of rice, cooked separately in broth from the pot, or the chicken may be cooled in the broth and served cold with mayonnaise and salad. The bread served in the broth may be replaced by vermicelli or soup pasta. The veal shank gives sweetness to the broth, but beef shank or ham hock may be used instead.

To serve 8

4 lb.	stewing chicken, trussed, with the liver reserved	2 kg.
2 to 2½ lb.	veal shank	1 kg.
4 quarts	water	4 liters
1 tbsp.	salt	15 ml.
4	carrots	4
4	leeks	4
1	turnip	1
1	large onion, stuck with 5 to 7 whole cloves	1
1	bouquet garni, including a 1-inch [2½-cm.] stick of cinnamon	1
	sliced dry bread	

Pork and liver stuffing

3½ oz.	lean salt pork with the rind removed, blanched in boiling water for 5 minutes, drained and finely chopped, or lean pork sausage meat	100 g.
	reserved chicken liver, finely chopped	
8	slices bread with the crusts removed, soaked in milk and squeezed dry	8
1 or 2	garlic cloves, finely chopped	1 or 2
2	eggs, lightly beaten	2
	salt and pepper	
	herbs and mixed spices	

Put the veal shank into a large pot with the water. Bring very slowly to a boil, skimming often. When the scum has almost ceased to rise, add the salt. Skim again. If you are finishing the soup the following day, leave to simmer overnight as slowly as possible, then add the vegetables and bouquet garni and simmer for about 2 hours. If you are serving the soup the same day, add the vegetables and bouquet garni as soon as you have skimmed the veal broth.

While the vegetables simmer, make the stuffing by mixing together all the ingredients until well blended. Stuff the chicken with this mixture and sew up the opening with strong thread. Put the chicken into the pot and simmer very gently for 2 to 3 hours or until the chicken is cooked.

Remove the chicken, strain the broth and serve it ladled over slices of dry bread. Carve the chicken and serve it at the same time as the broth or as a separate course. Slice the stuffing and serve it on a separate plate.

SIMIN PALAY
LA CUISINE DU PAYS

Gourmets' Pot-au-Feu

Pot-au-Feu des Gourmets

The chicken and beef that provide a main course to follow the soup may be kept warm — while the soup is being finished — by placing them in a large bowl or deep platter, draping foil over the top and putting the bowl or platter into an oven turned to its lowest setting.

To serve 6 to 8

4 lb.	stewing chicken	2 kg.
2 to 2½ lb.	beef brisket or boned beef shank, tied securely, any bones reserved	1 kg.
1	veal shank	1
4 to 5 quarts	water	4 to 5 liters
	salt	
2	carrots	2
1	turnip	1
1	large onion, stuck with 2 whole cloves	1
1	leek	1
1	small head lettuce	1
1	sprig chervil	1
2¼ cups	raw unprocessed rice	550 ml.
	ground saffron	
	Sausage stuffing	
¼ lb.	lean sausage meat, seasoned with dried herbs	125 g.
2	thick slices French or Italian bread, crusts removed, soaked in bouillon and squeezed almost dry	2
	salt and pepper	
2 tbsp.	chopped fresh parsley	30 ml.

Mix all of the stuffing ingredients together, blend well, and then stuff the chicken with the mixture. Sew up the opening with strong thread and truss the chicken.

Put the beef and beef bones, if any, into a pot (preferably a fireproof earthenware marmite) with the veal shank, the water, and a little salt; bring to a boil and skim, then partially cover and reduce the heat to keep the liquid at a slow simmer. After 1½ to 2 hours, add the chicken to the pot with the carrots, turnip and onion. Add the leek, tied in a bundle with the lettuce and chervil. Simmer very slowly until the beef and chicken are tender, about 1½ hours or longer, depending on the age of the bird. Remove the beef and chicken, and keep them warm.

Strain the pot-au-feu bouillon through a cloth-lined sieve into a clean bowl. Without degreasing it, pour 2 quarts [2 liters] of the bouillon into a saucepan. Bring the bouillon to a boil, and add the rice and a pinch of saffron. Cook the rice slowly over medium heat, adding more bouillon if this soup becomes too thick. When the rice is cooked, the soup — though thick — should be much more liquid than a risotto. You must be able to see the bouillon.

Pour the rice soup into a warmed tureen. Place the beef on a warmed platter; serve the chicken on another platter.

URBAIN DUBOIS
ÉCOLE DES CUISINIÈRES

Pot-au-Feu

As a rule, enough meat and vegetables are put in the pot-au-feu to last two meals and there is usually stock left for the base of soups or sauces to follow on other days. Rump roast, short rib or chuck are the best cuts of meat for pot-au-feu. In addition, every good housewife saves the carcasses of chickens she may have served and adds them to the pot. Or, if chicken salad, vol-au-vent or other cooked chicken dish is planned for another day, the fowl is cooked in the pot-au-feu because the chicken flavor makes the stock extra delicious.

To serve 10 to 12

3 to 3½ lb.	beef (meat and bones)	1½ to 1¾ kg.
4½ quarts	water	4½ liters
2 tbsp.	salt	30 ml.
2 or 3	carrots	2 or 3
1	turnip	1
1	small parsnip	1
5 or 6	leeks	5 or 6
2	ribs celery	2
1	onion	1
	thyme	
½	bay leaf	½
1	whole clove	1
	thin slices dry, crusty rolls	

Cover the meat and bones with water, bring to a boil and parboil for 5 minutes. Remove the meat and bones, discard the water and clean the pot. Put the meat and bones back in the pot, add the cooking water and the salt, and bring very slowly to a boil, skimming all the time until the scum stops rising to the top. Alternatively, you may place the meat and bones directly in the cooking water, reserving 2 cups [½ liter] to be added after the soup has begun to boil. This brings the scum more quickly to the top.

Simmer the soup very gently for 1½ hours, with the lid half on the pot. Add the vegetables — cut into pieces, if desired — and the seasonings, and cook for about 2½ hours longer or until the meat is tender. Skim off the fat and correct the seasoning. Remove as much stock as desired for serving, remove the meat, slicing enough for serving, and the vegetables. Strain the remaining stock through cheesecloth or a fine sieve, let it cool and keep it in the refrigerator for use in soups or sauces.

The meat, vegetables and soup may be served all together in the same bowl, or the soup may be eaten separately and followed by the sliced meat and vegetables. But always, very thin slices of small dry, crusty rolls are eaten in the soup.

LOUIS DIAT
FRENCH COOKING FOR AMERICANS

Bacon Broth

To serve 8

1½ lb.	slab bacon or ham hock, soaked in water overnight and drained	¾ kg.
1 lb.	beef shank	½ kg.
1	cabbage, quartered, cored and sliced	1
3	medium-sized parsnips (about ½ lb. [¼ kg.]), chopped	3
4 or 5	medium-sized carrots (about ½ lb. [¼ kg.]), chopped	4 or 5
½	small rutabaga, sliced	½
3	medium-sized potatoes (about 1 lb. [½ kg.]), diced	3
1½ to 2 quarts	water	1½ to 2 liters
	salt and pepper	
1	large leek, sliced	1
2 tbsp.	ground oatmeal, pulverized in a blender or food processor	30 ml.

Put the bacon, beef, cabbage, parsnips, carrots, rutabaga and potatoes into a large soup kettle or stewpan. Cover them with water. Add a little salt and pepper. Bring to a boil on top of the stove, then let the meats and vegetables simmer for 3 hours or longer (almost as long as you like, within reason) with the lid on either in a slow (300° F. [150° C.]) oven or on the hearth of a fireplace.

Ten minutes before eating the soup, transfer the kettle to the stove top and add the leek. Mix the oatmeal to a paste with cold water and stir this into the soup. Let the soup boil until thickened, then serve. The meat and vegetables are served separately, after the broth.

SHEILA HUTCHINS
ENGLISH RECIPES AND OTHERS FROM SCOTLAND, WALES AND IRELAND

Garbure

Each season determines what goes into this fine soup, for only freshly picked vegetables may be used. The classic garbure should contain, along with the vegetables, some preserved meat (goose, duck or pork) or at least some kind of salted meat (ham, salt pork, sausage or the carcasses of salted poultry). Traditionally, the soup is cooked on a wood fire. As it simmers gently in the hearth, a very thin layer of fat is spread on the surface of the soup and ignited; this creates a gratin, which is reinforced by putting a metal cover on the tureen and placing glowing embers on top.

To serve 8

3	medium-sized potatoes (1 lb. [½ kg.]), thickly sliced	3
1 cup	shelled broad beans, peeled	¼ liter
1 cup	freshly shelled large peas	¼ liter
1 cup	shelled fresh white beans	¼ liter
1	large green cabbage	1
1 lb.	preserved or salted meat	½ kg.
2 quarts	water	2 liters
	salt and pepper (preferably cayenne pepper)	
3	garlic cloves	3
1	bouquet garni of thyme, parsley and marjoram	1
	stale dark bread, very thinly sliced	

Put the water into a fireproof earthenware pot and bring it to a rolling boil. Throw in the potatoes, peas and beans and season with a little salt and pepper. Add the garlic and the bouquet garni. Cook, covered, for about an hour, making sure that the water never stops boiling.

Meanwhile, core the cabbage and separate the leaves. Cut the ribs out of the leaves, roll up he leaves and cut them crosswise into a chiffonade. Add the chiffonade to the boiling soup and cover the pot. As soon as the cabbage has begun to soften, which should be about half an hour before serving time, put in the preserved or salted meat, with its adhering fat. If you are not using preserved goose, a spoonful of goose fat added with the meat will greatly improve the soup.

Put the bread into a soup tureen. If you are using a poultry carcass, remove it from the soup. Cut the meat and serve it on a platter with the vegetables. Pour the broth over the bread in the tureen, and serve it separately. Tradition demands that when the meat is finished, one empties one's glass of red wine into the remains of the bread and broth.

SIMIN PALAY
LA CUISINE DU PAYS

Genoese Veal Soup with Fine Noodles

Zuppa di Cima alla Genovese con Linguine Fine

The pasta called for in this recipe is linguine fine, which is a flat, narrow noodle. Spaghetti may be used as a substitute.

To serve 4 to 6

3 lb.	veal breast, boned	1½ kg.
¼ lb.	*linguine fine*, broken into 2-inch [5-cm.] pieces	125 g.
1	large carrot, chopped	1
1	large onion, chopped	1
1	bay leaf	1
	salt	
1 tbsp.	finely chopped fresh marjoram	15 ml.
2	eggs	2

Pork and prosciutto stuffing

½ lb.	lean pork, ground	¼ kg.
¼ lb.	prosciutto, finely chopped	125 g.
4	slices bread, soaked in milk and squeezed dry	4
1 tbsp.	freshly grated Parmesan cheese	15 ml.
1 tbsp.	finely chopped pistachios	15 ml.
1½ tsp.	salt	7 ml.
	freshly ground pepper	
	grated nutmeg	
3	eggs, beaten	3

To make the stuffing, combine all the ingredients and mix them together well. Spread the breast of veal flat; spoon the stuffing onto the center of veal. Fold the meat in half over the stuffing, sewing the edges together with cotton string to seal in the stuffing completely. Then tie with string. Place the roll in a 6-quart [6-liter] pot and cover with water. Stir in the carrot, onion, bay leaf and salt. Cover and simmer for 1½ hours, or until the meat is tender. Remove the meat to a platter and place a heavy weight on top to press the meat into a flat shape.

Add the marjoram to the liquid remaining in the pot. Simmer, uncovered, for 20 minutes. Add the noodles to the pot and cook 5 to 10 minutes or until *al dente*. Beat the eggs and pour them gradually into the broth, stirring constantly. Bring the soup to a boil and, when the eggs have curdled into streaky threads or *stracciatelle*, remove the soup from the heat and ladle it immediately into hot bowls. Serve the stuffed meat, thinly sliced, as a main course, accompanied by a vegetable.

JACK DENTON SCOTT
THE COMPLETE BOOK OF PASTA

Fish Stew, Normandy-Style

Bouillabaisse Normande

Any firm-fleshed white fish such as cod, flounder, haddock, halibut or snapper may be used in this stew.

To serve 8

1½ lb.	live mussels (about 24), scrubbed and bearded	¾ kg.
1½ lb.	sole, cleaned and cut into pieces	¾ kg.
1½ lb.	turbot, cleaned and cut into pieces	¾ kg.
1½ lb.	brill, cleaned and cut into pieces	¾ kg.
2 tsp.	ground saffron or saffron threads	10 ml.
14 tbsp.	butter	210 ml.
1	large onion, sliced	1
2	garlic cloves, crushed	2
1	carrot, finely sliced	1
	crushed white pepper	
	grated nutmeg	
	salt	
2 quarts	water	2 liters
1	bouquet garni	1
16	thin slices French bread, toasted	16

Steam the mussels in a covered pan over high heat until they open—about 3 to 4 minutes. Remove and shell the mussels and keep them warm. Strain the mussel cooking liquor through a double thickness of dampened cheesecloth into a bowl, and reserve. In a small bowl, dissolve the saffron in a little of the hot liquor.

Melt the butter in a large pan, and add the onion, garlic, carrot, pepper, nutmeg and salt. Cook over medium heat for 5 minutes. Add the water, the bouquet garni and the remaining mussel cooking liquor. Bring to a boil and add the fish pieces. When the fish is cooked, in about 10 minutes, drain the pieces and place them on a warmed serving dish, surrounded by the mussels. Arrange the toasted bread around the edge of the dish.

Strain the broth into a warmed tureen, add the dissolved saffron mixture and serve the broth at the same time as the platter of fish.

JULES GOUFFÉ
LE LIVRE DES SOUPES ET DES POTAGES

Fish Soup with Garlic Mayonnaise

Bourride

To serve 4

1 lb.	angler, tail end, cleaned and sliced	½ kg.
1	small bass, cleaned and sliced	1
1 lb.	whiting, cleaned and sliced	¼ kg.
1	onion, thinly sliced	1
1	sprig thyme	1
1	stalk fennel	1
1	bay leaf	1
1	strip dried orange peel	1
	hot water	
	salt and pepper	
10	thick slices bread	10
4	egg yolks	4

Garlic mayonnaise

4	garlic cloves, cut up	4
	salt	
1	egg yolk, at room temperature	1
2 cups	olive oil, at room temperature	½ liter
2 to 3 tbsp.	fresh lemon juice	30 to 45 ml.
1 to 2 tsp.	lukewarm water	5 to 10 ml.

To make the garlic mayonnaise, put the garlic cloves in a large mortar. Reduce to a paste with a pestle, add a pinch of salt and the egg yolk, and begin pouring in the oil in a thin stream, turning the mixture with the pestle. Pour the oil very slowly and never stop turning.

After pouring in the first 3 or 4 tablespoons [45 or 60 ml.] of oil, add the lemon juice and a teaspoonful [5 ml.] of lukewarm water. Continue to add the oil, little by little, until the mixture is too stiff to turn easily. Add a little more water.

If the garlic mayonnaise breaks and the oil separates out, pour the whole mixture out of the mortar. Clean the mortar and put in another egg yolk and a few drops of lemon juice. Spoonful by spoonful, add the broken mayonnaise, turning the pestle continuously. This time, it should be successful. This is known as "lifting" the mayonnaise.

To make the soup, put the fish into a saucepan with the onion, thyme, fennel, bay leaf and orange peel. Add enough hot water to slightly more than cover the fish. Season with salt and pepper, and cook rapidly for 10 minutes.

Meanwhile, arrange the bread slices in a deep bowl or tureen. Remove the cooked fish from the pan and keep it warm. Strain the broth into a bowl. Moisten the slices with a few spoonfuls of broth, without letting them float.

In a clean saucepan, blend the egg yolks with ½ cup [125 ml.] of the garlic mayonnaise. Add the remaining broth very slowly to this mixture, stirring continuously. Cook over low heat until the soup begins to thicken. When it has thickened, the soup should coat a spoon. Be careful that the soup does not boil, because there is no hope of lifting it.

As soon as the soup is smooth and velvety, pour it over the soaked bread. The soup may be served first and followed by the fish slices served with the remaining mayonnaise, or both courses may be served together.

J. B. REBOUL
LA CUISINIÈRE PROVENÇALE

Fish Soup from Provence

Une Soupe Provençale

To serve 8

2 to 2½ lb.	conger eel, cleaned and cut into 8 slices	1 kg.
about 1½ lb.	live mussels (about 24), scrubbed and bearded	about ¾ kg.
⅓ cup	olive oil	75 ml.
1	small onion, thinly sliced	1
4	tomatoes, peeled and chopped	4
2	garlic cloves, crushed	2
1	large bouquet garni	1
1	small strip dried orange peel	1
2 quarts	water	2 liters
	salt and pepper	
	ground saffron	
	sliced homemade bread (recipe, page 165)	
	chopped fresh parsley	

In a large saucepan, heat half of the olive oil and cook the onion gently without letting it color. When it is soft, add the tomatoes, garlic, bouquet garni, orange peel and water. Season with salt, pepper and a pinch of saffron. Boil rapidly for 15 minutes. Strain the broth through a fine sieve into a bowl, pressing the vegetables to extract all of their juices.

Put the pieces of eel in the cleaned saucepan and season the eel with salt and pepper. Sprinkle on the remaining oil, then pour in the strained broth. Cook rapidly for 10 minutes. Meanwhile, put the mussels into another pan, cover and cook over high heat until they have all opened. Shell the mussels and strain their cooking liquor. Add the mussels and their liquor to the eel and cook for 3 minutes.

Arrange the pieces of eel and the mussels on a warmed serving platter. Put several large, thick slices of bread into a soup tureen, and pour in the soup. Sprinkle the soup with chopped parsley. The fish may be served at the same time as the soup, or as a second course.

70 MÉDECINS DE FRANCE
LE TRÉSOR DE LA CUISINE DU BASSIN MÉDITERRANÉEN

Breton Chowder

La Cotriade

Fish that are suitable for use in this dish include conger eel, mackerel, pollack, and (of the soft-fleshed varieties) sardine, skate, cod and wrasse.

This soup is at its best in its place of origin—the western coast of Cape Finistère. The fish should be perfectly fresh, and still wet with sea water. There are as many *cotriades* as there are varieties of fish and they vary with the seasons.

To serve 4 to 6

2 to 2½ lb.	mixed fish, cleaned and cut into slices if large	1 kg.
3 tbsp.	olive oil, butter or chopped salt pork fat	45 ml.
4	onions, quartered	4
6	medium-sized potatoes (about 2 lb. [1 kg.]), roughly cut up	6
1	bouquet garni	1
2 quarts	lightly salted boiling water	2 liters
2 tbsp.	coarse salt	30 ml.
	dried bread slices	
2 tbsp.	peppercorns, crushed	30 ml.
1 cup	wine vinegar	¼ liter

In a large, heavy saucepan, heat the oil or fat and add the onions. Cook over medium heat for a minute or two, add the potatoes and bouquet garni and continue cooking, stirring occasionally, for 10 minutes or until the onions begin to turn golden. Pour in the boiling water and cook for about 15 minutes or until the potatoes are just beginning to turn tender. Add the fish, reserving any soft-fleshed varieties to add 5 minutes later. Cook at a light boil for another 10 to 15 minutes. Remove the fish and vegetables to a hot serving dish, discarding the bouquet garni.

Dissolve the coarse salt in a quart [1 liter] of the broth, pour this brine over the fish, then pour it off. Pour the same brine onto the fish twice more, working carefully so that the fish absorb the salt but are not broken up in the process. Pour the remaining unsalted broth into a tureen lined with bread slices. Mix the peppercorns with the vinegar, and serve as a dipping sauce for the fish and potatoes.

Alternatively, serve bowls of the brine to the diners. A bite of fish and potato may be dipped first into the brine, then into the vinegar.

Serve the soup after the fish is eaten.

CURNONSKY
À L'INFORTUNE DU POT

Garnishes and Accompaniments

Recipes for basic garnishes appear in Standard Preparations, pages 163-167.

Brain Dumplings

To prepare the calf's brains called for in this recipe, first soak them in acidulated water for 2 hours, changing the water several times. Then drain them, and remove the membranes before sieving the brains.

To make 12 dumplings

3½ oz.	calf's brains, rubbed through a sieve	100 g.
1	bread roll, soaked in ⅔ cup [150 ml.] milk and squeezed dry	1
⅓ cup	bread crumbs	75 ml.
1	egg	1
1	egg yolk	1
1 tsp.	salt	5 ml.
	pepper	
	marjoram	
2 tbsp.	finely chopped fresh parsley	30 ml.

Mix the brains in a bowl until smooth, then add the soaked roll, the bread crumbs, egg and egg yolk, salt, pepper, marjoram and parsley. Mix well, form into small balls and poach, covered, in salted water for 10 minutes. Using a slotted spoon, remove the dumplings and drain them. Serve brain dumplings in clear meat soup.

JOZSEF VENESZ
HUNGARIAN CUISINE

Spaetzle

To make about 1½ cups [375 ml.] spaetzle

2 cups	flour	½ liter
1 tsp.	salt	5 ml.
	grated nutmeg	
	freshly ground pepper	
2	lightly beaten eggs	2
about ½ cup	milk	about 125 ml.

Mix the flour, seasonings and eggs together, then add enough milk to make a rather stiff batter. Beat quite well and let the batter stand for an hour before cooking. Pour the batter into a spaetzle sieve held over salted boiling water, let the batter drop into the water and cook for 10 to 15 minutes, according to your taste. Drain, and run cold or hot water through the spaetzle.

JAMES BEARD
JAMES BEARD'S AMERICAN COOKERY

Bread Balls

To serve 4

2	thick slices day-old firm-textured white bread, soaked in cold water	2
1 tbsp.	finely chopped onion	15 ml.
1 tbsp.	rendered chicken fat	15 ml.
2 tsp.	finely chopped fresh parsley	10 ml.
½	lemon peel, grated	½
	mixed herbs (optional)	
	salt and pepper	
1	egg, lightly beaten	1
	fresh bread crumbs	

Drain the soaked bread, squeeze it very dry and mash it in a bowl with a fork. Fry the onion in the fat until golden brown, then add it to the soaked bread, together with the parsley, lemon peel and, if liked, a pinch of mixed herbs. Season with salt and pepper, add the beaten egg and sufficient bread crumbs to absorb any excess moisture. Roll the mixture into tiny balls, drop them into boiling soup—any clear broth—and simmer, covered, for 15 to 20 minutes.

FLORENCE GREENBERG
JEWISH COOKERY

Potato Dumplings

Burgonyagombóc

To make 20 to 25 dumplings

1	large potato (about ½ lb. [¼ kg.]), boiled, peeled and mashed	1
1 tbsp.	semolina	15 ml.
1 tbsp.	finely chopped onion	15 ml.
2 tbsp.	rendered bacon fat	30 ml.
1½ tsp.	chopped fresh parsley	7 ml.
	salt and pepper	
2 tbsp.	beaten egg	30 ml.
1 to 2 tbsp.	flour	15 to 30 ml.

Mix the mashed potato with the semolina. Sauté the onion for 5 to 10 minutes in the bacon fat and add to the potato

mixture. Add the parsley and season with salt and pepper. Mix in the egg and gradually add enough flour to make a soft, but cohesive, dough. Roll the dough into balls between floured hands—a teaspoonful [5 ml.] at a time—or form the mixture into a fat sausage and slice into equal-sized pieces. Put the dumplings into the refrigerator for a few minutes to allow them to firm, then cook for 7 to 10 minutes in simmering salted water or broth.

FRED MACNICOL
HUNGARIAN COOKERY

Meat Dumplings

Frikadel'ki iz Govyadiny

Beef, veal or lamb may be used for these dumplings. Because the meat is chopped and pounded, it need not be a tender cut but it should be lean. Every trace of fat and gristle should be trimmed off before the meat is chopped.

To serve 6

½ lb.	lean boneless beef, veal or lamb, finely chopped	¼ kg.
4 tbsp.	beef suet, finely chopped	60 ml.
	salt and pepper	
	grated nutmeg	
2 tbsp.	finely chopped onion	30 ml.
2	slices bread with the crusts removed, soaked in milk and squeezed	2
2	eggs	2
2 tbsp.	heavy cream	30 ml.
3 to 4 tbsp.	bread crumbs, toasted in a 300° F. [150° C.] oven for about 10 minutes	45 to 60 ml.

In a bowl, mix the meat with the suet, seasonings, onion, soaked bread, eggs and cream. When the ingredients are thoroughly blended, pound the mixture a little at a time in a mortar, or chop it in a food processor until it becomes perfectly smooth.

Form the pounded dumpling mixture into walnut-sized balls, and roll them in the toasted bread crumbs. Add the dumplings to simmering soup or salted water and cook for 10 minutes or until they float to the top as a sign of doneness. If they are cooked in water, drain the dumplings in a slotted spoon and add them to the soup just before serving.

ELENA MOLOKHOVETS
PODAROK MOLODÝM KHOZYAĬKAM

Liver Dumplings

To make 12 dumplings

5 oz.	liver, preferably calf's or pig's, minced	150 g.
1	small onion, finely chopped	1
3 tbsp.	lard	45 ml.
1	hard roll, soaked in water and squeezed dry	1
	salt	
	freshly ground pepper	
1 tsp.	finely chopped fresh marjoram	5 ml.
1	egg, lightly beaten	1
¼ cup	fine bread crumbs	50 ml.
⅓ cup	flour	75 ml.
1	sprig parsley, finely chopped	1

Fry the onion in the lard until lightly browned. In a bowl, mix the liver, the hard roll, salt, pepper and marjoram. Add the fried onion, egg, bread crumbs, flour and parsley and mix well. Roll this mixture into 12 small balls and simmer them, covered, in hot soup for 15 to 20 minutes.

JOZSEF VENESZ
HUNGARIAN CUISINE

Baked Buckwheat

Kasha

This baked buckwheat is traditionally served with borscht, consommé or cabbage soup.

To serve 6 to 8

1 lb.	buckwheat groats	½ kg.
1 tsp.	salt	5 ml.
2 tbsp.	butter	30 ml.
about 1 quart	boiling water	about 1 liter

Put the buckwheat groats in a skillet without any fat or liquid and roast over medium heat, stirring, until the groats acquire a light golden color. Put the buckwheat into a 2-quart [2-liter] baking dish, season with salt, add the butter and pour in just enough boiling water to cover. Bake, uncovered, in a preheated 300° F. [150° C.] oven for 2½ to 3 hours, adding water if necessary. The buckwheat should have a thin crust on top but the groats should fall apart easily.

NINA AND GEORGE FROUD
THE HOME BOOK OF RUSSIAN COOKING

Pasta Stuffing with Ricotta and Spinach

Pasta con Ricotta e Spinaci

This stuffing may be varied almost endlessly. The spinach, for example, may be replaced by chard, or supplemented by leftover cooked meat, finely chopped, by sautéed chopped onion, or by poached, chopped brains. If meat is added, more whole eggs or egg yolks may be used to moisten it. The recipe for pasta dough appears on page 167. The techniques for stuffing, shaping and cooking pasta are shown on pages 16-17. The stuffed cooked pasta can be used as a soup garnish or, as suggested in the original version of this recipe, the pasta can be sauced with melted butter, scalded cream and freshly grated Parmesan cheese.

To serve 4 to 6

3½ oz.	ricotta	100 g.
½ lb.	spinach, parboiled, drained, squeezed and finely chopped	¼ kg.
1 tbsp.	butter (optional)	15 ml.
1	egg, or 2 egg yolks	1
	salt and pepper	
	grated nutmeg	
2½ tbsp.	freshly grated Parmesan cheese	37 ml.

If a buttery taste is desired, sauté the chopped spinach very briefly in the butter. Place the spinach in a mixing bowl and, if sautéed, allow it to cool. Sieve the ricotta into the bowl, or mash it into the spinach with a fork. Add the egg and season well with salt, pepper and nutmeg. Blend the mixture with a fork or with your hands, adding grated Parmesan cheese until the mixture is firm but still moist. Use the mixture to stuff small rounds of pasta dough.

ENRICA AND VERNON JARRATT
THE COMPLETE BOOK OF PASTA

Egg Balls

To serve 4

2	hard-boiled eggs, rubbed through a sieve	2
1	egg yolk	1
1 tbsp.	fresh bread crumbs	15 ml.
	salt and pepper	

Add the raw egg yolk to the sieved hard-boiled eggs; mix in the bread crumbs and seasoning. With floured hands, roll the mixture into tiny balls. Drop the balls into boiling soup, then simmer, covered, for 5 to 10 minutes. Alternatively, the egg balls can be cooked in boiling salted water, then added to soup just before serving.

FLORENCE GREENBERG
JEWISH COOKERY

Small Russian Meat Pies

Piroshki

Traditionally, piroshki are served with soup in Russian cooking. They may have a filling of meat, of sautéed mushrooms, eggs, and onions, or of browned onions and chopped cabbage. They may be made with any kind of dough, from puff paste to yeast dough.

To make 12 to 15 pies

Sour-cream dough

4 to 6 tbsp.	sour cream	60 to 90 ml.
1½ cups	flour	375 ml.
1 tsp.	salt	5 ml.
4 tbsp.	butter	60 ml.
	beaten egg or milk	

Meat filling

1 tbsp.	finely chopped onion	15 ml.
1 tbsp.	butter	15 ml.
1 cup	finely chopped cooked chicken or other meat	¼ liter
¼ cup	finely chopped fresh mushrooms	50 ml.
1	hard-boiled egg, finely chopped	1
¼ tsp.	Worcestershire sauce	1 ml.
1 tsp.	chopped dill or parsley, or dill seed	5 ml.
	salt and pepper	
1 to 2 tbsp.	stock (optional)	15 to 30 ml.

For the filling, sauté the onion in the butter until soft. Add the remaining ingredients and cook for 5 to 10 minutes over low heat. If the mixture seems too dry, add a little stock. Cool the filling before using.

For the pastry, sift the flour and salt together. Cut in the butter with a pastry cutter or two knives, leaving the mixture in coarse lumps. Add sour cream, a little at a time, until the dough holds together. Roll out the dough and fold it in three thicknesses. Chill for at least 1 hour.

Roll the dough out as thinly as possible. With a round cutter or the floured rim of a glass, cut out rounds 3 to 4 inches [8 to 10 cm.] in diameter. Put 1 to 2 teaspoons [5 to 10 ml.] of filling on each round. Fold over each round and pinch the edges together carefully, so that the filling will not ooze out during baking. Paint with beaten egg or milk.

Place the piroshki on a greased baking sheet. Bake in a preheated 425° F. [220° C.] oven for 15 to 20 minutes, or until golden brown. Serve hot or cold.

NIKA STANDEN HAZELTON
THE CONTINENTAL FLAVOUR

Standard Preparations

Meat Broth

This basic broth, based on beef with added chicken and veal, may be used in any recipe calling for beef broth. Almost any meaty veal, chicken or beef bones may be included.

To make 4 quarts [4 liters] broth

2 lb.	beef shank	1 kg.
2 lb.	beef short ribs	1 kg.
2 lb.	chicken pieces (backs, necks, wings)	1 kg.
1	chicken carcass, raw or cooked (optional)	1
1	meaty veal shank (optional)	1
5 quarts	water	5 liters
5	carrots	5
1	large onion stuck with 3 whole cloves	1
1	large garlic bulb	1
1	bouquet garni	1
	salt	

Place a round metal rack in the bottom of the stockpot to prevent the broth ingredients from sticking. Tie the thin cuts of meat into compact shapes with string. Starting with the largest pieces, fit all of the beef, chicken and veal into the pot. Add the water and bring it very slowly to the boil; it should take at least an hour for the water to reach the boiling point. With a slotted spoon, carefully lift off the surface scum as the liquid comes to a boil. Add the carrots, onion, garlic, bouquet garni and salt, and skim once more as the liquid returns to a boil.

Turn the heat down as low as possible, cover the pot with the lid askew, and leave the broth to simmer for 3½ hours, if you wish to serve the beef afterward, or for 5 hours if you wish to extract all of the goodness of the beef into the broth.

Strain the finished broth into a large bowl or clean pot through a colander lined with dampened cheesecloth. Degrease the surface thoroughly with paper towels, or allow the broth to cool and refrigerate it until the fat has solidified on the top and you can lift it off with a spoon.

Refrigerate the broth if you do not plan to use it immediately; it will keep safely for three or four days. To preserve the broth longer, lift off the last bits of fat and then warm the broth so that it may be poured into eight or nine 1-pint [½-liter] containers. The frozen broth will keep for six months while you use it—container by container—as necessary.

Game-Bird Broth

Game-bird broth may be prepared in the same way as meat broth, except that pheasants or partridges are used. Partially roast the pheasants for 25 minutes, the partridges for 15 minutes, in a preheated 450° F. [230° C.] oven. Add the game birds to the broth with the aromatic vegetables.

Alternatively, you can add game-bird trimmings and carcasses, raw or cooked, to a richly flavored broth already made from beef or chicken. Add fresh aromatic vegetables to the broth when you add the trimmings and carcasses, and simmer the broth for 2 to 3 hours before straining it.

Chicken Broth

Consommé de Volaille

The term *consommé de volaille* is also used for a broth made from chicken and beef. A richer result is obtained if broth replaces the water in this recipe.

To make 4 quarts [4 liters] broth

5 to 7 lb.	stewing chicken, trussed	2½ to 3 kg.
1	large onion, stuck with 3 whole cloves	1
2	carrots	2
1	large garlic bulb, unpeeled	1
1	bouquet garni	1
4 to 5 quarts	water or broth	4 to 5 liters
	coarse salt	

Place the chicken, breast uppermost, in the bottom of a heavy pot—preferably an oval-shaped pot—that is just large enough to hold the ingredients. Place the vegetables and the bouquet garni around the chicken. Pour in water or broth to cover and slowly bring to a boil. Using a slotted spoon, skim the surface until no more scum forms on top of the broth. As the fat from the bird melts and rises to the top, skim that off, too.

When the boiling point is reached, add a little salt and cover the pot, setting the lid ajar. Reduce the heat and cook undisturbed at a slow simmer for 1½ to 3 hours, depending on the age of the bird.

As soon as the thigh meat feels tender when prodded with the tines of a fork, remove the bird and the vegetables from the pot. Strain the broth through a colander, lined with several layers of dampened cheesecloth and placed over a large bowl or clean pot.

Fish Broth

To make 1 ½ quarts [1 ½ liters] broth

2 lb.	fish heads, bones and trimmings, rinsed and broken into pieces	1 kg.
1	onion, sliced	1
1	carrot, sliced	1
1	leek, sliced	1
1	rib celery, diced	1
1	bouquet garni	1
2 quarts	water	2 liters
	salt	

Place the fish, vegetables and herbs in a stockpot or large saucepan. Add the water and season lightly with salt. Bring to a boil over low heat. With a large, slotted spoon, skim off the scum that rises to the surface as the liquid reaches a simmer. Keep skimming until no more scum rises, then cover the pot, with the lid slightly ajar, and simmer the broth for 30 minutes. Without pressing down on the solids, strain the broth through a colander placed over a deep bowl.

Vegetable Broth

To make 1 ½ quarts [1 ½ liters] broth

2	leeks, thinly sliced	2
2	ribs celery with leaves, chopped	2
2	onions, thinly sliced	2
4	carrots, chopped	4
2	cabbage leaves, sliced thinly into chiffonade	2
1	head lettuce, cored and sliced thinly into chiffonade	1
4	sprigs flat-leafed parsley with stems, chopped	4
1 tsp.	thyme	5 ml.
1	bay leaf	1
	salt	
1 ½ quarts	water	1 ½ liters

Place all the ingredients in a large saucepan and bring very slowly to a boil. Skim, then cover with the lid ajar, and allow the broth to simmer undisturbed for about 45 minutes.

Strain the broth through a sieve into a bowl without pressing any of the vegetables through the sieve.

Bread

This recipe is for a basic crusty loaf, similar to French country bread *(pain de campagne)*. It can be varied by including dark flour (for example, 1 part whole-wheat and 1 part rye to 2 parts all-purpose or bread flour) and by allowing the yeast to ferment for 24 hours before making the bread. For a sourdough sponge, dissolve the yeast in 1 cup [¼ liter] of warm water and stir in 2 cups [½ liter] of the flour. Beat the mixture until smooth, cover tightly with plastic wrap and leave the bowl in a warm place overnight. Add the remaining ingredients and continue with the recipe.

To make 1 large loaf or 2 small ones — about 1 ½ pounds [¾ kg.] in all

1½ tsp.	dry yeast or cake compressed fresh yeast	7 ml.
2 cups	lukewarm water (100° F. [50° C.])	½ liter
	salt	
6 cups	flour, preferably bread flour	1½ liters
	farina, cornmeal or cracked wheat (optional)	

In a large bowl, dissolve the yeast in ½ cup [125 ml.] of the water and leave for about 15 minutes, or until foamy. Add the remaining water and the salt, and begin stirring in the flour. When the dough is stiff and starts to pull away from the sides of the bowl, turn it out onto a floured board. Knead, by folding the dough toward you, pushing it away with the heels of your hands and giving it a quarter turn; repeat vigorously until the dough is smooth and shiny and not sticky—after at least 10 minutes. Sprinkle the dough with more flour as necessary during kneading. Gather the dough into a ball, dust with flour and place the dough in a clean bowl; cover with a cloth and leave in a warm place until the dough has more than doubled in bulk—after 1 to 2 hours.

Turn out the dough onto the floured board and punch the ball down to expel all of the air. Knead again briefly and form the dough on a lightly floured baking sheet into a large round loaf or two long, tapered cylindrical French loaves. Or form one large or two small cylinders and put them into buttered loaf pans. Leave the bread to rise, covered loosely with a towel, until doubled in volume—about 1 hour. (If you are baking a large round loaf, you may leave it to rise for a second time on a board generously sprinkled with farina, cornmeal or cracked wheat.)

Preheat the oven to 400° F. [200° C.]. Place a baking sheet in the oven while it is preheating if you are not baking the bread in pans. To create steam, put a baking pan containing about 1 inch [2½ cm.] of hot water on the floor of the oven or the lowest shelf.

To bake the bread, slash the surface of each loaf in three or four places with a razor blade or razor-sharp knife, and transfer the loaf with a rapid jerk to the heated baking sheet. After the first 20 minutes of baking, remove the pan of water and turn the oven down to 350° F. [180° C.]. The bread will take about 1 hour to bake, depending on the size and shape of the loaves. When it is done, it will be golden brown all over and the bottom crust will sound hollow when you rap it with your knuckles. Cool on a wire rack.

Keep this bread in a bread box or wrapped snugly with foil for at least 1 or 2 days before using it for soups.

Red-Pepper Sauce

Rouille

There are many versions of this classic red-pepper sauce; some omit the basil and sweet red pepper, others moisten the sauce with fish broth as well as olive oil. To make the sauce somewhat milder tasting, remove the seeds of the dried chilies. The technique of making the sauce appears on page 51.

To make 1 ¼ cups [300 ml.] rouille

2	small, dried red chilies, stemmed but not seeded	2
	coarse salt	
	pepper	
1	small bunch basil leaves	1
2 or 3	garlic cloves	2 or 3
1	thick slice firm-textured white bread with the crust removed, soaked in warm water and squeezed dry	1
1	sweet red pepper, broiled, skinned, halved, deribbed and seeded	1
	olive oil	

In a large mortar, pound the dried chilies until they are reduced to a powder. Add salt and pepper and the basil and garlic, and continue to pound until the mixture is crushed to a paste. Add the bread, then the sweet pepper, pounding well to mix everything to a smooth purée. Add the oil in a thin, steady stream while constantly turning or stirring the mixture with the pestle. The *rouille* should be a smooth sauce with the consistency of mayonnaise.

Egg Threads

To serve 4		
1	egg	1
1½ to 2 tbsp.	flour	22 to 30 ml.
	salt	
1 quart	broth	1 liter

Put the flour and salt in a bowl, break in the egg, and whisk to amalgamate the mixture into a smooth batter. Strain the batter through a fine sieve into another bowl, preferably one with a lip for pouring.

Bring the broth to a boil in a saucepan. When the broth is bubbling, hold a perforated spoon over the pan and pour the batter from the bowl through the spoon. The batter will solidify into threads as it falls through the broth. Cook for 2 to 3 minutes more, then serve.

Croutons

To prepare croutons as a garnish for delicate-tasting soups, you can substitute clarified butter for the combination of butter and oil specified in this recipe. If the croutons are to accompany strong-flavored soups, you may prefer to sauté the bread cubes in olive oil. If you want to toast the croutons instead of sautéing them, spread the cubes on an ungreased baking sheet and toast them for 2 to 3 minutes on each side in a preheated 400° F. [200° C.] oven.

To make about 1 cup [¼ liter] croutons		
2	bread slices, ½ inch [1 cm.] thick, cut from a day-old, firm-textured white loaf	2
4 tbsp.	butter	60 ml.
¼ to ½ cup	oil	50 to 125 ml.

Remove the crusts from the bread and cut the slices into cubes. Combine the butter and ¼ cup [50 ml.] of the oil in a large skillet. Melt the butter over medium heat and, as soon as the butter and oil mixture is hot, add the bread cubes and increase the heat to high. Turn the cubes frequently with a broad metal spatula so that they brown evenly on all sides, and add more oil as necessary to keep the cubes from burning. Before serving, drain the croutons on paper towels.

Crepes

For crepes to cut into strips as a soup garnish, 1 to 2 tablespoons [15 to 30 ml.] of chopped fresh parsley or of fines herbes may be added; or a pinch of ground saffron may be dissolved in a little hot water and the mixture used as part of the liquid for the batter.

To serve 8		
½ cup	flour	125 ml.
3	eggs	3
3 tbsp.	melted butter	45 ml.
2 tbsp.	Cognac (optional)	30 ml.
	salt (optional)	
about 1 cup	milk or water	about ¼ liter

Place the flour in a bowl, make a well in the center of the flour and in it put the eggs, butter and the Cognac and/or the salt if used. Whisk while gradually adding enough milk or water to make a batter the consistency of light cream. Do not whisk more than necessary.

To make the crepes, heat a crepe pan or small frying pan over medium-low heat and grease it lightly with butter for the first crepe only. Pour in a small ladleful of the batter, tilting the pan to form a thin layer of batter all over the bottom. Cook the crepe for 1 to 2 minutes or until the edges separate from the pan, then turn the crepe and briefly cook the other side. The crepes may be stacked on a plate and kept warm, or they may be stacked and covered with plastic wrap for refrigeration until needed.

Royales

These custard garnishes for consommé may be colored and flavored in a variety of ways. Adding about ¼ cup [50 ml.] of cooked, squeezed and puréed spinach to the custard mixture before straining it will make green royales; the same quantity of thick puréed tomato will make the royales red. If you add spinach or tomato, also add an extra egg yolk to preserve the consistency of the custard.

To serve 6 to 8		
1	egg	1
3	egg yolks	3
1 cup	lukewarm broth	¼ liter

Beat the egg and the yolks together until they are well blended, and gradually beat in the warm broth. Strain the custard mixture through a fine-meshed sieve and then ladle it into small buttered molds not more than 2½ inches [6 cm.] deep, filling the molds to a depth of only ½ inch [1 cm.].

Place the molds on a rack set in a wide saucepan or large skillet, and pour enough hot water into the pan to reach to within ½ inch of the tops of the molds. Cover the pan and poach the custards, either in a preheated 300° F. [150° C.] oven, or over low heat. Never letting the water in the pan come to a boil, cook for 12 to 15 minutes, or until the custards are set and a knife inserted into the center of one of them comes out clean.

Remove the molds from the pan and let them cool. Then invert each mold over a plate and give the bottom of the mold a sharp tap to unmold the custard. Cut the custards into dice with a knife, or into ornamental shapes with special cutters.

Quenelles

This mixture can be made with partridge or pheasant breast, lean veal or skinned fish fillets instead of the chicken. The meat may be puréed in a food processor or with the finest blade of a food mill instead of in a mortar, but the purée should still be sieved after processing.

	To serve 6	
½ lb.	lean, raw boneless chicken breasts, skinned	¼ kg.
	white pepper	
	cayenne pepper	
	grated nutmeg	
1	egg white	1
⅔ cup	cold heavy cream	150 ml.
	salt	

In a large mortar, season the meat with a pinch of white pepper, cayenne pepper and nutmeg. Pound the meat with a pestle until it forms a smooth paste. Add the egg white, little by little, continuing to pound the paste until the egg white is amalgamated. Purée the mixture, in small batches, through a fine-meshed sieve set over a plate, scraping the sieve clean after each batch. Pack the purée into a metal or glass bowl, set in a larger bowl of crushed ice.

Cover the purée with plastic wrap or foil to prevent a crust from forming on the top and refrigerate it for 1 hour. Then, with the bowl still over ice, use a wooden spoon to work the cream gradually into the stiffened purée. Season to taste with a little salt. Refrigerate the purée (you can dispense with the large bowl of ice at this stage) until you are ready to make the quenelles.

Put the mixture into a pastry bag with a metal tip, or a wax paper cone with the end snipped off. Press out small, oval quenelles into a buttered shallow pan or large skillet. Carefully pour in just enough boiling water to cover the quenelles and place the pan over low heat so that the water continues to simmer very gently. When the quenelles float to the surface of the simmering water—after about 10 minutes—they are done and may be transferred with a perforated spoon to hot broth for serving.

Pasta Dough

The techniques of making, stuffing and cooking pasta are demonstrated on pages 16-17. To make green pasta, omit the saffron from this recipe and use ¼ cup [50 ml.] of spinach or chard purée to replace one of the eggs called for. For the purée, parboil ½ pound [¼ kg.] of the greens for 3 to 5 minutes, or until just tender. Drain, squeeze completely dry by hand, and chop finely, or purée in a blender.

	To garnish 6 to 8 servings	
1½ to 2 cups	flour	250 to 375 ml.
	ground saffron (optional)	
2	large eggs, lightly beaten	2
1 tsp.	olive oil	5 ml.
½ tsp.	salt	2 ml.
	semolina or farina	

Put 1½ cups [375 ml.] of flour into a bowl and blend with a pinch of saffron, if using. Add the eggs, oil and salt and mix with your fingers or a fork. Knead with your fingers until a pliable dough forms, adding more flour, a little at a time, if necessary. Wrap the dough in plastic wrap or a dampened cloth, and let it rest at room temperature for 30 minutes.

Sprinkle the remaining flour evenly over a cutting board. With a rolling pin, roll and stretch the dough until it is very thin. During the rolling, the pasta will absorb the remaining flour. Alternatively, set a pasta machine at the desired thickness and put the dough through the machine repeatedly—sprinkling the dough with flour after each rolling—until the pasta loses its stickiness and is smooth.

If making noodles by hand, dust the surface of the dough with a little semolina or farina and roll up the sheet of dough loosely from both long sides until the two rolls meet in the center. Cut across the rolls with a sharp knife to make noodles of the desired width. If you are using a pasta machine, set the cutters to the desired width and roll the sheet of dough through the machine to cut it. Separate the noodles and let them dry for a few minutes on a cloth or board, lightly sprinkled with semolina or farina. Cook the noodles in a large pot of boiling, salted water before adding them to soup.

Recipe Index

All recipes in the index that follows are listed by their English titles except in cases where a soup of foreign origin, such as pot-au-feu, is universally recognized by its source name. Entries also are organized by the major ingredients specified in recipe titles. Foreign recipes are listed by country or region of origin. Recipe credits appear on pages 173-175.

General Index/Glossary

Included in this index to the cooking demonstrations are definitions, in italics, of special culinary terms not explained elsewhere in this volume. The Recipe Index begins on page 168.

Acorn squash panades, 60-61
Aioli, preparing, 80-81
Al dente: *an Italian term, literally translated as "to the tooth." Used to describe the texture of cooked pastas or vegetables when they are firm to the bite: not too soft on the outside and barely cooked through.*
Almonds, in *potage à la reine,* 34
Aromatic vegetables: in *bourride,* 80; in broth, 8-11; browning with meat, 46; with fish, 50, 80; in garbure, 82-83; in jellied consommé, 64-65; leftovers, 30-31, 46-47; in meat and chicken soup, 76-77; in pork and bean soup, 78-79; in *poule au pot,* 76-77; in purées, 24-31; in Scotch broth, 42-43; in squash panade, 60-61; with tripe, 48-49
Aromatics: *all substances —such as vegetables, herbs and spices —that add aroma and flavor to food when used in cooking.*
Artichokes, puréeing, 23, chart 36
Asparagus, puréeing, chart 36
Avocados: in cold soup, 66-67; peeling, 66; puréeing, chart 36
Bain-marie: *a French term often translated as "water bath." Used to describe any large vessel partly filled with hot or simmering water into which smaller vessels of food can be placed to cook or warm them.*
Barley, in Scotch broth, 42-43
Beans: in mixed-vegetable soup, 40-41; pork and, 78-79; puréeing, 23, 24, 26, chart 36-37; shelling, 83
Beef: in borscht, 84-86; broth, 6, 8-11; and chicken, 76-77; in jellied consommé, 64-65; poaching, 76-77; in *poule au pot,* 75; tripe, 48-49
Beets: baking, 85; greens in cold soup, 68-69; liquor, 84; puréeing, chart 36; soups, 84-86
Belgian endive, puréeing, chart 36
Blanch: *to plunge food into boiling water for a short period. Done for a number of reasons: to remove strong flavors, such as the excess saltiness of some salt pork; to soften vegetables before further cooking; to facilitate the removal of skins or shells. Another meaning is "to whiten."*
Blender, puréeing with, 23, chart 36-37
Borscht: cold, 86; preparing, 84-86
Botvinya, preparing, 68-69
Bouillon. See Broth
Bouquet garni: *a bunch of mixed herbs —the classic three being parsley,*

thyme and bay leaf —tied together or wrapped in cheesecloth, and used for flavoring stocks, sauces, braises and stews; 8, 42-43, 46, 77-79
Bourride, preparing, 80-81
Bread: as garnish, 21; layering, 56, 57, 59; in onion panades, 58-59; panades, 55-61; puréeing, 30, 32, 34, chart 36-37; and stuffing, 21, 76
Bread soups. See Panades
Broccoli, puréeing, 36
Broth: basic, 8-11; and bread, 55-57; chicken, 8-9; clarifying, 64; cleansing, 10; compound, 39-53; defined, 6; fish, 9, 50, 80; freezing, 11; meat, 8-11; preparing, 8-11; rapid and slow, 10-11; Scotch, 42-43; simple, 8-11; straining, 11; vegetable, 8-11
Browning: aromatic vegetables, 46; onions, 59; oxtails, 46
Brunoise, 13
Brussels sprouts, puréeing, chart 36
Buckwheat: *a variety of grain much used in Russian cooking;* 84
Butter: in clam chowder, 53; in crayfish bisque, 32; in leek and potato soup, 26-27, 40; in onion soups, 26-27, 58-59; in panades, 56, 61; in pea purées, 25; puréeing with, chart 36-37; in purées from leftovers, 30-31; in squash panade, 61; in velouté, 28-29
Cabbage: in beet soup, 85; in garbure, 82-83; in *poule au pot,* 76-77; puréeing, chart 36; stuffed for garnish, 76
Caramelize: *heating sugar until it turns brown and syrupy. Also, evaporating meat or vegetable juices to leave a brown caramel-like residue on the bottom of the pan.*
Caramelizing: meat, 6, 46; vegetables, 6, 46, 58
Carrots: in mixed-vegetable soup, 40-41; in panades, 56-57; puréeing, 24-25, chart 36; in vegetable purées, 24-25
Casserole, panade, 56-57
Cauliflower, puréeing, chart 36
Celeriac, puréeing, 23, chart 37
Cheese: and bread, 21; as garnish, 40; in onion panade, 58-59; in *pistou,* 41; in squash panade, 60-61
Cherry, Hungarian, soup, 62-63; preparing, 73
Chestnut, puréeing, chart 37
Chick-peas, in menudo, 48
Chicken: and beef, 76-77; broth, 6, 8-11; in jellied consommé, 64-65; in panades, 56-57; poaching, 76-77; in *poule au pot,* 75-77; puréeing, chart 37; quenelles, 20; à la reine, 34-35; in Senegalese soup, 70-71
Chiffonade: *a French term for any leafy herb or vegetable that has been sliced into fine ribbons;* 13
Chilling borscht, 86
Chorizo: *spicy, garlicky Spanish sausage. Any other spicy, fresh sausage may be substituted.*

Chouriço: *spicy, garlicky Portuguese sausage similar to chorizo.*
Chowders, preparing, 52-53
Cider: *apple juice. Fermented apple juice produces hard cider, or apple wine. In Spain and England, hard cider is occasionally fermented a second time to produce a champagne cider. In America and France, hard cider is fermented and distilled to produce apple brandies known as applejack and Calvados.*
Clam chowder, preparing, 52-53
Clarifying: broth for jellied consommé, 64; consommé, 6
Cleansing: compound broths, 42; pork and bean soup, 79; purées from leftovers, 30-31; simple broths, 10-11
Coconut, in Senegalese soup, 70
Cold soups, 62-73; avocado and cream, 66-67; borscht, 86; *botvinya,* 63, 68-69; cherry, 62-63, 73; gazpacho, 63, 66-67; jellied consommé, 64-65; pear and watercress, 72-73; Senegalese soup, 63, 70-71
Compound broths, 39-53; clam chowder, 39, 52-53; Creole gumbo, 44-45; defined, 6; fish, 50-51; leek and potato, 40; leftovers, 46-47; *menudo,* 39, 48-49; mixed-vegetable, 39, 41; mussels in velouté, 52-53; oxtail, 46-47; Scotch broth, 39, 42-43; shellfish, 52-53; tripe, 48-49; velouté, 39, 52-53
Consommé: chilled, 63-65; clarifying, 6, 64; cold jellied, 64-65; defined, 6; garnishes for, 6, 12-21
Corn, puréeing, chart 37
Court bouillon: *a flavored cooking liquid, usually made by adding aromatic vegetables and seasonings — and sometimes wine or other acid liquid —to water.*
Crab, disjointing, 44
Crayfish bisque, preparing, 32-33
Cream: in *bourride,* 80-81; in carrot purée, 24-25; in cold avocado and cream soup, 66-67; in cold purées, 63; in leek and potato soup, 27; in mussel velouté, 53; in pear and watercress soup, 72-73; in *potage à la reine,* 34; puréeing with, 23-25, 27-31, 34, chart 36-37, 63; purées from leftovers, 30-31; in quenelles, 20; in Senegalese soup, 70-71; soup, defined, 6; in squash panade, 61; in velouté, 28-29, 53
Creole gumbo, preparing, 44-45
Croutons, 21
Cucumber, puréeing, chart 37
Curry spices, 71; in Senegalese soup, 70-71
Custard, preparing, 15
Cutting: bread, 21; custard for garnish, 15; dumplings, 19; fish, 69, 80; pasta, 16; squash, 60; tripe, 48; vegetables, 13, 26, 40
Deglazing oxtail soup, 47
Degrease: *to remove the fat from cooking juices and broths;* 11, 86

Disjointing crabs, 44
Dough, pasta, 16
Dumplings: as garnish, 18-20; marrow, 18-19; meat, 18-19; potato, 18-19; quenelles, 20
Egg: custards, 14-15; in dumplings, 18; garnish, 12, 14-15; poaching, 14; puffs, 14; puréeing with, 28-29, 34, chart 36-37; sieving yolks, 15; to strain consommé, 64; stuffing for *poule au pot,* 77; threads, 15; whites in quenelles, 20; yolks in aioli, 80; yolks in bread panades, 55, 57; yolks in *potage à la reine,* 34; yolks in sorrel purée, 28-29; yolks in velouté, 28-29, 52
Eggplant, puréeing, chart 37
Endive. See Belgian endive
Enrichments: in avocado and cream soup, 66-67; in bread panades, 55-57; in *bourride,* 80-81; in carrot purées, 24-25; in clam chowder, 53; in crayfish bisque, 32; for fish soup, 50; in jellied consommé, 64-65; in leek and potato soup, 26-27, 40; in mussel velouté, 53; in onion soups, 26-27, 59; in pea purées, 25; in pear soup, 72-73; in *potage à la reine,* 34; puréeing, chart 36-37; in purées from leftovers, 30-31; in Senegalese soup, 71; in sorrel purées, 28-29; in squash panade, 60-61; in velouté, 28-29, 52
Farina. See Semolina
Fennel: *an herb grown for its feathery anise-flavored leaves or a vegetable grown for its white, bulbous and mild-tasting (though still anise-flavored) stalk;* 12, 37
Fermented beet liquid: *a tart flavoring made by steeping raw grated beets, rye bread and sugar water for 3 or 4 days. The fermented liquid is strained before being used;* 84
Fines herbes: *a mixture of finely chopped fresh herbs —the classic herbs being parsley, chives, tarragon and chervil.*
Fish: in broth, 6, 8-9; in compound broths, 50-51; poaching, 68, 80; puréeing, chart 37; quenelles, 20; steaks, 80-81; and vegetable soup, 68-69
Flour: in dumplings, 18; in onion soup, 26-27; in pasta, 10; in purées, 36-37; roux, 28, 39, 44, 52; in velouté, 28, 39
Fond brun, defined, 6
Fonds blanc, defined, 6
Food mill, puréeing with, 23, 36-37
Food processor, puréeing with, 23, 37
Freezing broth, 11
Fruit, in cold soups, 63, 72-73
Frying bread cubes, 21
Full-meal soups, 74-86; beef and stuffed chicken, 76-77; borscht, 75, 84-86; *bourride,* 75, 80-81; garbure, 82-83; pork and bean, 75, 78-79; *poule au pot,* 74-77
Garbure, preparing, 82-83

Recipe Credits

The sources for the recipes in this volume are listed below. Page references in parentheses indicate where the recipes appear in the anthology.

Acton, Eliza, *Modern Cookery.* Published by Longman, Brown, Green and Longmans, London. 1856 edition(91, 102, 129).

Allen, Jana and Margaret Gin, *Innards and other Variety Meats.* Copyright © 1974 Jana Allen & Margaret Gin. Published by 101 Productions, San Francisco. By permission of 101 Productions(124).

American Heritage, The editors of, *The American Heritage Cookbook.* Copyright © 1964 American Heritage Publishing Co., Inc., New York. By permission of American Heritage Publishing Co., Inc.(135).

The Art of Cookery, Made Plain and Easy. By a Lady. The Sixth Edition, 1758(142).

Audot, L. E., *La Cuisinière de la Campagne et de la Ville, ou la Nouvelle Cuisine Économique.* Published by Librairie Audot, 1881 edition(112, 148).

Aznar, Marina Pereyra de and Nina Froud, *The Home Book of Spanish Cookery.* First published in 1956 by Faber and Faber Limited, London. New material © Marina Pereyra de Aznar and Nina Froud 1967, 1974. By permission of Nina Froud(104, 111, 131, 146).

Beard, James, *James Beard's American Cookery.* Copyright © 1972 by James A. Beard. Published by Little, Brown and Company, Boston. By permission of Little, Brown and Company(160).

Berjane, J., *French Dishes for English Tables.* Copyright © F. Warne (Publishers) Ltd. Published by Frederick Warne & Co. Ltd., London. By permission of Frederick Warne & Co. Ltd.(102).

Besson, Joséphine, *La Mère Besson "Ma Cuisine Provençale."* © Editions Albin Michel, 1977. Published by Editions Albin Michel, Paris. Translated by permission of Editions Albin Michel(90).

Blanchard, Marjorie Page, *Treasured Recipes from Early New England Kitchens.* Copyright © 1975 by Harrington's in Vermont, Inc., Richmond, Vermont. Published by Garden Way Publishing Co. in association with Harrington's of Richmond, Vermont, Inc. By permission of Writers House, Inc., author's agents(131, 135).

Boni, Ada, *Italian Regional Cooking.* Copyright © 1969 s.c. by Arnoldo Mondadori. English translation, copyright ©1969 s.c. by Thomas Nelson & Sons Ltd. and E. P. Dutton and Company, Inc. Published by Bonanza Books, a division of Crown Publishers, Inc., New York. By permission of Arnoldo Mondadori Editore(131).

Boulestin, X. Marcel, *Recipes of Boulestin.* © The Estate of X. M. Boulestin 1971. Published by William Heinemann Ltd., London. By permission of William Heinemann Ltd.(96).

Brandon, Leila, *A Merry-Go-Round of Recipes from Jamaica.* Revised edition. Published by Novelty Trading Co., Ltd. Jamaica. By permission of Leila E. Brandon(127).

Brera, Gianni and Luigi Veronelli, *La Pacciada.* © 1973 by Arnoldo Mondadori Editore. Published by Arnoldo Mondadori Editore, Milan. Translated by permission of Arnoldo Mondadori Editore(112, 118, 142).

Breteuil, Jules, *Le Cuisinier Européen.* Published by Garnier Frères Libraires-Editeurs c. 1860(103, 142).

Brissenden, Rosemary, *South East Asian Food.* Copyright © R. F. and R. L. Brissenden, 1970. Published by Penguin Books Ltd., London. By permission of Penguin Books Ltd.(106).

Brown, Helen Evans, *Helen Brown's West Coast Cook Book.* Copyright © 1952 by Helen Evans Brown. Published by Little, Brown and Company, Boston. By permission of Little, Brown and Company(121, 143, 145).

Bugialli, Giuliano, *The Fine Art of Italian Cooking.* Copyright © 1977 by Giuliano Bugialli. Published by Times Books/Quadrangle — The New York Times Book Co. Inc., New York. By permission of Times Books, a Division of Quadrangle/The New York Times Book Co. Inc.(117, 139).

Carême, Antonin, *L'Art de la Cuisine Française au Dix-Neuvième Siècle.* Published in Paris 1833(105, 106, 111).

Carnacina, Luigi, *Great Italian Cooking,* edited by Michael Sonino. Published in English by Abradale Press Inc., New York. By permission of Aldo Garzanti Editore and Abradale Press(124, 139, 153).

Cass, Elizabeth, *Spanish Cooking.* Copyright © Elizabeth Cass 1957. First published by André Deutsch Ltd., 1957. Also published by Mayflower Books Ltd., 1970. By permission of André Deutsch Ltd.(144).

Chantiles, Vilma Liacouras, *The Food of Greece.* Copyright © 1975 by Vilma Liacouras Chantiles. Published by Atheneum Publishers, New York. By permission of Vilma Liacouras Chantiles(118).

Chen, Joyce, *Joyce Chen Cook Book.* Copyright © 1962 by Joyce Chen. Published by J. B. Lippincott Company, New York. By permission of J. B. Lippincott Company(128).

Clarisse ou la Vieille Cuisinière. Copyright © 1922 by Editions de l'Abeille d'Or. Published by Editions de l'Abeille d'Or, Paris. Translated by permission of Editions Rombaldi, Paris(110).

Conran, Terence and Maria Kroll, *The Vegetable Book.* © Conran Ink 1976. Published by Collins Publishers, Glasgow and London. By permission of Collins Publishers and Crescent Books, New York(93, 98).

Corbitt, Helen, *Helen Corbitt's Cookbook.* Copyright © 1957 by Helen Corbitt. Published by Houghton Mifflin Company, Boston. By permission of Houghton Mifflin Company(149).

Costa, Margaret, *Margaret Costa's Four Seasons Cookery Book.* Copyright © Margaret Costa. Published by Thomas Nelson & Sons Ltd., 1970. By permission of Margaret Costa(104).

La Cuisine Naturelle à l'Huile d'Olive. © 1978 Editions De Vecchi S. A. Paris. Published by Editions De Vecchi, Paris. Translated by permission of Editions De Vecchi S. A. Paris(146).

Curnonsky, *A l'Infortune du Pot.* Copyright Editions de la Couronne 1946. Published by Editions de la Couronne, Paris(160). *Recettes des Provinces de France.* Published by Les Productions de Paris(132).

Cutler, Carol, *The Six-Minute Soufflé and Other Culinary Delights.* Copyright © 1976 by Carol Cutler. Published by Crown Publishers Inc., New York. By permission of Clarkson N. Potter, Inc.(104, 116, 138, 144).

Dannenbaum, Julie, *Menus for All Occasions.* Copyright © 1974 by Julie Dannenbaum. Published by Saturday Review Press/E. P. Dutton and Company, Inc., New York. By permission of Edward Acton, Inc.(93, 96, 109).

David, Elizabeth, *A Book of Mediterranean Food.* Copyright © Elizabeth David, 1958, 1965. Published by

Penguin Books Ltd., London. By permission of Penguin Books Ltd.(99). *French Provincial Cooking.* Copyright © Elizabeth David, 1960, 1962, 1967, 1970. First published by Michael Joseph Ltd., London 1960. Also published by Penguin Books Ltd., London. By permission of Elizabeth David(97). *Italian Food.* Copyright © Elizabeth David, 1954, 1963, 1969, 1977. Published by Penguin Books Ltd., London. By permission of Penguin Books Ltd.(91, 111).

Davidson, Alan, *North Atlantic Seafood.* Copyright © Alan Davidson, 1979. Published by Penguin Books Ltd. and Macmillan London Ltd. By permission of Penguin Books Ltd. and Alan Davidson(150).

de Gouy, Jean, *La Cuisine et la Pâtisserie Bourgeoises.* Published by J. Lebègue & Cie., Libraires-Éditeurs, Paris 1896(126).

De Gouy, Louis P., *The Soup Book.* Copyright © 1949 by Mrs. Louis P. De Gouy. Published by Dover Publications Inc., New York. By permission of Dover Publications, Inc.(122, 125, 128).

de Pomiane, Edouard, *Le Carnet d'Anna.* Published by Les Éditions Paul-Martial, Paris, 1938(106).

Diat, Louis, *French Cooking for Americans.* Copyright 1941, 1946 by Louis Diat. Copyright © 1969, by Mrs. Louis D. Diat. Published by J. B. Lippincott Company, New York. By permission of J. B. Lippincott Company(98, 100, 156).

Driggs, Louise, *Soups and Stews the World Over.* Copyright © 1971 by Louise Driggs, edited by Eleanor Porter. Published by Hastings House, Publishers, New York. By permission of Hastings House, Publishers(120).

Dubois, Urbain, *Ecole des Cuisinières.* Published by Dentu, Paris, 1876(156).

Duff, Gail, *Fresh All the Year.* © Gail Duff 1976. First published by Macmillan London Ltd., 1976. Also published by Pan Books Ltd., 1977. By permission of Macmillan London Ltd.(93).

Durand, Charles, *Le Cuisinier Durand.* Privately published by the author, 1843(107).

Escoffier, A., *Le Carnet d'Epicure* (magazine). 1912, no. 12 and 1913, no. 15. Translated by permission of Pierre Escoffier(123).

Farmer, Fannie Merrit, *The Fannie Farmer Cookbook.* (Edited by Wilma Lord Perkins.) Copyright © 1965 by Dexter Perkins Corporation. Published by Little, Brown and Company, Boston. By permission of the Fannie Farmer Cookbook Corporation, Bedford, Mass.(133).

Field, Michael, *All Manner of Food.* Copyright © 1965, 1966, 1967, 1968, 1970 by Michael Field. Published by Alfred A. Knopf, New York. By permission of Jonathan Rude-Field(147). *Michael Field's Cooking School.* Copyright © 1965 by Michael Field. By permission of Holt, Rinehart, Winston, Publishers, New York(144, 149).

Foods of the World, *The Cooking of Italy, Middle Eastern Cooking.* Copyright © 1968 by Time-Life Books Inc. Copyright © 1969 by Time Inc. Published by Time-Life Books Inc., Alexandria(88, 143).

La France à Table (French magazine). No. 7 June 1935, No. 11 Feb. 1936(115, 139).

Froud, Nina and George, *The Home Book of Russian Cooking.* © Nina and George Froud. Published by Faber and Faber Limited, London. By permission of Nina Froud(162).

Gouffé, Jules, *Le Livre des Soupes et des Potages.* Published by Librairie Hachette et Cie. Paris, 1875(154, 158).

Gould-Marks, Beryl, *The Home Book of Italian Cookery.* Beryl Gould-Marks 1969. Published by Faber and Faber Limited, London. By permission of Faber and Faber Limited(154).

Graves, Eleanor, *Great Dinners From Life.* Copyright © 1969 Time Inc. Published by Time-Life Books Inc., Alexandria(89, 113, 132, 147).

The Great Cooks' Guide to Soups. Copyright © 1977 by Arthur Weinberg. Published by Random House and Bernard Glaser Wolf Ltd. By permission of Emanuel and Madeline Greenberg(120 — Emanuel and Madeline Greenberg).

Greenberg, Florence, *Jewish Cookery.* Copyright © The Jewish Chronicle Ltd. 1963. Published by Penguin Books Ltd., London. By permission of Penguin Books Ltd.(105, 161, 162).

Grigson, Jane, *English Food.* Copyright © Jane Grigson, 1974. First published by Macmillan 1974. Published by Penguin Books Ltd., London, 1977. By permission of Macmillan London Ltd.(122). *Fish Cookery.* Copyright © Jane Grigson, 1973. Published by the International Wine and Food Publishing Company. By permission of Overlook Press.(137). *Jane Grigson's Vegetable Book.* Copyright © 1968 by Jane Grigson. Published by Atheneum Publishers, New York. By permission of Atheneum Publishers(94). *Observer Magazine* (June 26, 1977). By permission of David Higham Associates Limited for the author(148).

Haitsma Mulier-Van Beusekom, C.A.H., Van (Editor), *Culinaire Encyclopedie.* Published by Elsevier © 1957. Revised edition 1974 by N. V. Uitgeversmaatschappij Elsevier Nederland and E.H.A. Nakken-Rövekamp. Translated by permission of N. V. Uitgeversmaatschappij Elsevier Nederland(116).

Hazelton, Nika Standen, *The Continental Flavour.* Copyright © Nika Standen Hazelton, 1961. Published by Penguin Books Ltd., London. By permission of Curtis Brown Ltd.(163).

Hewitt, Jean, *The New York Times Natural Foods Cookbook.* Copyright © 1971 by Jean Hewitt. Published by Times Books, a Division of Quadrangle/The New York Times Book Co., New York. By permission of Times Books, a Division of Quadrangle/The New York Times Book Co.(146). *The New York Times New England Heritage Cookbook.* Copyright © 1972 and 1977 by The New York Times Company. Published by G. P. Putnam's Sons, New York. By permission of G. P. Putnam's Sons(95). *The New York Times Weekend Cookbook.* Copyright © 1975 by Jean Hewitt. Published by Quadrangle/The New York Times Book Co., New York. By permission of Jean Hewitt(126).

Hutchins, Sheila, *English Recipes and Others from Scotland, Wales and Ireland.* © 1967 by Sheila Hutchins. Published by The Cookery Book Club. By permission of Sheila Hutchins(157).

Irwin, Florence, *Irish Country Recipes.* Published by The Northern Whig Limited, Belfast(127).

Isnard, Léon, *La Cuisine Française et Africaine.* Copyright 1949, by Editions Albin Michel. Published by Editions Albin Michel, Paris. Translated by permission of Editions Albin Michel(89, 90, 92).

Jans, Hugh, *Vrij Nederlands Kookboek.* © 1973 Unieboek/C. A. J. van Dishoeck, Bussum. Published by Unieboek/C. A. J. van Dishoeck, Bussum. Translated by permission of Unieboek B.V.(118).

Jarrat, Enrica and Vernon, *The Complete Book of Pasta.* © 1969 by Enrica and Vernon Jarratt. English translation © 1975 by Vernon Jarratt. Published by Michael Joseph, London. By permission of Michael Joseph(162).

Jewry, Mary (Editor), *Warne's Model Cookery and Housekeeping Book.* © Copyright F. Warne (Publishers) Ltd. Published by Frederick Warne & Co. Ltd., London. By permission of Frederick Warne & Co. Ltd.(100, 127).

Junior League of New Orleans, *The Plantation Cookbook.* Copyright © 1972 by The Junior League of New Orleans, La. Published by Doubleday & Company, Inc., New York. By permission of Doubleday & Company, Inc.(136).

Kahn, Odette (Editor), *Cuisine et Vins de France* (magazine). Published by Société Française d'Éditions Vinicoles. Translated by permission of Odette Kahn(96).

Kennedy, Diana, *The Cuisines of Mexico.* Copyright © 1972 by Diana Kennedy. Published by Harper and Row Publishers, Inc., New York. By permission of Harper and Row Publishers, Inc.(102).

Knight, Jacqueline, E., *The Cook's Fish Guide.* Copyright © 1973 by Jacqueline E. Knight. Published by E. P. Dutton and Company Inc., New York. By permission of E. P. Dutton and Company(134).

Lassalle, George, *The Adventurous Fish Cook.* © Caroline Lassalle 1976. Published by Pan Books Ltd., London. By permission of Pan Books Ltd.(137).

Leyel, Mrs. C. F. and Miss Olga Hartley, *The Gentle Art of Cookery.* © The Executors of Mrs. C. F. Leyel 1925. Published by Chatto & Windus Ltd. London. By permission of Chatto & Windus Ltd.(95, 111).

Lin, Florence, *Florence Lin's Chinese Vegetarian Cookbook.* Copyright © 1976 Florence S. Lin. Published by Hawthorn Books, Inc., New York. By permission of Hawthorn Books, Inc.(109).

MacMiadhachàin, Anna, *Spanish Regional Cookery.* Copyright © Anna MacMiadhachàin, 1976. Published by Penguin Books Ltd., London. By permission of Penguin Books Ltd.(128, 138).

Macnicol, Fred, *Hungarian Cookery.* Copyright © Fred Macnicol, 1978. Published by Penguin Books Ltd., London. By permission of Penguin Books Ltd.(161).

McNeill, F. Marian, *The Scots Kitchen.* Published by Blackie and Son Limited, London. By permission of Blackie and Son Limited(101, 121, 129).

Martin, Peter and Joan, *Japanese Cooking.* Copyright © 1970 Peter and Joan Martin. Published by Bobbs Merrill Co. Inc., New York. By permission of Bobbs Merrill Co. Inc.(89, 107).

70 Médecins de France, *Le Trésor de la Cuisine du Bassin Méditerranéen.* (97, 153, 159).

Menon, *La Cuisiniere Bourgeoise.* 1746(99).

Molokhovets, Elena, *Podarok Molodým Khozyaĭkam.* Published in St. Petersburg, 1892(150, 151, 152, 161).

Montagné, Prosper, *The New Larousse Gastronomique.* English translation © 1977 by Hamlyn Publishing Group Limited. Published by Crown Publishers, Inc., New York. By permission of Crown Publishers, Inc.(103).

Montagné, Prosper and A. Gottschalk, *Mon Menu — Guide d'Hygiène Alimentaire.* Published by Société d'Applications Scientifiques, Paris(151).

Murray, Janet, *With a Fine Feeling for Food.* Copyright © Janet Murray, 1972. By permission of Janet Murray(121 130).

Nelson, Kay Shaw, *Soups and Stews.* Copyright © 1974 by Kay Shaw Nelson. Published by the Henry Regnery Company, Chicago. By permission of Kay Shaw Nelson(146).

Nignon, Edouard, *Les Plaisirs de la Table.* Published by the author c. 1920. Translated by permission of Daniel Morcrette, B. P. 26,95270-Luzarches, France(89).

Norberg, Inga, *Good Food from Sweden.* Published in 1935 by Chatto & Windus, London. By permission of Curtis Brown Ltd.(155).

Ohio Housewives, *Ohio Housewives Companion,* 1876(123).

Olney, Judith, *Summer Food.* Copyright © 1978 by Judith Olney. Published by Atheneum Publishers, New York. By permission of Atheneum Publishers(92, 145).

Olney, Richard, *Simple French Food.* Copyright © 1974 by Richard Olney. Published by Atheneum Publishers, New York. By permission of Atheneum Publishers(110, 114).

Ortiz, Elizabeth Lambert, *The Complete Book of Caribbean Cooking.* Copyright © by Elizabeth Lambert Ortiz, 1973, 1975. Published by M. Evans and Company, Inc., New York. By permission of John Farquharson Limited(125).

Palay, Simin, *La Cuisine du Pays.* © 1970 Marrimpouey Jeune-Pau. Published by Editions Marrimpouey Jeune et Cie., Pau. Translated by permission of Editions Marrimpouey Jeune et Cie.(155, 157).

Paradissis, Chrissa, *The Best Book of Greek Cookery.* Copyright © 1976 P. Efstathiadis & Sons. Published by P. Efstathiadis & Sons, Athens. By permission of P. Efstathiadis & Sons(117).

Peck, Paula, *Paula Peck's Art of Good Cooking.* Copyright © 1961, 1966 by Paula Peck. Published by Simon & Schuster, a division of Gulf & Western Corporation, New York. By permission of Simon & Schuster, a division of Gulf & Western Corporation(99, 101, 115).

Peter, Madeleine, *Grandes Dames de La Cuisine.* Copyright © 1977 by Editions Robert Laffont, S. A. Published by Editions Robert Laffont, S. A. By permission of Holt, Rinehart and Winston(108).

Petersen, Bengt, *Delicious Fish Dishes.* © Bengt Petersen/Wezäta Förlag 1976. Published by Wezäta Förlag, Göteborg. By permission of Wezäta Förlag(130).

Les Petits Plats et les Grands, © 1977, by Editions Denoël, Paris. Published by Editions Denoël Sarl, Paris. Translated by permission of Editions Denoël Sarl(132 — Mrs. Henry Cabot Lodge, 142).

Petits Propos Culinaires, © 1979, Prospect Books. Published by Prospect Books, Washington, D.C. February 1979. By permission of the publisher(105 — Tante Ursule, 149 — Jeremiah Tower).

Platt, June, June Platt's New England Cook Book. Copyright © 1971 by June Platt. Published by Atheneum Publishers, New York. By permission of Atheneum Publishers(91, 110).

Portinari, Laura Gras, Cucina e Vini del Piemonte e della Valle d'Aosta. © Copyright 1971 Ugo Mursia Editore — Milan. Published by Ugo Mursia Editore S.p.A. Milano. Translated by permission of Ugo Mursia Editore(141).

Les Princes de La Gastronomie, © 1.2. 1974 — Les Éditions Mondiales. Published by Modes de Paris. Translated by permission of Les Éditions Mondiales(130).

Progneaux, Jean E., Les Spécialités et Recettes Gastronomiques Bordelaises et Girondines. Published by Quartier Latin, La Rochelle. Translated by permission of Quartier Latin(108).

Reboul, J. B., La Cuisinière Provençale. Published by Tacussel, Marseilles. Translated by permission of Tacussel, Éditeur(154, 159).

Renaudet, B., Les Secrets de la Bonne Table. Published by Editions Albin Michel, Paris. Translated by permission of Éditions Albin Michel(94, 98, 141).

Richter, M. and W. Bickel, Suppen. Copyright © M. Richter, W. Bickel. Published by Fachbuchverlag Dr. Pfanneberg and Co. Giessen. Translated by permission of Fachbuchverlag Dr. Pfanneberg and Co.(113).

Robaglia, Suzanne, Margaridou. Published by Éditions Creer, Nonette. Translated by permission of Éditions Creer(100, 140).

Romagnoli, Margaret and G. Franco, The Romagnolis' Table. Copyright © 1974, 1975 by Margaret and G. Franco Romagnoli. Published by Little, Brown and Company, Boston in association with the Atlantic Monthly Press. Reprinted by permission of Little, Brown and Company(88, 119).

Rombauer, Irma S. and Marion Rombauer Becker, Joy of Cooking. Copyright © 1931, 1936, 1941, 1942, 1943, 1946, 1951, 1952, 1953, 1962, 1963, 1964, 1975 by The Bobbs Merrill Company, Inc., New York. Reprinted by permission of The Bobbs Merrill Company(121).

Root, Waverly, The Best of Italian Cooking. Copyright © 1974 by Edita S. A. Published by Helvetica Press, Inc. Reprinted by permission of Helvetica Press, Inc.(133).

Ross, Janet and Michael Waterfield, Leaves from our Tuscan Kitchen. Copyright © Michael Waterfield, 1973. Published by Atheneum Publishers, New York. By permission of Atheneum Publishers(94, 143).

Saint-Ange, Madame, La Cuisine de Madame Saint-Ange. © Éditions Chaix. Published by Editions Chaix, Grenoble. Translated by permission of Editions Chaix(94, 114, 138).

Sarvis, Shirley, Simply Stews. Published by Signet. By permission of Shirley Sarvis(120).

Savarin, Jeanne Mme. (Editor), La Cuisine des Familles (magazine). No. 19 October 29, 1905, No. 7 August 6, 1905, N. 131 December 22, 1907, No. 12 September 10, 1905(92, 109, 140, 152).

Scott, Jack Denton, The Complete Book of Pasta. Copyright © 1968 by Jack Denton Scott. Published by William Morrow & Company, Inc., New York. Reprinted by permission of Jack Denton Scott and William Morrow & Company, Inc.(119, 158).

Seranne, Ann, Ann Seranne's Good Food & How to Cook It. Copyright © 1972 by Ann Seranne. Published by William Morrow & Company, Inc., New York. Reprinted by permission of William Morrow & Company, Inc.(135).

Sigurdardóttir, Helga, Matur Og Drykkur. Published by Isafoldarprentsmidja H. F. Reykjavik. 4th edition 1966. Translated by permission of Isafoldarprentsmidja (136).

Skipwith, Sofka, Eat Russian. © Sofka Skipwith 1973. Published by David and Charles (Holdings) Ltd., Devon. By permission of David and Charles (Holdings) Ltd.(148).

Standard, Stella, Stella Standard's Soup Book. Copyright © 1978 by Stella Standard. Published by Taplinger Publishing Company, New York. By permission of Taplinger Publishing Company, Inc.(103).

Szathmary, Louis, The Chef's Secret Cookbook. Copyright © 1971 by Louis Szathmary. Published by Quadrangle Books, Chicago. Reprinted by permission of Times Books, a Division of Quadrangle/The New York Times Book Co.(108).

Tarr, Yvonne Young, The New York Times Bread and Soup Cookbook. Copyright © 1972 by Yvonne Young Tarr. Published by Quadrangle/The New York Times Book Co., New York. Reprinted by permission of Times Books, a Division of Quadrangle/The New York Times Book Co.(134).

Tobias, Doris and Mary Merris, The Golden Lemon. Copyright © 1978 by Doris Tobias & Mary Merris. Published by Atheneum Publishers, New York. By permission of Atheneum Publishers(143).

Ungerer, Miriam, Good Cheap Food. Copyright © 1973 by Miriam Ungerer, A William Cole Book. Published by Viking Penguin Inc., New York. By permission of Viking Penguin Inc.(101, 145, 147).

Varenne, La, Le Vray Cuisinier François, 1651(102, 123).

Venesz, Jozsef, Hungarian Cuisine. © Jozsef Venesz, 1958. Published by Corvina Press(160, 162).

Women's Committee of The Walters Art Gallery, Private Collections: A Culinary Treasure. Copyright © 1973 by The Walters Art Gallery, Baltimore. By permission of The Walters Art Gallery, Baltimore(95, 148).

Wason, Betty, The Art of German Cooking. © Elizabeth Wason Hall 1967. Published by Doubleday and Company, Inc., New York. By permission of Doubleday and Company, Inc.(141).

Willinsky, Grete, Kochbuch der Büchergilde. © Büchergilde Gutenberg, Frankfurt am Main 1958. Published by Büchergilde Gutenberg. Translated by permission of Büchergilde Gutenberg(90, 97, 119).

Witwicka, H. and S. Soskine, La Cuisine Russe Classique. © Éditions Albin Michel, 1968 et 1978. Published by Editions Albin Michel, Paris. Translated by permission of Éditions Albin Michel(88, 107).

Wright, Carol, Portuguese Food. Copyright © 1969 by Carol Wright. Published by J. M. Dent & Sons Ltd., Publishers, London. Reprinted by permission of Deborah Rogers Ltd., on behalf of Carol Wright(140).

Acknowledgments

The indexes for this book were prepared by Michael J. Sullivan. The editors are particularly indebted to Pat Alburey, Hertfordshire, England; Alan Davidson, London; Elizabeth Lambert Ortiz, London; and Jeremiah Tower, Berkeley, California.

The editors also wish to thank: Joseph Beck, Elizabeth S. Crosby, Poultry and Dairy Quality Division, United States Department of Agriculture, Washington, D.C.; Erika Bertrang, Alexandria, Virginia; Karen Caplan, Frieda's Finest, Los Angeles, California; Gene Cope, National Marine Fisheries Service, Washington, D.C.; Sue Crowther, London; Jennifer Davidson, London; Pamela Davidson, London; Peggy Eastman, Chevy Chase, Maryland; Dr. George J. Flick, Mary C. Holliman, Jean Brewer, Department of Food Sciences and Technology, Virginia Polytechnic Institute and State University, Blacksburg, Virginia; Dorothy Frame, London; Diana Grant, London; Maggie Heinz, London; Marion Hunter, Surrey, England; Brenda Jayes, London; H. Kenneth Johnson, National Live Stock and Meat Board, Chicago, Illinois; John Leslie, London; Agneta Munktell, London; Jo Oxley, Surrey, England; Joanna Roberts, London; Alice Salmon, London; Shirley Sarvis, San Francisco, California; Henry Sauter, Larimer's Inc., Washington, D.C.; Eileen Turner, Sussex, England; Lillie Vincent, United States Department of Agriculture, Washington, D.C.; Betty Wason, Arlington, Virginia.

Picture Credits

The sources for the pictures in this book are listed below. Credits for each of the photographers and illustrators are listed by page number in sequence with successive pages indicated by hyphens; where necessary, the locations of pictures within pages are also indicated — separated from page numbers by dashes.

Photographs by Tom Belshaw: 4, 10-11 — top, 12, 16, 18-19 — center, 21 — top and bottom, 22, 26-27, 28-29 — bottom, 30-33, 40, 46-51, 52 — bottom, 54, 56-57 — bottom, 58-59, 62, 64-65, 68-69, 73, 78-79, 80 — top and bottom right, 81, 84-85.
Photographs by Alan Duns: 10-11 — bottom, 13 — top left, center left and bottom (3), 15 — except top left, 17 — top, 18-19 — top and bottom, 20, 21 — center, 24-25, 28-29 — top, 34, 35 — top, 38, 42-43, 52 — top, 53, 56-57 — top, 66-67, 70-72, 74, 76-77, 80 — bottom left.
Other photographs (alphabetically): Gina Harris, 13 — top right and center right, 41, 86. Richard Jeffery, cover. Louis Klein, 2. Aldo Tutino, 14, 15 — top left, 17 — center and bottom, 35 — bottom, 44-45, 60-61, 82-83.
Illustrations (alphabetically): Mary Evans Picture Library and private sources, 7, 88-167. Whole Hog Studios, Atlanta, Georgia, 8-9.

Library of Congress Cataloguing in Publication Data
Time-Life Books.
   Soups.
   (The Good cook, techniques and recipes)
   Includes index.
   1. Soups. I. Title. II. Series: Good cook, techniques and recipes.
TX757.T55   1979   641.8'13   79-17129
ISBN 0-8094-2868-7
ISBN 0-8094-2867-9 lib. bdg.

176